The Japanese Mind

A one-time senior editor at *Time*, Robert C.
Christopher also served as foreign editor and
executive editor at *Newsweek* for nearly a decade,
and was the first editor of *Newsweek International*.
Now the Administrator of the Pulitzer Prizes, he
holds a degree in Oriental Studies from Yale and
has written on Japanese affairs for such
publications as the *New York Times Magazine*,
the London *Sunday Times*, *Asia*, and *Foreign
Affairs*.

The Japanese Mind

THE GOLIATH EXPLAINED

ROBERT C. CHRISTOPHER

Pan Original
Pan Books London and Sydney

First published in Great Britain 1984 by
Pan Books Ltd,
Cavaye Place, London SW10 9PG
9 8 7 6 5 4 3 2 1
© Kriscon Corporation 1983
ISBN 0 330 28419 3

Phototypeset by Input Typesetting Ltd, London
Printed and bound in Great Britain by
Cox & Wyman Ltd, Reading

This book is for my wife, Rita,
who first persuaded me to undertake it—
and then gallantly endured the consequences.

Contents

Foreword   ix

SECTION ONE: *The Japanese Tribe*   xiii

1   The Oddest Couple: Japan and America   15
2   The Heart and Mind of Japan   34

SECTION TWO: *Growing Up Japanese*   53

3   All in the Family   55
4   The Education Race   70
5   A Woman's Place   91
6   "My Home"   106

SECTION THREE: *The Social Animal*   125

7   Masses and Classes   127
8   Automatic Controls   142
9   The *Gaijin* Complex   153

SECTION FOUR: *Work and Power*   173

10 The Information Society   175
11 Machines and Mandarins   191
12 The Fruits of Industry   216
13 Mom, Pop and the Robots   240

SECTION FIVE: *Looking Ahead*   265

14 A Talent for Survival   267

Index   296

Foreword

Since Japan first began to emerge as a significant factor in world affairs, Britain has never wanted for perceptive students of that country and its culture. The elegant translations of Arthur Waley and Sir George Sansom's seminal explorations of the Japanese past, to cite merely two of the most obvious examples, still stand as landmarks in the history of Western scholarship on Japan, and the ground that men such as Waley and Sansom broke continues to be very actively tilled by contemporary British scholars. To be sure, the work done by some of Britain's present-day Japanologists verges on the arcane and occasionally seems designed more to demonstrate the author's intellectual virtuosity than to enlighten his readers. But that, of course, is true of a certain amount of all academic writing on any subject; and what is far more important is that a notable amount of intelligent and original analysis of Japan and matters Japanese is today available to anyone in Britain who wishes to take advantage of it.

The difficulty is that, relatively speaking, not very many people in Britain actually do take advantage of the wealth of specialized material on Japan available to them. Largely, I believe, because Japan's rise to its present importance has been so rapid and was foreseen by so few of those who present themselves as experts on Japanese affairs, most educated people in Britain today possess little knowledge of Japan beyond that which they are able to extract from the media. And that is simply not enough to enable anyone to form intelligent judgments about the policies toward Japan that the United Kingdom might most usefully pursue.

This is not a state of affairs purely confined to Britain. The situation is little if any better in the United States and Canada and, so far as I can determine, is even worse in the countries of continental Europe. Everywhere in the Western world, in short, it is more often than not the case that otherwise well-informed people possess lamentably little understanding or knowledge of a country which, amongst non-Communist nations, now stands second only to the United States in terms of economic power.

Given that fact, I long ago concluded that even if I were able to do so, it would make little sense for me to add one more title to the long and excellent list of scholarly works on Japan already available in English. What was more urgently needed, it seemed to me, was a psychic and institutional guidebook to today's Japan that might capture the interest of busy, intelligent and responsible Westerners whose previous exposure to things Japanese had been relatively minimal.

This is the book I have tried to write. And since that was my purpose, I have made every effort not to commit the sin which, according to legend, once led an American schoolchild to write: "This book told me more about penguins than I wanted to know." Specifically, I have almost entirely shunned the use of such scholarly paraphernalia as footnotes and have confined the amount of historical detail imposed upon readers to that which I consider absolutely essential to an understanding of contemporary Japan.

My decision to omit academic citations, however, is in no way intended to conceal the fact that I am deeply indebted to a vast company of previous students of Japan, both academic and otherwise. Because this book has been quite literally forty years in gestation, it inevitably contains facts, figures and insights drawn from hundreds of other books, monographs, articles and statistical studies. To list all of these would require inordinate space; and the same, unhappily, is true of the hundreds of individuals who have helped to shape my thinking on Japan over the decades. But there are a few people and institutions whose influence and/or assistance have been of such central importance that I cannot fail to mention them. Among non-Japanese, in order of my exposure to them, these include:

● Professor Emeritus Edwin O. Reischauer of Harvard University, who commanded the US Army school in which I received my initial instruction in the Japanese language and who—without, I suspect, ever being aware of my existence—first opened my eyes to the fact that Japanese are no more mysterious than Occidentals, just different.

● Professor Chitoshi Yanaga, formerly of Yale University, who, with marvellous clarity, introduced me to the intricacies of Japanese history.

● Bernard Krisher, now chief editorial adviser to Japan's *Focus* magazine, who was my colleague at *Newsweek* magazine for fourteen years and who generously shared with me not only his insights into Japanese affairs but his extraordinary access to the movers and shakers of contemporary Japan.

● The Japan Society of New York, whose able and indefatigable executives—most particularly, David MacEachron and Ms Ruri Kawashima—have provided me (and countless others) with invaluable continuing exposure to significant figures in present-day Japan and to nearly every conceivable aspect of Japanese life and society.

As for Japanese, the majority of those to whom I am most indebted are mentioned one way or another in the body of this book. Those who are not will, I hope, understand that they have gone unnamed because of my fear that some of the views I have expressed might cause them personal or professional embarrassment. I trust that I shall create no such problems, however, by mentioning some organizations whose members have been unfailingly and uncommonly helpful over the years: the Japanese Foreign Office, the Ministry of International Trade and Industry, the Japanese Information Center in New York, the Foreign Press Center/Japan and International House of Japan.

Finally, I owe special gratitude to my agent, Melanie Jackson, whose enthusiasm converted this project into something more than a gleam in the eye, and to my editors, Joni Evans and Marjorie Williams, who miraculously transformed the customary carrot-and-stick relationship between editors and writers. With them, it was carrots all the way. For that and for their invariably wise advice, I salute them.

Old Lyme, Connecticut
November 8, 1983

SECTION ONE

The Japanese Tribe

1

The Oddest Couple:
Japan and America

Sitting on my desk as I write this is a small bronze casting of a crouching animal, vaguely feline in appearance but with the square head and broad, fanlike tail of a Chinese dragon. Each time I look at this enigmatic little figure, as I have done almost daily for the past thirty-five years, I feel a faint twinge of guilt. For fond of it as I am, it is not really mine. Once, with others like it, it must have adorned the uprights of a wrought-iron fence that set off the home of a prosperous Japanese merchant or professional man. I acquired it by plucking it out of the sea of rubble which was all that remained of western Tokyo in September 1945.

To speak of a sea of rubble is a cliché, but that is precisely how I recall the Tokyo I first saw a few days after Douglas MacArthur accepted the surrender of the Imperial Japanese Government on the battleship *Missouri*. In those days, you could drive for miles through Tokyo without seeing anything but undulating heaps of debris, a foot deep here, three feet deep there. In all this vast empty expanse, once home to hundreds of thousands of people, the only thing raising its head above the wreckage, the only thing vaguely reminiscent of human habitation, was an occasional burnt-out safe—a forlorn reminder of the illusory prudence of some businessman or householder now as likely as not dead.

It was the most melancholy and horrifying landscape imaginable—so much so that once when I was driving through it with a major general on MacArthur's staff, he suddenly turned to me and said in a soft Georgia drawl: "You know, Lieutenant, I have no cause to love the Japs. But I come from a conquered people myself, and sometimes I just can't help sympathizing with these folks."

Even if you had spent the previous two or three years in the jungles of the South Pacific helping roll back the tide of Japanese aggression, it was hard not to feel that way in the Japan of late 1945. With the solitary exception of the ancient capital of Kyoto, which had been spared on cultural grounds, every major Japanese city had been mercilessly pounded by American bombers. In that process, 40 percent of all Japan's urban buildings had been destroyed, and nearly 700,000 Japanese civilians (out of a total population of 72 million) had perished. And that was only part of the toll. Three months after the war was over, I encountered in a village north of Tokyo a sad, straggling little funeral procession whose members carried much-enlarged photographs of a plump, rather bewildered-looking young man—one of the last of the more than 1.3 million Japanese soldiers, sailors and airmen killed during World War II.

The arrival of the U.S. occupation forces put a merciful end to the bombings and the casualties, but it by no means marked the end of Japan's travail. For all practical purposes, the Japanese economy was at a standstill. Such factories as remained more or less intact stood idle for want of raw materials. Fuel of any kind was so scarce that the few taxis still running operated on the gases generated by unwieldy charcoal burners mounted on their tails. Public buildings went unheated, and as the first bitter postwar winter set in, a Japanese family counted itself fortunate if its members were able to huddle around a small, barely glowing charcoal brazier.

Most terrible of all was the hunger. Food was so short that American G.I.s could—and did—buy anything from cherished family heirlooms to a woman for a few boxes of K rations or a couple of cartons of cigarettes. An acquaintance of mine, now the chairman of a major Japanese manufacturing company, recalls that once during that winter he was unable to find any food at all for himself or his family for a solid week. A big man for a Japanese, he had weighed nearly 190 pounds at the time of Pearl Harbor; by the fall of 1945, he was down to 105 pounds.

Thus weakened, the people of Japan became unnaturally vulnerable to disease, but for those who fell ill there was scant help available. Once, while driving through a rural area sixty or seventy miles from Tokyo, I encountered an American counterintelligence captain who was pursuing some mysterious investigation there. Shortly before, he told me, cholera had broken out in the district—at which point it developed that the local authorities had no medical supplies with which to treat the victims or inoculate their families and neighbors. Only through the intervention of the American CIC officer who managed by highly illicit means to "requisition" vaccine from a U.S. Army medical unit was the epidemic finally checked.

Living amid the ruins of what had clearly been, even before the war, a far poorer and less technologically advanced country than the United States induced in most of the American G.I.s I knew a universal reaction. Over and over again, I remember hearing members of the Occupation forces ask incredulously: "What in Christ's name ever made these people think they could take on the United States?" And no American I know of who served in the Occupation imagined for a moment that Japan would ever again pose any kind of challenge to the United States. Instead, the general view was that expressed by Lindesay Parrott in an article he published in the Sunday *New York Times Magazine* in late 1945. The economy of Japan, Parrott wrote, was not ever "likely to expand sharply. . . . The prospect is for a return to Japan's status as a small, self-contained nation."

I conjure up these memories of the stricken Japan of 1945 because I believe they are essential to an understanding of the 118 million people who make up today's Japan. In my own case, what I experienced in the ruins of Tokyo inspired a lifelong fascination with things Japanese. When, in 1946, I was abruptly demoted from an officer and an adult to a junior at Yale College, I abandoned my prewar major in English Literature to take a degree in Oriental Studies. And ever since, Japan has been an integral part of my existence. I returned there for a second tour of Army duty during the Korean War and from the mid-1960s on have visited the country almost annually, blessed on most of these occasions with the special access accorded a representative of an influential American publication. In a certain sense, I can claim, to borrow Dean Acheson's phrase, to have been present at the creation of contemporary Japan—a small, inherently unpromising country which today, improbably enough, stands shoulder to shoulder with the United States as one of the two dominant economic powers in the non-Communist world.

Yet so overwhelming is the bustling reality of today's Japan that I sometimes find it hard to recall the physically and psychically shattered nation of 1945. And if that gap is hard for me to bridge, I very much doubt that anyone who did not see Japan at its postwar nadir can fully comprehend the magnitude of what the Japanese people have accomplished since then. Many Japanese, in fact, will argue that this is true even of their own young people—that no one born in Japan since the mid-'50s really appreciates the herculean efforts involved in transforming a clutch of mountainous islands with no significant natural resources into the world's second-greatest power in the space of thirty-five years.

If even young Japanese can be charged with failing to comprehend the forces that have propelled their society to its present heights, it is surely understandable that most Americans do not comprehend them either. But even an understandable weakness is nonetheless a weakness. And there is, in my view, great danger in the prevailing American ignorance of Japan and the true nature of its accomplishments.

Paradoxically perhaps, this danger does not stem from any lack of scholarly expertise on Japan in this country. Since World War II there has emerged in the United States a very substantial body of Japanese linguists and perceptive specialists on everything from Japanese films to Japanese economic history. But with a few notable exceptions, the specialists have not played a key role in shaping Japanese–American relations. When their expertise has been made available to industrial and political decision makers, it has frequently been brushed aside. And more often than not, the decision makers have plunged ahead without expert advice and in something approaching total ignorance of Japan and its people.

What is particularly worrisome about the general misunderstanding of Japan by our decision makers—and by the great majority of ordinary Americans as well—is that it is different both in nature and in its potential consequences from the ignorance we often display of European, Latin American, African or Middle Eastern countries. A Lyndon Johnson, a Jimmy Carter or a Ronald Reagan may speak no language other than English and have only the most superficial knowledge of the economic and political problems of any country outside the United States. Nonetheless, as far as most of the world goes, Americans cope as well as can reasonably be expected. In greater or lesser degree, the thought processes of Germans, Russians, Saudis or Nigerians resemble our own sufficiently closely that when we put our minds to it we can usually deal with them, commercially and diplomatically, with a reasonable degree of sophistication.

Between Americans and Japanese, however, the gulf is both wider and deeper. Except for the little-heeded minority who make Japan a lifetime study—and who sometimes do so out of romantic attachment to a vanished world that bears about as much relation to contemporary Japan as Elizabethan England does to Mrs. Thatcher's England—Americans have no idea how Japanese think and feel. Because we cannot conceive that they could be radically different from our own, we cannot duplicate the logical processes of the Japanese or grasp the value system that underlies Japanese behavior.

The fact is, however, that Japanese logic and Japanese values *do* differ radically from our own—and precisely because most of us decline to recognize this, we consistently blunder in our attempts to influence the way in which Japan and the Japanese behave. Nor are our blunders confined to the much-publicized economic competition between the two countries; they extend to cultural, political and social dealings as well.

Inevitably, the most flagrant American blunders in dealing with the Japanese are committed by people who not only lack knowledge of Japan but see no need to acquire any. Not long ago, an American who for many years represented a major U.S. media conglomerate in Tokyo told me the sad story of his own company's flounderings in Japan. At some point in the mid-'70s, his bosses back in the United States came up with the notion of entering into a joint venture with a leading Japanese publishing firm. When preliminary negotiations at long range failed to produce results, top executives of the U.S. firm decided—logically enough by American lights—to fly to Tokyo and make a direct approach to the president of the Japanese company they were wooing.

When he learned of this plan, my friend in Tokyo strongly urged that it be abandoned. No Japanese chief executive, he explained, would take a decision of such importance without first making sure that it had been thoroughly considered and accepted by everyone in his company from the middle management level up. What was more, my friend warned his bosses, any attempts to circumvent this process—which could occupy anything up to a couple of years—was almost sure to be counterproductive.

The response to this warning back at corporate headquarters in the United States was outright incredulity. With considerable impatience, the American company's top brass pointed out that good businessmen, no matter what their nationality, simply didn't operate in that fashion. So off the American executives went to Tokyo, where the president of the Japanese company welcomed them warmly, entertained them lavishly—and courteously declined to make any commitment. In the end, to the continuing mystification of the American executives, the deal never came off.

Variations on this error stud the whole history of Japanese–American relations, and often enough the damage amounts to something considerably more serious than simply the loss of a bit of corporate profit. At a seminar on U.S.–Japanese relations a few years ago, W. Michael Blumenthal, then Secretary of the Treasury, wryly noted that whenever he proposed a change in Japanese policy to Prime Minister Takeo Fukuda, he never got the definitive response he wanted. Instead, Fukuda would reply that the idea sounded interesting and that Blumenthal ought to try to sell it to the four Japanese cabinet officers primarily responsible for economic affairs. Unlike many Americans, Blumenthal was too sophisticated to jump to the conclusion that he was getting the runaround. Clearly, however, he did regard the collective decision-making process that is the essence of Japanese government as an almost insurmountable built-in stalling mechanism—which helps to explain why the Carter Administration which Blumenthal served had so little success in achieving any significant change in Japanese economic policies.

In a sense, the errors committed by Americans who have had little or no exposure to Japan and Japanese culture are forgivable. What is less forgivable is that even Americans who have had such exposure often betray an almost impervious incomprehension of the realities of Japanese life and psychology. A number of years ago, the then U.S. Ambassador to Tokyo, a career Foreign Service officer who had painstakingly acquired the requisite professional knowledge of the Japanese political scene, blandly assured me that if it weren't for Japanese trade restrictions, there would be an excellent market in Japan for large American refrigerators. I could only conclude that in all his years in Japan, the Ambassador had never laid eyes on an ordinary Japanese kitchen, which simply does not have room enough for a standard U.S. refrigerator.

An isolated incident, perhaps? Not at all. Some years later, I discussed with a subsequent U.S. Ambassador to Tokyo the inability of U.S. automakers to sell cars in Japan. Part of the trouble, I suggested, might stem from the attitude expressed by the chief executive officer of one of Detroit's Big Three, an outspoken man who had declared on one occasion that his company didn't "give a damn" about the Japanese market. What was more, I went on, since the Japanese, like the British, drive on the left, it might be helpful if U.S. auto companies equipped the models they sent to Japan with right-hand drive.

When I had finished, the Ambassador threw me a frosty glance which made it plain that he regarded me as some sort of traitor to my people. All the points I had raised, he declared, were simply Japanese-inspired obfuscation. The real villain of the piece, once again, was the Japanese Government's trade restrictions.

Though they would never admit it, both the ambassadors I have mentioned were indulging in the deplorably common American habit of blaming on the Japanese problems which in fact are largely of our own making. This, of course, is a common pattern of behavior in all human relationships: none of us likes to face up to our own shortcomings. But in the relationship between Japan and the United States, there is another factor at work as well: a deeply ingrained superiority complex which makes it hard for a great many Americans to concede that we could ever be in error or at fault in our dealings with the Japanese.

To some degree, this superiority complex clearly reflects plain, old-fashioned racism. The historic tendency of Caucasians to dismiss non-Caucasians as "lesser breeds without the law" was powerfully reinforced in the United States by the incessant drumfire of anti-Japanese propaganda to which Americans were exposed during World War II; and though they are dwindling in number, there are still people in this country who find it inconceivable that a nation of "little yellow men" could ever outstrip Americans in anything except duplicity. Less numerous but almost equally inconducive to a healthy Japanese–American relationship are the China-lovers—people like Henry Kissinger, who, shortly after his first visit to Peking, held forth at a Washington dinner party on how much more gratifying it was to deal with a subtle and sophisticated man like Chou En-lai than with "economic animals" like the leaders of Japan. Probably the most important source of American condescension toward Japan, however, is a less conscious emotion—the lingering remnants of a "Big Brother knows best" attitude engendered back in Occupation times when Americans quite literally ruled Japan.

It is, I believe, undeniable that the American occupation of Japan following World War II was one of the most successful such ventures in history. Far more richly endowed with enthusiasm and self-confidence than with political or economic expertise, the members of what the Japanese came to call *Ma shireibu* (MacArthur's head-quarters) nonetheless succeeded in the space of a few short years in radically reshaping Japanese society; from family life to corporate law, there was almost no aspect of Japanese life in which the "American samurai" did not decree sweeping changes. For the Japanese, most of whom assumed that American military superiority betokened moral and political superiority as well, this was in a sense a liberation—an externally imposed revolution that endowed them with a more equitable and dynamic society. But upon the United States itself the impact of the Occupation was much more ambiguous. Many of the predominantly youthful Occupationaries—I recall one twenty-three-year-old who was for a time the ideological watchdog of the Japanese film industry—went on to become pillars of the American establishment. And they carried with them a tutorial attitude toward the Japanese which I believe still insensibly pervades U.S. officialdom in most of its dealings with Japan.

Taken in combination with the traditional inclination of Americans to conceive of their society as a model for all others, the special blind spots in American thinking about Japan have had one supremely serious consequence: for years now, the Government of the United States has characteristically treated the Government of Japan with a mixture of arrogance and disregard. This pattern first reached full flower during the Nixon Administration, when Washington took a series of decisions that directly affected Japanese interests—among them de facto devaluation of the dollar and recognition of Communist China—without any consultation with Tokyo or even anything much in the way of prior notice to the Japanese. And from the days of the "Nixon shocks" on, each successive American administration has calmly assumed that whenever the interests of the United States and Japan seemed to diverge, it was up to the Japanese to give way and make all the concessions.

That, of course, is a standard enough initial bargaining position in any set of diplomatic negotiations. But some of the demands the United States has made upon Japan have been of a kind we would never consider making of any other great nation. Jimmy Carter, for example, saw nothing untoward in sending a mission to Tokyo to propose that in order to reduce its perennial trade surpluses, Japan should basically restructure its domestic economy.

While admittedly not in a class with Jonathan Swift's "modest proposal" that Ireland's famines could be ended if only Irish peasants would market their babies for the table, the Carter Administration's recommendations to Japan did have some of the same sweeping simplicity. The difference, of course, is that where Swift was being deliberately ridiculous, Jimmy Carter and his emissaries were deadly serious.

So far, the high-handed tone which American officialdom has consistently adopted toward Japan has not had any really catastrophic results. At bottom, this is because the Japanese, while fending off the most outrageous American demands, have repeatedly made concessions substantial enough to avert an ultimate test of wills. Contemporary Japanese–American relations strongly recall the manner in which the late Herman Hickman, a famed Yale football coach, dealt with Yale alumni. "Keep 'em sullen but not mutinous" was Hickman's rule—and that is precisely how the Japanese Government has handled the United States Government for nearly fifteen years now.

For two allies to deal with each other on this uneasy basis is clearly less than ideal. More disturbing yet, it is doubtful that this kind of relationship between Japan and the United States will prove to be workable indefinitely. If the economic frictions between the two countries continue to multiply—as they surely will without farsighted management on both sides—American frustration and anger are bound to mount. And if the concessions we demand of Japan become even more costly and painful than they have been in the past, Japanese rebelliousness will grow as well. Ultimately, these twin processes could undercut the current close relations between the two nations—and that would pose for the United States dangers too enormous to risk.

Unhappily, as I have suggested earlier, there are still a great many Americans who don't understand or accept the overriding import- ance of the Japanese alliance to our country. In the autumn of 1977, when the Carter Administration was engaged in almost daily denunciation of Japan for running a $9-billion trade surplus with the United States, Nobuhiko Ushiba, then Japanese Minister of State for External Economic Affairs, flew to Washington to try to defuse the situation. During that visit, Ushiba held a private meeting with some of the more influential members of the U.S. Senate and, as one of his aides confided to me bitterly a few weeks later, was stunned when they told him: "Remember, Mr. Minister, the United States doesn't need Japan, but you do need us."

Along with an embarrassing lack of elementary courtesy, that statement reflected inexcusable ignorance. Japan's dependence upon American military protection and upon access to American markets is so great and so obvious that it needs no spelling out. But the woes of Detroit and Pittsburgh notwithstanding, it should not be necessary either to spell out to anyone who sits in the United States Senate the extent to which America's economic well-being and inter- national security rest upon Japan.

Any United States Senator ought to know, for example, that year in and year out, Japan is the world's largest importer of American agricultural products—which are the products the United States exports most successfully nowadays. In a normal year, in fact, Japan buys better than 15 percent of all U.S. farm exports—more than twice as much as any other nation—and there is now more acreage in the United States devoted to producing food for Japan than there is in Japan itself.

Any U.S. Senator ought to know too that potentially Japan is a major market for American coal and oil. In fact, a very large part of the persistent American trade deficit with Japan could be wiped out at one stroke if Congress would repeal the foolish law that prohibits Alaskan oil producers from selling their crude in Japan, thereby obliging them to market much of it on the U.S. East Coast at prices substantially higher than it would cost to import an equivalent amount of Mexican or Venezuelan oil.

Direct trade between Japan and the United States, moreover, is only one facet of the two countries' inescapable economic interdependence. Perhaps even more important in the long run is the fact that as the possessors of the world's two most advanced economies, the United States and Japan are both threatened by a worldwide phenomenon which Fereydoon Hoveyda, a former Iranian Ambassador to the United Nations, has aptly christened "disorderly industrialization."

By disorderly industrialization, Hoveyda means the helter-skelter growth all around the globe of the capacity to produce manufactured goods—a process that has been particularly notable in recent years in the nations of the Third World. In their all-out drive for economic development, a number of nations that were economic primitives until relatively recently are now emerging as strong contenders for world markets for industrial products.

So far, this fact has not made itself felt very conspicuously in the United States, but in some other parts of the world it is highly visible. While traveling in the Middle East a couple of years ago, I was startled to find Korean cars jostling their way through the streets of Amman and Bahrein right alongside the Mercedes-Benzes, Fords and Toyotas. And in Tokyo a few months later, a salesman for a Japanese steel company gave a wry smile when I mentioned the bitterness U.S. steelmakers felt about being undersold in their own markets by Japanese competitors. "I can understand how they feel," he said. "We Japanese are beginning to feel the same way about Korean steel. There's still not too much of it being sold here, but it's the thin end of the wedge, and a few years from now it will be giving us—and you Americans—plenty of trouble."

Korea, of course, is only one of the new industrial powers, and more will inevitably emerge in the years to come. Already, in fields ranging from shipbuilding to the production of certain synthetic fibers, there exists on a global basis enough manufacturing plant to turn out far more goods than world markets can possibly absorb. And since the newer factories and lower labor costs of Third World producers often give them a competitive edge in these fields, it seems clear that neither the United States nor Japan can hope to retain indefinitely their onetime dominance in industries that depend on traditional, relatively unsophisticated technologies.

Most of the men who manage the Japanese economy—and a number of thoughtful Americans as well—believe that there is only one intelligent response to this challenge: both Japan and the United States must deemphasize some of their traditional industries and reorient their economies around highly sophisticated new technologies in which Third World nations cannot hope to make themselves competitive for a long time to come.

But such a course, assuming both countries actually chose to pursue it, could impose a whole new set of strains on Japanese–Aamerican relations. It would be likely, in fact, simply to transfer the field of economic combat from the auto and electronics industries to such areas as genetic engineering and advanced information systems. And because the transition to new and unfamiliar industrial patterns must inevitably create social and political tensions in both America and Japan, the two countries could as a result find themselves even more at loggerheads in the future than they have been in the past.

All this makes it imperative for Japan and America to achieve much closer cooperation in the economic sphere than they have ever had before. If they do not do so, the strains on the Japanese–American alliance could eventually become insupportable—and that would be catastrophic. For Mr. Ushiba's tormentors to the contrary notwithstanding, it is vital to American interests that the military ties between Japan and the United States endure.

That Japan plays a key role in our own national security will strike many Americans as a highly dubious proposition. For years now, successive American administrations have publicly complained that the Japanese are not pulling their weight in terms of defense spending. Barely six months after it took office, the Reagan

Administration faithfully observed this tradition by publishing a Defense Department study which pilloried Japan for ranking last or next to last among all U.S. allies "regardless which measure of military burden-sharing is used."

By repeatedly belaboring Japan in this fashion, Washington has helped make it an article of faith for many Americans that Japan's current prosperity rests heavily upon the fact that it is getting a "free ride" militarily. Inevitably, this prompts frustrated American businessmen and astigmatic editorial writers to demand indignantly from time to time why the United States should pour out its treasure to defend people who are unwilling to defend themselves.

The short answer to that question is that we have no other sensible choice. Without the air and naval bases that Japan affords us, our most advanced Pacific bases would be so far from the mainland of Asia as to make it close to impossible for us to offer any meaningful assistance to our Asian allies or any serious deterrent to our enemies in the region. More important yet is the fact that however weak they may be militarily, the Japanese ultimately hold the balance of power in Asia.

To test the truth of this statement, all that is necessary is to turn the present state of affairs in East Asia on its head. Suppose that instead of being allied with the United States, Japan with its immense industrial and technological power chose to strike up an alliance with Russia—or, more likely, with an anti-American regime in Peking. At that point, the American voice in Asian affairs would dwindle to a mere whisper, and the potential threat to the security of the United States would become almost too fearsome to contemplate.

The conventional wisdom among American policymakers is that there is no realistic danger that the Japanese will ever decide to leave the shelter of the U.S. nuclear umbrella. And it is perfectly true that a change of alliances or even a shift to neutralism would involve radical and highly painful changes in Japan's economic and political life. Japan's high level of prosperity and its enviably low unemployment rate, not to speak of the democratic government and open society Japanese currently enjoy, would surely be among the probable casualties of such a step.

By American standards, all this would seem to make any major change in Japan's present international posture logically inconceivable. But by Japanese lights things aren't that simple. Historically, the Japanese have shown themselves to be an extremely volatile and highly adaptable people. Twice in little more than a century they have totally transformed their society. In 1853, when Commodore Matthew Perry and the "black ships" of the U.S. Navy forced the Japanese to open their country to foreigners, Japan was a kind of fly in amber—the world's last surviving feudal society of any consequence. Japanese feudalism was, admittedly, of a rather special variety: the country's great feudal magnates were kept on a very tight leash by a centralized military bureaucracy in Tokyo ruling in the name of the shogun, or generalissimo of the imperial armies—who, in turn, theoretically derived his authority from a shadowy emperor safely tucked away in impotent obscurity in Kyoto. But for all its complex governmental structure, the Japan of the mid-nineteenth century undeniably remained a premodern state, economically, politically and socially.

With the shock of exposure to the outside world, however, it rapidly became apparent to the Japanese that they had only two choices: either to create a modern industrial state or to fall prey to Western imperialism as most other Asian nations had. Characteristically, the Japanese chose to transform themselves, and with the overthrow of the last shogun and the "restoration" of the Emperor Meiji in 1868–69, Japan embarked on a pell-mell drive to emulate the great imperial powers of Europe in every possible respect. In this consuming national effort, the behavior patterns of centuries were ruthlessly cast aside in favor of "Westernization," and by the beginning of this century Japan had achieved sufficient industrial and military might to inflict a stunning defeat upon the forces of the Russian Empire and become a significant element in the world power game in its own right.

But because it had been so hastily constructed and rested upon so limited an economic base, the new Japanese polity was shallow-rooted. In the 1930s, the ravages of the Great Depression, together with the social, political and psychic strains created by the frantic pace of Westernization, brought to a halt Japan's progress toward meaningful parliamentary government. Instead, all power fell into the hands of a military oligarchy, which, in its parochial self-assurance, proceeded to lead the country down the path that led to Pearl Harbor. Yet when, at Hiroshima and Nagasaki, the folly of that course became, quite literally, blindingly apparent, the Japanese wasted little time on regrets; instead, they did another 180-degree turn and embraced democratic capitalism no less abruptly and no less wholeheartedly than they had previously embraced imperialism.

Given that track record, it would be folly to assume that another radical transformation of Japanese society is a total impossibility—

particularly under the kind of outside impetus that a breach with the United States would provide. And there is an important aspect of the Japanese character that makes such a turnabout even less of an impossibility. Contrary to the impression most Westerners have of them—and contrary to the impression that they seek to give the world—the Japanese are not a stolid, unemotional people. They are, in fact, exactly the opposite. "You always have to remember," a Japanese editor once told me in an attempt to explain why he opposed strong military forces for Japan, "that we Japanese are hysterics."

That, of course, was overstatement in the heat of argument. But there is undeniably a traditional highly emotional Japanese response to a continuing pattern of slights and injuries. That response is to bear one's grievances quietly, even courteously, for a prolonged period of time—and then to explode in a frenzy of destructive rage with no heed for consequences.

Obviously, what I have been drawing here is a worst-case scenario. The Japanese are not yet at the explosive state in their relations with the United States; they aren't even, I believe, very close to that stage. But for too long now, the drift of Japanese–American relations has been in the wrong direction. Over and over again, unnecessary tensions have been created—some by careless acts of omission such as the Nixon Administration's failure to help Japan cope with its total dependence on imported crude during the oil crisis of 1973, others by equally careless acts of commission such as Jimmy Carter's sabotage of Japan's nuclear energy program by his attempt to enforce a worldwide ban on breeder reactors. Even the most pro-American Japanese, in short, now have a mental list of grievances against the United States—grievances which Japanese leaders forbear to recite publicly but which continue to fester away somewhere in the national consciousness.

In America's own interest, this drift must be reversed—and it cannot be reversed simply by occasional ritual proclamations of affection for Japan on the part of Presidents and Secretaries of State. It will be reversed only if the people who make American policy can be brought to recognize just how the Japanese differ from us, that it is important to treat those differences respectfully and that it is not only possible but necessary to turn them to our own advantage in dealing with the Japanese.

Invoking the national interest as a justification for any particular course of action is always a chancy business; what one person sees as a patriotic obligation may strike another as rampant imperialism—or simply irrelevant pomposity. Not long ago when I was discussing Japan with a highly successful American businessman, he finally said impatiently: "Listen, I don't know much about the strategic importance of Japan to the U.S., and to tell you the God's honest truth, I don't care that much about it. What I do know is that in my industry the Japanese are coming on like gangbusters and I either have to lick 'em or join 'em—or maybe a little bit of both."

For a rapidly mounting number of Americans, in other words, there is the most compelling reason of all to acquire greater understanding of Japan: self-interest.

In the years since World War II, Japan and the United States have become perhaps the world's oddest couple—totally dissimilar in their ethnic and cultural heritages, yet deeply involved with each other in ways both obvious and not so obvious. Even the most casual visitor to Tokyo cannot fail to be struck by the degree to which the superficial aspects of Japanese life have been Americanized. The young people strolling through Tokyo's entertainment districts of an evening affect the same uniform as their contemporaries in the United States; if designer jeans, down vests and peasant skirts are "in" in SoHo, they're "in" in Shinjuku too. When these children of what a popular Japanese novelist has labeled "the crystal mood" of comfort and affluence feel like a snack, they are apt to do the same thing young Americans do: drop in at McDonald's or Kentucky Fried Chicken. (Many of the latter chain's Tokyo outlets boast life-size statues of the late Colonel Sanders, and at Christmastime—which is widely observed in predominantly non-Christian Japan—these are decked out in Santa Claus suits.) When they want a drink, young Tokyoites are much more likely to order beer or whiskey than sake; sake consumption in Japan, in fact, has fallen by nearly 25 per cent since 1973. And in the mornings, the broad avenues around the Imperial Palace are just as thickly infested with joggers as the sidewalk alongside Manhattan's F.D.R. Drive.

But Japan's conscious imitation of the United States is by no means confined to consumer fads and pop culture. These, in fact, are merely the most visible manifestations of a process which extends to some of the most basic aspects of Japanese society and the Japanese economy. While American businessmen search frantically for the unique Japanese secrets that will enable them to counter competition from Japan, Japanese businessmen accurately insist that most of what they know about modern managerial techniques they have learned from the United States. Even more important is the fact that Japanese democracy is essentially American-inspired. To oversimplify only slightly, it reflects a national judgment by the Japanese back in the late 1940s that since the awesome economic and military machine that crushed Japan in the Pacific War was the creation of a democratic society, democracy was clearly the only way to go.

At first, this postwar Japanese passion for everything American went almost totally unrequited. Whatever the Japanese were willing to take, the United States, secure in its economic and military preeminence, somewhat absentmindedly gave. And why not? The Japanese were, in effect, wards of the United States, and their imitativeness was flattering.

In essence, this attitude, mixed with occasional irritation, persisted into the '70s, even as one Japanese product after another—high-quality cameras, textiles, TV sets, motorcycles, calculators—made increasing inroads into the American market. Not until the Japanese challenge suddenly threatened Detroit, the ultimate citadel of Yankee know-how, did most Americans begin to perceive how powerfully our relationship with Japan could affect us. And by then the Japanese, a half-step ahead as always, had begun to build themselves a solid base in the domestic economy of the United States. As of mid-1981, Japanese interests controlled wholly or in part some 225 U.S. manufacturing companies, and nearly 10 percent of all U.S. exports were being shipped abroad by the American subsidiaries of Japan's giant trading companies. By that point too, nearly 90,000 Americans, ranging from production-line workers to heavy-hitting Washington lobbyists, were working directly for Japanese companies, and at least another quarter of a million indirectly owed their livelihoods to Japanese patrons.

Inevitably, this mounting economic interdependence has had its impact on the domestic life of the United States—an impact admittedly less conspicuous than the American influence on Japanese living habits, but significant nonetheless. An extraordinary number of the gadgets most favored by today's with-it Americans have been inflicted on us by the Japanese. Pac-Man, mini-tape recorders, video-cassette recorders and those handy-dandy earphones that enable growing throngs to stalk out cities vacant-eyed as they solace themselves with Mozart or Mick Jagger—all these originated in Japan, and even when manufactured in the United States are mostly made by Japanese-owned companies or under license from Japanese firms. Meantime, shrewdly capitalizing on the American passion for svelteness and the fad for "natural" food, Japanese entrepreneurs have converted their national cuisine into a growth industry in this country. In 1946 there was precisely one Japanese restaurant in New York City, and as recently as fifteen years ago there were only thirty; today there are well over two hundred, and the end is not in sight. And while it is still mainly the Beautiful People who find it chic to lunch on raw fish, such Japanese treats as instant noodles and teriyaki sauce now turn up right alongside the canned chicken chow mein on supermarket shelves.

Some people may argue that the Sony Walkman, the sushi craze and the fact that American galleries are selling Japanese prints and folk art in record numbers are minor and probably transient phenomena. But there is one aspect of the increasingly reciprocal nature of the Japanese–American relationship that no one can dismiss as unimportant: as a consequence of the Japanese economic challenge, more and more Americans are reexamining the operations of our own economic and social systems and, at least in some cases, altering their behavior as a result.

The most dramatic example of this has been furnished by Detroit—and there is considerably more to this story than just the fact that Japanese competition has driven American automakers to make a multibillion-dollar investment in "down-sizing" their own cars. In a display of humility that would have been inconceivable even a decade ago, the once-haughty titans of Detroit are openly drawing on Japanese know-how. The Plymouth station wagon that I bought in mid-1981 is powered by a Mitsubishi engine; in emulation of Nissan and Toyota, the major U.S. automakers are pushing the use of robots on their assembly lines; and in an attempt to match the vaunted reliability of Japanese cars, at least one Detroit auto plant has organized its workers into Japanese-style "quality-control circles." (This last device, ironically, is one that Japanese industrialists insist was originally conceived by American management theorists.)

What is happening in Detroit, however, is only the tip of the iceberg. Like sushi making, the study of Japanese managerial techniques has become a growth industry in the United States. Small fortunes are being made by authors and consultants who are prepared to instruct American business as to just what lessons it should learn from Japanese business—and the notion that Japan has things to teach us is by no means confined to the business sphere alone. Increasingly, sober commentators suggest that Americans could profitably study everything from Japanese methods of crime control to the unique nature and role of the Japanese bureaucracy.

The impulse behind all this is sound, and the growing American tendency to look at Japan with respect instead of indifference or condescension is surely healthy. But many of the remedies for America's malaise that have been prescribed ostensibly on the basis of Japanese experience are, in my view, misguided. And they are misguided for precisely the same reason that so many of our past judgments about Japan have been misguided: they are based on only superficial knowledge of the Japanese and their society.

In the complex interaction between Japan and the United States over the past thirty-five years, it is clearly the Japanese who have profited more—and they have done so essentially because so many of them have observed the United States in such minute detail. At times, indeed, the dogged manner in which Japanese scholars, journalists and businessmen pursue even the most trivial piece of information about American life borders on the absurd. Some years ago, a young Japanese businessman who was studying English in a class taught by my wife interrupted her disquisition on past participles to inquire whether she wore underwear. When her initial indignation subsided, it dawned on my wife that the young man, who worked for a major Japanese textile firm, was simply conducting a little on-the-spot market research. Americans to whom I have told this story invariably find it funny or a bit pathetic. What most of them overlook is that it is tireless investigation of the tastes, habits and needs of American consumers—generally conducted, to be sure, on a considerably more scientific basis—that has so often enabled Japanese industry to outcompete American companies in their own market.

Similarly, both Japanese industry and the Japanese Government have developed a certain number of men who have made it their business to learn exactly where the levers of power lie in the American economic and political establishments—and how to manipulate those levers. One such Japanese, a man I have known for a number of years, is on first-name terms with the governors of at least half a dozen U.S. states. "They all hope my company will invest in their state," he explains with a small smile.

More important yet, my friend regularly has breakfast or drinks with the key members of the various Congressional committees whose operations affect his firm's interests. His knowledge of the motives, mind-sets and aspirations of top U.S. politicians comes close to being encyclopedic, and whenever I see him he regales me with unpublicized but unfailingly accurate information about what is going on in the arcane recesses of the U.S. Government.

There are, in short, a considerable number of Japanese who know pretty clearly what makes America tick, and Japanese institutions, public and private, have made shrewd use of that knowledge in their dealings with the United States. Unhappily, however, I know of no American businessman who has the same kind of access to political circles in Tokyo that my Japanese friend enjoys in Washington. If the United States is to begin holding its own vis-à-vis Japan—if, to put it in the most basic terms, Americans are to profit more from their dealings with Japanese—a great many more of us must come to understand what makes Japan tick. Given the diffuse way in which power is exercised in the United States, it simply will not do for such understanding to be confined to a relatively small corps of scholars and specialists; it must become part of the mental furniture of as many as possible of the nonscholarly Americans who, on a day-to-day basis, conduct our business with Japan.

2

The Heart and Mind of Japan

One noontime a few years ago, I had a luncheon date in Tokyo with a Japanese Government official who in all visible respects was extraordinarily Westernized. Unlike most Japanese bureaucrats, who are clean-shaven and sober-suited, he sported a beard and was turned out in a Harris tweed jacket and gray flannel trousers—souvenirs, apparently, of his several years of residence in Britain. When I began to question him about his field of expertise, which happened to be Japan's nuclear energy program, his answers not only were delivered in impeccably idiomatic English but were remarkably frank and explicit.

Suddenly, on an impulse, I interrupted him to ask: "Otasan, could you possibly talk with another Japanese on the same terms on which we are talking?"

"Certainly not," he answered with no hesitation. "Whenever I begin to speak with a Westerner, I first have to shift mental gears, so to speak. Then, if I find myself talking with Japanese again, I have to be careful to shift back into my Japanese gear. Otherwise, they will probably disregard what I have to say—and may even be irritated by it."

Mr. Ota's point was that certain aspects of Japanese thought and of the Japanese character are so different from Western thought and mores that even a person highly familiar with both cultures must make a conscious effort to bridge the gap. And contrary to what many Americans assume, these differences are not confined to relatively peripheral matters of style and social manners; they are so fundamental and make themselves felt in so many facets of Japanese behavior that without an awareness of them it is impossible to figure out why a Japanese conducts himself as he does in any particular situation. So the first necessity for anyone who wishes to understand Japan is to establish an overall framework that will help to make sense of the countless specific manifestations of Japan's "differentness."

The framework I have constructed for myself over the years involves seven basic propositions:

The Japanese language is so complex that it has been called "the Devil's language." Since the Japanese as a people distrust and shun straightforward verbal communication, this suits them just fine.

The logical place to begin any analysis of the Japanese mind is with the language in which Japanese think. They themselves sometimes refer to it as "the Devil's language"—a phrase apparently coined by Saint Francis Xavier, the great sixteenth-century Jesuit missionary to Japan—and few who have ever tried to learn Japanese will quarrel with that description.

To begin with, Japanese does not have the kind of close kinship with any other language that English has with German or Spanish with French. Philologists generally believe that Japanese belongs to the Altaic family of languages—a group that includes Korean, Mongolian, Turkish and, in more remote fashion, probably Hungarian and Finnish as well. But even with these somewhat esoteric tongues, Japanese does not have a relationship close enough to be of much practical value to the ordinary Turk, Finn or Japanese. When a foreigner sets out to learn Japanese, there is little useful carry-over from his own language, whatever it may be. And the same is true in reverse for the Japanese.

More troublesome yet, present-day Japanese is essentially the offspring of a highly unsuitable marriage between the original unwritten Japanese language of fifteen centuries ago and archaic Chinese. What made this marriage so unfortunate is that grammatically and in other important respects, Chinese and Japanese are utterly dissimilar. Roughly speaking, the blending of them that has occurred in Japan is comparable to the result you might get if you decided to write English in Arabic script and to create compound words in spoken English by jamming together three or four syllables from medieval Arabic.

Irrational as all this sounds—and is—spoken Japanese has absorbed the Chinese infusion reasonably successfully. In fact, the most difficult aspect of spoken Japanese for foreigners to master is not borrowed from Chinese but reflects a distinctively Japanese phenomenon: an obsession with comparative status in all personal relationships. Confusingly, verb forms in Japanese—and even basic verb stems—alter sharply depending upon the speaker's hierarchical relationship to the person being spoken to. Thus, a man who wants to ask his younger brother or a subordinate whether he has already gone somewhere will say: "*Mo itta ka?*" But if he wishes to ask his boss the same question, he will employ totally different words: "*Mo oide ni naremashita ka?*"

These honorific usages are not the only thing about spoken Japanese that requires considerable adjustment on the part of the fledgling American student of the language: the equivalent of prepositions in Japanese follows the noun they modify instead of preceding it, and verbs, which come at the very end of a sentence in the German fashion, are inflected by the attachment of a seemingly infinite variety of added syllables to the stem. But in general, Japanese grammar, once you have mastered its principles, is reasonably straightforward, and the pronunciation of the language is simple, closely resembling Italian in vowel sounds. (The fact that both "l" and "v" are missing from the list of Japanese consonants, however, creates a problem for Japanese in learning other languages, and in attempting to cope with that problem, they sometimes over-compensate: on one occasion a Japanese friend who was trying to convince me that a recent government announcement had been made only for public relations purposes impatiently declared: "Believe me, Bob, that was just a piece of P.L.")

All in all, then, spoken Japanese is not an unduly complex or difficult language. But written Japanese is an entirely different kettle of fish. It is, in fact, quite certainly the most difficult system of written communication in general use in the contemporary world.

Since the sixth century, when they first began to feel a need for a written language and turned to Chinese to meet that need, the Japanese have borrowed thousands upon thousands of Chinese pictographs, or *kanji*, each of which stands for a different object or concept. The most extensive Japanese dictionary lists nearly 50,000 different characters, some consisting of more than forty separate brushstrokes. In practice, however, the great majority of these are rarely if ever used. Since 1946, in fact, youngsters completing Japan's nine years of compulsory education have been required to learn "only" 1,850 characters, and with that number it is possible to make your way through a Japanese newspaper—though not through a college textbook on economics or most serious works of literature.

Even the minimal task of memorizing 1,850 different *kanji*, however, requires enormous initial effort and constant subsequent reinforcement. A well-educated Japanese woman who has lived for some years in the United States confessed to me recently that because she has not continued to read extensively in Japanese, she has forgotten hundreds of *kanji* she once knew. And there is more to forget than just the physical appearance of a particular *kanji*: for each new character learned, a Japanese must also learn multiple pronunciations, one or more of them drawn from Chinese and the rest consisting of native Japanese words similar in meaning to the original Chinese pictograph but quite different from it—and from each other—in sound.

If this sounds daunting, it is. And the final outrage is that it isn't even possible to write Japanese in *kanji* alone. To handle the inflections and connectives that exist in Japanese but not in Chinese and to cope with such things as foreign words and place names, written Japanese employs two different phonetic alphabets, each consisting of forty-eight symbols and two diacritical marks.

When first confronted with this witches' brew, the innocent foreigner almost invariably asks why the Japanese don't just scrap *kanji* in favor of the Latin alphabet—or *romaji*, as the Japanese call it. But although a great many Japanese as well as Westerners have proposed exactly that over the last century or so, it isn't going to happen any time soon and probably won't ever happen.

Some of the reasons a shift to *romaji* isn't in the cards are essentially illogical. These include the sheer aesthetic appeal of *kanji*, the huge investment of time and energy that educated Japanese have made in learning the present system and the fact that precisely because foreigners find it so hard to master, that system feeds the cherished Japanese sense of belonging to a unique and impenetrable culture.

But there is at least one practical objection to writing Japanese in the Latin alphabet—which is that Japanese has fewer sounds than any other major language and therefore has to ascribe a lot of meanings to the few it does have. If you look up the sound *ki* in a Japanese-English dictionary written in *romaji*, for example, you find that it has a score of different meanings ranging from "a tree" to "undiluted." And even two or more sounds used in combination can be tricky; I've always been particularly enchanted by the word *seikan*, which can mean, among other things, sexual feeling, naval construction, can manufacturing or serene contemplation.

The upshot of all this is that when one uses a particular sound or set of sounds in conversation, it may or may not be clear from the context what meaning was intended. When it isn't clear, the only way to make it so is to indicate to the person with whom you are speaking the *kanji* that represent the particular meaning you want to convey. One method of doing this is by sketching the characters in question on the palm of your left hand with the index finger of your right hand—a habit so ingrained in some Japanese that they occasionally fall into it even when the person they are talking to is on the other end of a telephone line.

If the Japanese were to decide to abandon *kanji,* in short, they would also have to abandon the use of many words whose meaning can't be made clear by sound alone. And unless those words were somehow replaced by new words with the identical meaning, their loss would make it impossible to read the great works of Japanese literature and history in even a remote approximation of their original form—which would deprive future Japanese of much of their cultural heritage. Inevitably, too, the loss of so many words would render Japanese an even less precise language than it now is—and perhaps the most serious of the many criticisms that can be made of the Japanese language is that it is already excessively vague and imprecise.

Even Japanese themselves frequently complain of this and ascribe all sorts of unfortunate consequences to it. An eminent lawyer, Takeyoshi Kawashima, argues, for example, that written law in Japan is too easily manipulated—and even essentially changed—by individual judges simply because Japanese words "do not in general have meanings that are clear and limited." Similarly, the late Hideki Yukawa, a Nobel Laureate in physics, admitted that whenever he did scientific work he thought in English because he could think things in English that it was impossible for him to think in Japanese.

To be fair, there are also highly knowledgeable people who reject out of hand the notion that Japanese is an inherently vague language; the most distinguished of contemporary American Japanologists, former Ambassador to Tokyo Edwin O. Reischauer, staunchly insists that there is nothing about Japanese that prevents clear, concise and logical presentation of ideas "if that is what one wishes to make." But the catch there is in Dr. Reischauer's final clause: the great majority of Japanese simply do not wish to speak in clear, concise and logical fashion. In their conversations with each other—and more often than not in their conversations with foreigners—Japanese religiously shun explicit, carefully reasoned statements in favor of indirect and ambiguous ones basically designed not to communicate ideas but to feel out the other person's mood and attitudes. As the Japanese see it, plain speaking has one overwhelming drawback: it tends to commit the speaker to a hard-and-fast position, and thus can easily provoke direct confront-ation—which all Japanese dread. Accordingly, straight talk disturbs the typical Japanese—so much so that in a scholarly paper that he did on this phenomenon, Masao Kunihiro, a Harvard-trained cultural anthropologist, included a footnote confessing that even to write about it openly made him uncomfortable.

At bottom, in fact, Japanese prefer whenever possible to avoid verbal communication entirely. Their language abounds in proverbs such as "Words are the root of all evil," and among themselves they rely to a remarkable degree on something called *haragei*—which can be translated as "visceral communication" or, less elegantly, as "belly language."

The essence of *haragei* is that because of the racial homogeneity and almost identical social and cultural conditioning of the Japanese people, it is often possible for one Japanese to determine the reaction of another to a particular situation simply by observing the second man's facial expressions, the length and timing of his silences and the ostensibly meaningless grunts he emits from time to time. Among Japanese of the same generation and occupation, this process can become so sophisticated that words are expended only on court-esies and badinage, and the art of direct verbal communication almost atrophies.

Just how addictive *haragei* can be was fully driven home to me a few years ago when a friend of mine, an American journalist long resident in Tokyo, reported on an interview he had just had with one of the elder statesmen of Japan's ruling Liberal Democratic Party. Toward the end of the conversation, my friend asked how many months the politician thought it would be until the then Prime Minister of Japan would be forced to resign. For his own reasons, the politician apparently wanted my friend to have the right answer to that question and to publish it. But that posed a problem: the old man clearly felt that with a foreigner, even a knowledgeable foreigner, he could not rely on *haragei*, and yet a lifetime of habit prevented him from giving the answer straight out. In the end, what he did was mutter repeatedly *"Muzukashii ne"* ("A difficult question"), meanwhile using his forefinger to trace very conspicu-ously on his desktop the number 7.

This, admittedly, was an extreme case. But the seeming inability of many Japanese to give a straight answer to a straight question is a perennial source of frustration to foreigners. If you wish to communicate successfully with Japanese, however, that kind of reaction is self-defeating. The things to cultivate are patience, persistence, a knack for indirection, an ear for nuance—and a sharp eye for the occasional moving finger.

Racially and culturally, Japan is the most homogeneous of the world's major nations—which is a prime reason Japanese have been able to Westernize their society yet still preserve a keen sense of their own special identity.

The notion that Japanese can read one another's minds—or at least, faces—simply because they share a common background may at first blush seem improbable. But that is only because outsiders commonly fail to appreciate what a truly extraordinary degree of ethnic and cultural homogeneity prevails in Japan. To say that Japan is not an avowedly pluralistic society like the United States or Switzerland is to understate the case to the point of absurdity. By comparison with Japan, even nations such as Italy or Germany that Americans normally think of as homogeneous are hotbeds of ethnic, cultural and linguistic diversity.

Simply from observing the highly varied facial types in contemporary Japan—there are occasional Japanese who could pass for southern Europeans and many who could be Malay or Polynesian—it is clear that a number of different peoples contributed genes to the present-day population of Japan. The bulk of the progenitors of the modern Japanese were Mongoloid peoples who apparently came to the islands from northeast Asia by way of Korea. But judging from the nature of a number of Japanese institutions, there presumably was some influx from south China and other parts of southern Asia as well. And over the centuries these immigrants intermingled with and almost totally absorbed the original inhabitants of the Japanese islands—a proto-Caucasian race known as the Ainu.

All that, however, took place a very long time ago. Not since the eighth century A.D. has there been any major new element injected into the Japanese gene pool—which means that for more than a thousand years a great ethnic blender has been whipping the originally diverse components of the Japanese race into a single uniform substance.

Probably even more important than the ethnic unity of the Japanese, however, is the fact that until quite recent times Japanese society and culture developed in comparative isolation. This is by no means to say that the Japanese nation somehow emerged from a vacuum, uninfluenced by external forces. Its system of writing is only a part of the enormous cultural debt Japan owes China—a country which in the most formative period of Japanese history unquestionably possessed the most advanced civilization in the world. As early as the sixth century, when Japan still consisted of a clutch of semiautonomous tribes under the hegemony of the ruling family of Yamato, a plain east of modern-day Osaka, a remarkable statesman named Prince Shotoku sent embassies to China to study the glories of Chinese culture. And from then until the ninth century, the Japanese in a conscious orgy of self-improvement tirelessly imported Chinese arts, technology, scholarship and social and political institutions. In everything from the site plan of the first Japanese capital at Nara to the concept of the emperor as standing at the apex of both religious and political life, the Japanese of those early centuries almost slavishly followed Chinese models.

Of all the Japanese importations from China, the most enduring in their influence were spiritual and intellectual. The native Japanese religion, which eventually came to be called Shinto, or "the way of the gods," was a brand of animism centering around the worship of natural phenomena and mythological ancestors such as the sun goddess Amaterasu Omikami, the alleged progenitress of the Imperial Family. Lacking any real ethical system or meaningful concept of an afterlife, it was a folk faith whose essentially primitive nature is suggested by the fact that its word for a god—*kami*—basically means simply "up."

Shinto, in short, was inadequate to meet the spiritual needs of the increasingly sophisticated society that Prince Shotoku and his successors created in Japan. That void was filled by the arrival from China of Buddhism, with its concern for individual salvation and its complex philosophical overtones. Carrying with it dynamic impact on architecture, the arts and literature, Buddhism in its manifold forms rapidly became the dominant faith in Japan. From the ninth century on, it pervaded the intellectual and political life of the country much as Christianity did in medieval Europe.

In the end, though, Buddhism in Japan suffered much the same fate that Christianity has in Europe. Partly for political reasons and partly because, in my view, the Japanese are not inherently a mystical people, it began to wane in strength as early as the sixteenth century. In a sense, its place was taken by another gift from China: Confucianism. Essentially an ethical system rather than a religious

faith, Confucianism, with its emphasis on loyalty, personal relationships and etiquette and with the high value that it places on education and hard work, is ideally suited to the pragmatic Japanese
character. Few if any Japanese today would describe themselves as
Confucian, but Confucian values still permeate the thinking of virtually the entire Japanese population. Here, as in many other things,
late-twentieth-century Japanese are still very much the heirs of
ancient China.

To put that fact in its proper perspective, however, it is vital to
bear in mind that most of Japan's borrowings from China were
conducted at arm's length—and all of them were entirely voluntary.
Thanks to Japan's island location and its relative remoteness from
most of the major power centers of the premodern world, the
country was not an inviting target for invaders. Indeed, until the
arrival of the American occupation forces in 1945, the only time
Japan had been seriously threatened by a major foreign incursion
was in 1281, when Kublai Khan tried to make a landing, only to
have his fleet driven off by what Japanese immortalized as
kamikaze—the divine wind. In short, unlike most other major
nations in today's world, Japan throughout most of its long history
escaped having alien institutions and cultures imposed on it by
force.

It would be selling the Japanese short to suggest that this was
purely a result of Japan's geographic location. There was also a
strong dose of xenophobia and cultural self-defensiveness involved.
By the late sixteenth century, less than a hundred years after the
first Portuguese missionaries reached Japan, some 300,000 Japanese
had been converted to Catholicism—which, as a percentage of the
total population, made them far more numerous than Christians are
in today's Japan. Potentially at least, this constituted an entering
wedge for Western colonialism, and in the early seventeenth
century, Japan's rulers, who were keenly conscious of this threat,
responded to it in draconian fashion. Thousands of Christians were
martyred or massacred, nearly all those who weren't killed were
forced to recant and by 1638 Japan had been effectively sealed off
from the rest of the world. For nearly two hundred years thereafter,
no Japanese were legally permitted to go abroad, and the only
Europeans allowed to live in Japan were a handful of Dutch traders
confined to a small island in Nagasaki harbor.

This self-imposed isolation did not mean that Japan remained
totally ignorant of developments abroad. Even after 1638, the Dutch
trading post off Nagasaki served Japan as a kind of window on

the world. Somewhat improbably, Dutch became the language of Western learning in Japan, and through books brought in from Holland, Japanese scholars managed to keep at least partially abreast of scientific and intellectual progress in the West. As a result, when Japan finally did rejoin the world and was exposed to the full force of Westernization, it was in the fortunate position of possessing at least a small corps of men capable of handling Western technologies and concepts with some sophistication.

However misguided the motives for it, in fact, the seclusion in which Japan lived between 1638 and the arrival of Commodore Perry in 1853 gave the country an invaluable breathing spell. During these years, which are known as the Tokugawa Era, the increasing complexity of Japanese economic life sparked the emergence of an entrepreneurial class—which meant that the country's subsequent industrialization could be managed by Japanese rather than by foreigners. Even more important, it was under the highly centralized government of the Tokugawa shoguns that Japanese developed a strong national consciousness—a deep-seated awareness of and pride in their unique identity as a people.

None of this is to say that Westernization, when the Japanese finally embraced it, was a comfortable process. The breathtaking speed with which Japan set out to transform itself into a "modern" nation following the ouster of the last Tokugawa ruler in 1868 caused enormous social, economic and psychic disruptions—disruptions which, as I have suggested, ultimately contributed in indirect form to Japan's suicidal march into war with the United States. Nonetheless, because of the internal strengths they developed during their two centuries of isolation, the Japanese, unlike so many other Asian and African peoples, acquired a vital ability: instead of swallowing destabilizing and often unsuitable Western ideas and institutions whole, they were—and still are—remarkably successful in adapting importations from the West to their own needs and imperatives.

The way in which almost all things foreign are subtly transformed when they are absorbed into Japanese culture is not easy to generalize about, but some notion of how the process works can be found in the way in which the Japanese use some of the massive number of words they have borrowed from Western languages, above all English. One such word is *pinku* (pink), which has somewhat the same chic flavor in Japanese that use of the French word chartreuse for lime green has in English. Another word borrowed from English is *waishatsu* (white shirt), which Japanese adopted as their word for a Western-style shirt back in the days when nobody dreamed of wearing anything but a white shirt with a business suit. But in our degenerate age, a Japanese gentleman may decide that he wants a pink shirt for office wear—and if he does, he will ask the salesclerk for a *pinku waishatsu*.

To English-speakers, that phrase sounds utterly ridiculous, but in a Japanese context it is both logical and serviceable. And essentially the same kind of sea change occurs in far more complex Japanese borrowings from the West. In Britain, a Prime Minister with a ten-vote majority in the House of Commons feels free to ram his or her program through with total disregard for the most deeply held convictions of the opposition parties. But in Japan, whose parliamentary institutions are in theory very similar to Britain's, any sensible Prime Minister will go to extreme lengths to avoid such action. The reason: in the Japanese ethic it is abhorrent for anyone, even if he is legally entitled to do so, to brush aside the feelings of his opponents and decline to make at least token concessions to them.

Though Japanese rarely admit it, their society is an exclusionary one. The only way to win complete acceptance by Japanese is to be born into their tribe.

It is, then, a prolonged process of cultural as well as ethnic blending that has rendered Japan as homogeneous as it is today. But it would be misleading to imply—as Japanese sometimes do—that the great national blender has succeeded in removing all the lumps from Japanese society.

There is, to start with, the ugly fact that quite a lot of Japanese—probably more than two million—are hereditary outcasts. Originally called *Eta* (full of filth) and now known by the euphemism *Burakumin* (the people of the hamlets), these unfortunates are ethnically indistinguishable from other Japanese and in theory enjoy the same legal rights as their fellow citizens. But in fact, the majority of them live in the impoverished ghettos known as *buraku* and are the victims of systematic economic and social discrimination. Nobody is quite sure why: one theory is that they are descended in part from long-ago prisoners of war; another is that they earned obloquy by engaging in particularly grisly or un-Buddhist occupations such as butchering, leatherworking and gravedigging—all fields in which they still predominate. Whatever the reason, other Japanese shun contact with them as much as possible and carefully check the pedigrees of prospective sons-in-law or daughters-in-law to make sure that they do not carry the taint of *Burakumin* blood.

The other chief minority in Japan consists of "the Koreans." Currently, there are something over 600,000 Korean Japanese, the great majority of whom were born in Japan and a considerable number of whom are third-generation. They too are discriminated against, often on the strength of the same kind of racist stereotyping from which blacks and Chicanos in the United States suffer: uncouth, violent, prone to crime and the like.

All told, the *Burakumin*, the Koreans and such even smaller minorities as the Eurasians and people of Chinese birth or ancestry make up less than 3 percent of Japan's total population. To an American or even an Englishman, this would suggest that it should be relatively easy to assimilate them into the mainstream of Japanese life. But with some exceptions, that hasn't happened. The way most Japanese deal with "the *Burakumin* problem" is simply to decline to acknowledge that it exists. (It is a reasonable bet, for example, that when this book is translated into Japanese, this particular portion of it will be quietly omitted.) And when it comes to people born in Japan of Korean or Chinese parents, the solution is equally simple. At a cocktail party I once attended in New York, a Japanese businessman commented to me with what he clearly regarded as flattering astonishment on the impeccable Japanese spoken by our hostess, whom I shall call Miss Chen. Since Miss Chen had been born, brought up and largely educated in Japan, I should have found it strange if her Japanese had not been fluent, but not so for a Japanese: since her parents were Chinese, Miss Chen in Japanese eyes will remain automatically and forever an outlander.

In short, while it is possible—though not particularly easy—for a foreigner to acquire Japanese citizenship, it is not possible for an immigrant or the children of immigrants to "become Japanese" the way such people can "become American." The way you get to be Japanese is the same way you get to be Zulu or Shona in Africa: you have to be born into the tribe. For that is what the people of Japan—or at least more than 97 percent of them—really are: members of a single great tribe united not just by common citizenship or common language but by common bloodlines, common racial memory and common tribal codes, some of which stretch back into prehistory. The eminent Japanese industrialist who once told me "We Japanese are a hundred million brothers" wasn't boasting or indulging in some sort of intellectual conceit. He was just trying to help me understand what it means to be Japanese.

> *Far more than the citizens of most collectivized societies, Japanese are dominated by a sense of responsibility to the various groups to which they belong—their country, their company and so on. Paradoxically, this helps to account for their drive and efficiency.*

Along with the Japanese sense of tribal identity goes an acute awareness of the vulnerability of the tribe. To foreigners, Japan sometimes seems enviably strong—possessor of the world's most effectively functioning economy, master of the most advanced technologies and, potentially at least, a major military power. But to Japanese themselves their society seems constantly threatened with a staggering variety of catastrophes.

In its most basic form, the perennial Japanese conviction that there is almost certainly trouble around the corner probably was inspired by the typhoons and earthquakes that have been ravaging the Japanese islands for all of recorded history. And that conviction can scarcely have failed to be reinforced by the fact that it was the Japanese who in 1945 became the first—and so far only—people in the world to suffer atomic attack.

Whatever its origins, the strength of the Japanese vulnerability complex is undeniable. One of the most successful movies ever made in Japan—in box-office terms, at least—involves a situation in which the Japanese archipelago is being swallowed up by the sea and the other nations of the world show a marked disinclination to give refuge to any escapees from this disaster. It was not, I believe, just a taste for doomsday sci-fi that made Japanese stampede to see this piece of fantasy. Most Japanese moviegoers, I suspect, were half prepared to accept the idea that something like that really could happen to their country.

More important yet, there are disasters only slightly less mind-boggling than the physical disappearance of their islands that most Japanese actively fear. Because of Japan's almost total dependence on imported energy and the fact that it possesses so few of the other resources required by modern industry, Japanese never forget that any prolonged interruption of their imports—or for that matter, foreign rejection of the Japanese exports that pay for those imports—would thrust Japan back into an economic status roughly comparable to that of Yemen. Similarly, the small size of the Japanese islands and their proximity to such titans as China and the Soviet Union give the Japanese a sense of helplessness about their ability to withstand any major military assault, nuclear or conventional.

It can be argued that while all the dangers Japanese worry about really do exist, the odds are that none of them will materialize—or at least, not in truly catastrophic form. Nonetheless, the constraints these fears impose upon the Japanese national psyche are very real. And they serve, I believe, to reinforce other important aspects of the Japanese character: tribal values, Confucian ethics and a heavy emphasis on hierarchy and loyalty stemming from the fact that feudalism survived in Japan until little more than a century ago.

Between them, all these factors have produced a society in which the individual's responsibility to the group assumes a preeminence it does not have in any Occidental nation, not even in such avowedly collectivist ones as the Soviet Union. In Moscow, to cite a mundane example, service in restaurants and stores is slow, discourteous and inefficient because waiters and salesclerks see no personal advantage to be gained from performing their jobs well. In Tokyo, service is swift, efficient and courteous because waiters and salesclerks would be letting down the group to which they belong if they performed their jobs badly.

Americans, of course, tend to think of a preoccupation with the collective as a negative factor, something that inhibits initiative and delays progress. But Japan is living proof that this need not be so. As my friend Jiro Tokuyama of the Nomura School of Advanced Management once pointed out to me, there is an important difference between Lord Nelson's historic order of the day "England expects every man to do his duty" and the one that Japan's Admiral Heihachiro Togo handed down at the battle of Tsushima Strait in the Russo-Japanese War: "The future of our nation and our empire depends upon the performance of each one of you." Of the two exhortations, Togo's is clearly far more demanding, embodying as it does the principle that there is no limit to the duty an individual Japanese owes to the group. "It didn't happen on my watch" is simply not an excuse that cuts any ice in Japan. Both failure and success are team affairs in Japanese eyes, and every member of a team, regardless of the quality of his personal performance, must share in the onus or the glory earned by the team as a whole.

Japanese abhor direct personal confrontation and, to avoid it, almost always operate by consensus. Though often a handicap, this is also a source of strength.

Effective though it is as a spur to high performance, there's no denying that the sense of collective responsibility felt by Japanese does inhibit certain forms of individualism cherished in the West. Probably the single most important thing to know about Japanese is that they instinctively operate on the principle of group consensus.

For an individual to achieve self-gratification at the expense of the collective welfare is regarded as unspeakably reprehensible, and individual self-assertion in almost any form is rigorously discouraged. "The nail that sticks up gets pounded down," says one of the most famous of Japanese proverbs. So it does—with the result that only in very rare cases does an individual, however brilliant or charismatic, unilaterally make decisions for an entire group or organization. Under normal Japanese practice, before a group is committed to any new course of action, all its members—or at least, all those with any claim to competence in the matter—must have examined the proposal and acceded to it.

The manner in which such a consensus is achieved is known as *nemawashi*, or "root-binding"—a term taken from *bonsai* culture, in which, whenever a miniature tree is repotted, its roots are carefully pruned and positioned in such a way as to determine the tree's future shape. In the human context, *nemawashi* involves a cautious feeling-out of all the people legitimately concerned with an issue, a highly tentative process in which no firm stands are openly taken and argument is implicit rather than explicit.

From a Japanese point of view, the overriding advantage of this indirect approach is that it all but rules out the possibility of direct personal conflicts. The extent to which Japanese dread such conflicts is not always evident from the way in which they deal with Westerners; because they are intellectually aware that in the West confrontation is regarded as healthy and useful, a certain number of Japanese now try to accommodate this strange foreign taste. Their efforts to do so are often enough both forced and inept—an extreme case in point being a Japanese businessman of my acquaintance who, after a few years' residence in Texas, has seemingly concluded that any fruitful intercourse with Americans must begin with an exchange of insults. Such behavior, however, is highly misleading. No matter how they conduct themselves with foreigners, in their dealings among themselves Japanese all operate on the same premise: a resort to confrontation tactics automatically signifies that you have lost the game.

When they first learn of *nemawashi*, most Westerners instinctively dismiss it as an impossibly clumsy and ineffectual way to do business—and it can in truth be tedious and time-consuming. It also sometimes leaves Westerners confused as to who the key figures on the other side really are: in one set of negotiations between a European and a Japanese company with which I became involved, the Europeans never quite grasped the fact that their strongest ally in the Japanese company was about three notches down its executive totem pole and was floating trial balloons rather than making firm business propositions.

Still, for all its drawbacks, *nemawashi* has at least one great merit even by Western standards: by performing the function known to American businessmen as "getting everyone on board," it ensures that once a course of action has been agreed upon, it can be executed rapidly and with a minimum of the foot-dragging and intramural sniping that often impedes the progress of our own institutions.

> *Since their primary commitment is to the well-being of their tribe rather than to ideology or religion, Japanese find it easier than most peoples to accept change—and sometimes do so simply so that Westerners won't think them "backward."*

Paradoxical as it may sound, the supreme emphasis that Japanese place upon consensus and the great pains they take to achieve it also help give their institutions an extraordinary adaptability. In their heart of hearts, the Japanese people as a whole have only one absolutely immutable goal—which is to ensure the survival and maximum well-being of the tribe. Neither political ideologies nor formal religious creeds have the same absolute and unalterable grip upon most Japanese that they have on many Westerners. There are many institutions elsewhere in the world—established religions, collectivized economies, internal exile—which can accurately be described as "un-American" and which in the ultimate philosophic sense would remain un-American even if they were somehow imposed upon this country. But in the philosophic sense, it is not really possible to speak of an un-Japanese society: a truly Japanese society—like truly Japanese behavior—is whatever the Japanese consensus holds it to be at any given period.

This remarkable degree of flexibility clearly has its potential dangers. Nearly twenty years ago, when he was Undersecretary of State, George Ball enraged a number of old Japan hands by arguing against massive rearmament of Japan on the ground that "you never know when the Japanese will go ape." The statement was undeniably overdrawn and perhaps lacked some of Mr. Ball's customary felicity of expression, but it is nonetheless true that there is no nation whose social and political course over the long term is as chancy to predict as Japan's.

At the same time, it is also true that this flexibility has been one of the cornerstones of Japan's survival and economic success. It serves at least in part to explain the fact that the Japanese were able to adjust to the massive changes imposed upon their society by the U.S. Occupation without something approaching a national nervous breakdown. And certainly, it has contributed greatly to what we have already seen to be one of Japan's great strengths—the relative ease with which the Japanese absorb and adapt ideas, practices and technologies from abroad.

American bitterness over the fact that so many of Japan's economic triumphs have rested on research and development work done in the United States always baffles me somewhat: after all, we made the technology available, and from the Japanese point of view it would have been purely foolish to refuse to capitalize on that fact and to squander time and money reinventing the wheel. Besides, although relatively few Americans have yet registered the fact, the nature of Japanese borrowing from the West is in the process of change. In the past, that borrowing for the most part reflected a realistic recognition on the part of the Japanese that they had a lot of catching up to do. That, however, is no longer nearly so true as it used to be; increasingly, Japan is engendering its own technologies, and in the future Japanese industrialists will have to worry more about other people copying them and less about what they can usefully copy themselves.

This in no way means that Japanese borrowing from the West will cease; rather, it means that to an increasing degree the motives for it will be social and psychological rather than economic. One of the strongest of these motives is the almost childlike fascination anything foreign—and particularly American—holds for Japanese. There is, for example, no development in American life-styles or pop culture so small or esoteric that it does not promptly find imitators in Japan. At the tail end of the '70s, shortly after I had idly noted a modest resurgence of American interest in swing music of the Big Band Era, I flew off to Tokyo and found myself listening to a Japanese band playing old Glenn Miller hits with such faithfulness that if you closed your eyes, it was possible to imagine you were listening to the original recordings.

Another motive for Japanese borrowing from the West has always been the fear that foreigners will dismiss Japan as a "backward" nation. To avoid that humiliation, Japanese society, or at least some element within it, picks up almost every new social or intellectual trend that appears in the United States—consumerism, environmentalism, feminism, what have you. Not all of these alien plants flourish in Japanese soil, but all are cultivated there in at least scraggly form. And the mere fact that a particular movement has been accepted as an essential element of modernity by "progressive thinkers" in the United States and Western Europe can be a powerful weapon in the hands of its Japanese advocates. As we shall see when we look into the lot of Japanese women, feminists in Japan have successfully employed just this device to bludgeon the Japanese Government into public endorsement of policies which the old men who rule Japan privately find totally repugnant.

> *Despite their readiness to adopt foreign ideas, institutions and techniques, most Japanese don't welcome too much personal contact with foreigners and, in their hearts, feel superior to the rest of the world.*

Japan's fascination with things foreign and the Japanese craving for foreign approval are easy to ridicule—and even easier to misinterpret. One thing they emphatically do not imply is that Japanese, particularly those over the age of twenty-five or so, have any overwhelming desire for a lot of contact with foreigners. While foreign visitors to Japan are typically treated with great courtesy and hospitality, any Westerner who concludes from this that he can move easily into the mainstream of Japanese life is making a serious mistake. Though there are increasingly numerous exceptions to the rule, the majority of Japanese still find personal dealings with foreigners something of a strain. And reluctant though they are to admit it, nearly all Japanese are rendered even more uncomfortable by Westerners who speak fluent Japanese and have mastered the nuances of Japanese society and culture.

In part, this reflects a kind of Cosa Nostra mentality—a subliminal fear that a foreigner who seeks to penetrate Japanese society is, in a sense, spying into things that properly concern only the members of the tribe. But it also reflects a rarely articulated but deeply rooted conviction that *wareware Nihonjin* ("we Japanese") are the pick of the human crop.

As is frequently true with individuals, in other words, Japan's national sense of vulnerability and fear of being regarded as inferior go hand in hand with a certain arrogance—the kind of arrogance which holds, to paraphrase an old U.S. Army saying, that there are three ways to do things: the right way, the wrong way and the Japanese way.

This superiority complex, if one can call it that, was deeply shaken by the debacle of World War II and has never since reasserted itself in the ugly guise it wore in the years before the war. But it is only natural that Japan's present extraordinary achievements have left Japanese less disposed to humility now than they were in the '50s and '60s. Though on most occasions they remain by Western standards excessively polite and mired down in ritual courtesies, Japanese Government officials no longer automatically assume a low posture in their dealings with other nations. Unthinkable as it would have been in the '50s and '60s, it was possible by the first year of the Reagan Administration for a senior Japanese bureaucrat to publicly blast some aspects of U.S. trade policy as "cynical" and "unrealistic."

This is not the kind of talk the world has grown accustomed to hearing from the Japanese. But it is, I believe, the kind of talk the world is going to hear more and more of in the years ahead—particularly in situations where the Japanese feel themselves to be leading from strength.

SECTION TWO

Growing Up Japanese

3

All in the Family

At a casual glance, the crowds that jam the beaches south of Tokyo on a hot summer Sunday could almost as well be at Jones Beach, Sanibel Island or Malibu. The typical family strolling across the sand—Mommy, Daddy and two kids—is clearly a product of the age of universal birth control and easy abortion. And the processional order is the one to which dutiful U.S. husbands have long since become accustomed: Mommy walks ahead holding five-year-old Junior by the hand; struggling along behind them comes Daddy, laden down with the baby, the pails and shovels, the inflatable rubber duck, the plastic cooler and the portable TV. If it weren't for the uniform skin color of the participants (Japanese, by the way, describe themselves as "wheat-colored" rather than yellow), the scene would be as American as a Big Mac.

But only superficially. As with so many other things, family life in Japan has been Americanized in some of its externals, yet the psychic environment in which Japanese spend their childhood differs in extremely important ways from the atmosphere in which most American children grow up.

To start with, Japanese attach far more importance to marriage as an institution than contemporary Americans do. The notion that it is acceptable for young men and women to live together without getting married is one American social trend that has yet to be widely imitated in Japan. During a visit to Japan in late 1980, I asked a young Japanese woman of avowedly feminist views how she felt about "living together"; her modernism forced her to declare that she approved of the idea in principle, but it was clear that she had no intention of entering into any such arrangement herself and didn't know anyone who had.

I don't mean to suggest by this that premarital sexual activity is unknown in Japan. In Western societies, under the lingering influence of Christianity, "illicit" sex is still surrounded in the minds of many people with overtones of guilt, acknowledged or unacknowledged. But in Japan sex is not a moral issue per se; even homosexuality does not disturb Japanese in the way that it still does many Westerners.

What in fact determines the acceptability of any particular sexual act in Japan is its social consequences, and with the changes in the social environment that have occurred in Japan in the last thirty years have come changes in permissible sexual behavior. It is true that men, whether married or unmarried, are still accorded far more sexual freedom in Japan than women—particularly married women, who are expected to protect the sanctity of the family by remaining unshakably faithful to their husbands. But it is no longer the case, as it was before World War II, that an unmarried woman who engages in sexual activity irretrievably cuts herself off from respectability. Today, unmarried women—especially the young working women known as O.L.s (for "office ladies")—do sometimes have affairs. As a rule, however, they are far more discreet about such involvements than their American counterparts—and considerably less likely to indulge in them at all. And among girls of high school and university age, sexual indulgence is, by contemporary American standards, astoundingly infrequent.

The reasons for this, as I have said, are essentially pragmatic. A proper Japanese bride is still expected to be a virgin, and for the vast majority of Japanese women, marriage and childbearing remain life's supreme objectives. Japanese society simply assumes that women will be married by the time they are twenty-four or twenty-five and men by the time they are twenty-seven or twenty-eight. "Japanese think anyone over thirty who is still unmarried is a little bit crazy," I was told by Father Joseph Pitau, an Italian Jesuit with more than twenty years' residence in Japan. "In fact," he added wryly, "they find the idea so unthinkable that I often get invitations addressed to 'Father and Mrs. Joseph Pitau.' "

Once married, moreover, Japanese are far more apt to stay that way than Americans. Though Japanese men in general indulge in more extramarital sexual activity than American men and make less effort to conceal the fact, the divorce rate in Japan is still less than a quarter what it is in the United States. In part, this is doubtless because Japanese men often demand and get custody of their children and because alimony awards are less frequent and generally smaller than in this country. But it is also because most Japanese still regard marriage not as the culmination of a romance but as a commitment that is primarily social and practical in significance.

How strong that attitude remains is clearly indicated by the fact that, according to the most recent surveys, 40 percent of all Japanese marriages are still arranged by go-betweens—and the real figure, according to at least one Japanese sociologist, is probably considerably higher than that. (Some "modern" Japanese couples, he theorizes, are embarrassed to admit that they didn't marry for love.)

To be sure, arranged marriages in today's Japan are relatively humane affairs: if the two young people involved turn out to dislike each other, they are under no compulsion to go through with the deal. Nonetheless, most Americans are outraged by the mere thought of marrying a semi-stranger chosen for suitability by a third party. Yet even the most sophisticated and outwardly Westernized Japanese generally defend the practice. "It's not a bad system," argues Professor Sadako Ogata, one of Japan's top women academics, in flawless American English acquired during years of graduate study in the United States. "It helps young people to make a rational choice—and love can follow after."

Despite these fundamental differences, there are two important respects in which marriage in Japan has become increasingly similar to marriage in America. For one thing, the large families that characterized prewar Japan have virtually disappeared. Primarily for economic reasons, today's typical Japanese couple rarely has more than two children. (Statistically, in fact, the average Japanese family now includes only 1.7 children.) Increasingly, this state of affairs is achieved through contraception—more often by the use of condoms than by use of the pill, whose potential side effects worry Japanese more than they do Americans. But where contraception fails or is not practiced, Japanese women can—and frequently do—fall back upon abortions, which can be legally obtained for either medical or "economic" reasons.

The other great change in the nature of marriage in Japan is another of the legacies of the U.S. Occupation. Until 1945, the oldest son in a Japanese family was legally obligated to support his parents in their old age, and even after that formal obligation was rescinded during the MacArthur era, most Japanese households continued for a long time to include members of three generations: grandparents, parents and children. Nowadays, however, it is less and less common for three generations of a family to live under the same roof. In recent years, the number of new households formed in Japan has been running at twice the rate of population increase—which means that particularly in Japan's cities, the so-called nuclear family has become the norm. This has badly damaged one of the economic safety nets that elderly people in Japan used to be able to rely upon and has been particularly hard psychologically upon elderly women, who traditionally ruled the roost in Japanese homes, lording it over their daughters-in-law and pampering their grandchildren. So thoroughly have the tables been turned, in fact, that older women now write to advice-to-the-troubled columnists in Japanese newspapers complaining that when they visit their sons' homes, their daughters-in-law scornfully refuse even to listen to their advice.

The power that has been lost by *Obasan* (Grandma), however, does not reflect any overall setback for her sex. On the contrary, the single most significant fact about the Japanese family today remains what it has been for most of Japan's modern history: the typical Japanese household is a disguised matriarchy—and a rather thinly disguised one at that.

For nearly all Japanese, the matriarchal nature of the environment in which they spend their earliest years has consequences that endure for the rest of their lives—and that stems in large part from a central anomaly in sexual roles in Japan.

A great many Westerners, probably the majority of them, live in the illusion that the Japanese male is lord of all he surveys. In fact, that has not been the case for a long time. Even back in pre-World War II days when they had almost no legal rights at all, Japanese wives were rarely the powerless, purely decorative creatures Westerners so often mistook them for. There is a perfectly good Japanese phrase for "henpecked"—*kaka denka*—and it is not one of recent coinage. Consider, for example, the case of former Prime Minister Takeo Miki, whose wife once publicly proclaimed that her man "hardly knows how to wash his face properly" and on another occasion felt obliged to assure an interviewer that she had never struck Miki.

Admittedly, this isn't your run-of-the-mill Japanese wife. In the majority of Japanese families, the husband is still nominally the unchallenged boss. Great attention is paid to his well-being, his ego is assiduously nourished and if, after finishing work, he chooses to gamble at mah-jong with the boys for a couple of hours or to drop in at his favorite bar for a few drinks and an exchange of suggestive repartee with the hostesses, he is most unlikely to face any reproaches when he finally does wander home. In public, moreover, most Japanese wives, no matter how highly educated or able in their own right, are careful to treat their husbands with deference. I know of one thoroughly intelligent Japanese woman, an artist of outstanding talent, who almost never opens her mouth on social occasions. Her husband, who in other respects parades his cosmopolitanism, holds that the modesty historically expected of Japanese women requires that when in company, they should speak only when spoken to—and then briefly.

To the casual Western observer, in fact, the typical Japanese wife of childbearing age seems horridly oppressed. Particularly in the lower income brackets and in socially conservative groups where the use of baby-sitters is still considered shameful neglect, a young Japanese mother is essentially the prisoner of her children. She enjoys none of the freedoms her husband accepts as his God-given right, and the social high point of her day is likely to be an excursion to the supermarket—with the children in tow.

But in a sense, it is the very freedom that men enjoy and women lack that is the undoing of the Japanese husband. Between their gregarious habits and the inordinate amount of time they spend on the job—it is not particularly remarkable for a Japanese man to work ten hours a day five days a week and then go back to the office for a few hours on Saturday—the majority of Japanese husbands spend relatively little time at home. A young Foreign Ministry official, who saw nothing unusual about his lot, confessed to me once that his regular pattern was to arrive home between 11p.m. and midnight, eat, sleep and rise at 7a.m. to catch his commuter train. So far as his family is concerned, the Japanese father often comes close to being simply a nocturnal boarder.

Almost inevitably, the power vacuum created by this situation is filled by the woman of the house. In the great majority of Japanese families the husband turns over his entire salary to his wife, who then doles out to him a daily allowance—usually a rather modest one—for cigarettes, drinks and sundries. Though I have heard of cases in which men who work overtime ask to be paid from petty cash so that they can keep their extra earnings for themselves, Japanese males for the most part seem to see nothing confining or humiliating about letting their wives control the purse strings.

To a remarkable degree, Japanese men also seem content to accept the corollary principle that she who pays the piper calls the tune.

In most Japanese households, it is basically the wife who makes the major decisions such as where the family will live, what car it will buy and what schools the children will attend. Generally, a woman will make at least a show of consulting her husband on these matters, but not always: in one 1979 survey a startling 41 percent of the men polled admitted that they left the education and disciplining of their children entirely to their wives.

At bottom, many Japanese men actually seem to want to play only a minimal role in the management of their families—and they pay for that in loss of real authority. One highly successful Tokyo businesswoman who talks of her own mate with unconcealed condescension insists that "what most Japanese women really think about their husbands is 'Oh, he's just a child and can't be expected to take big responsibilities.' " As individuals, very few Japanese wives are incautious or undiplomatic enough to make such a statement publicly. But as a group they come pretty close to doing so: a proverb much favored by Japanese women holds that "a good husband is healthy and absent."

If Japanese society were uniformly matriarchal, the relatively weak role of the traditional Japanese father might pose no particular problem. What makes it a very real problem indeed is the fact that while male dominance is only a polite fiction in most Japanese homes, it is an overwhelming reality in professional and public life. As a result, from birth on male children in Japan get favored treatment. In today's Japanese family, the discrimination in favor of boys is not as extreme as it was twenty or thirty years ago: the kind of crown-princely status that the eldest male child used to be accorded by his parents and younger siblings is now pretty much a thing of the past. But boys in general still get more education than girls, and even in the most modern of Japanese families they tend to occupy a special place. Even Yoriko Kawaguchi, who is a rising star in the Ministry of International Trade and Industry and who stands a good chance to become the first woman to exercise real power in the upper ranks of the Japanese bureaucracy, tacitly admits as much. "From the time they were born," she says, "I was determined not to differentiate between my son and my daughter. For example, I had decided never to say 'Boys shouldn't cry' to my son. But now I do. He has to live in this society, and for his sake I have to equip him for that."

The degree to which Japanese mothers favor their sons and take masculine superiority for granted undeniably has unfortunate effects on their daughters. Reminiscing about her youth, an extremely capable Japanese woman in her early forties remarked to me: "Of course, my brother was more intelligent than I, and so he went to a more prestigious secondary school and an elite university." Then, seemingly for the first time in her life, she suddenly reflected: "But perhaps my education was also tailored, so to speak. Perhaps if I had been sent to a better secondary school than I was, I could have gotten into an elite university too."

Hard as it may be on girls, however, the conventional Japanese upbringing also creates basic problems for boys. In a thousand ways, they are led to believe that maleness automatically endows them with superiority. Yet the person who totally shapes their lives in their preschool years and in whom as children they put all their trust is female.

To complicate things even more, Japanese children when they are very small bask in maternal love that is utterly supportive and uncritical. In Japan as everywhere else in the contemporary world, elderly curmudgeons complain that the younger generation is being ruined by too much parental permissiveness. But anyone who harbors this fear about Japanese toddlers is simply ignoring historical reality. In *The Century Magazine* for June 1913, an American woman named Frances Little wrote of the typical Japanese baby of the time: "He lives neither by rule nor regulation, eats when, where and what he pleases, then cuddles down to sleep in peace. . . . There is really no reason why he should ever cry. . . . Rarely denied a wish, he blossoms like a wild rose on the sunny side of the hedge."

In this respect at least, things haven't changed much in Japan since 1913. Today as then, little children are rarely given cause to cry, and if they do are automatically picked up and comforted. When it's time for bed, Mama croons them to sleep. When they go out in public, they are dressed up within an inch of their lives and indulgently forgiven behavior that would earn most American or European children a quick parental reproof if not a spanking.

This combination of constant maternal attention and all-embracing love gives Japanese children an enviable sense of security in their early years, but it has other and more controversial results in the longer run. In my own view, it considerably complicates male–female relations in Japan, since Japanese men are always unconsciously trying to find someone who will love and cherish them as uncritically as Mama professed to—which, in most cases, is obviously a foredoomed effort. It is partly, I am convinced, because they rarely find such an undemanding, ego-warming relationship in their marriages that so many Japanese men take mistresses and find psychic satisfaction in the banal attentions of bar hostesses.

Beyond all this, the mother–son relationship in Japan breeds in most Japanese boys a taste for dependence that subsequently manifests itself in their professional lives. Every Japanese man has or strives to acquire what in my part of the United States would be called his "rabbi." Such mentor relationships, however, are far more universal in Japan than in America, play a considerably more important role in Japanese psychology and are quite different in nature from the normal interplay between an up-and-coming American and his patron.

Basically, a Japanese expects his rabbi (who can be an older relative, someone who graduated from his college a year or two earlier, a corporate superior or the leader of a political clique) to help him cope with all of life's challenges—emotional, social and economic. The rabbi may well arrange his protégé's marriage; he will certainly give counsel on all sorts of personal problems and, above all, intercede with the powers-that-be to get the younger man promotions and to advance his career ambitions generally. But in sharp departure from the usual situation in the United States, a protéé in Japan does not necessarily feel obliged to justify such intercessions in his behalf by performing his job with uncommon competence or even by effective office politicking in support of his rabbi. All he feels his rabbi can legitimately expect of him is that he be loyal, sincere and dutiful. Mama, after all, did what she did out of love and not—ostensibly at least—because she expected any payback.

By Western standards, this dependency syndrome, which the Japanese call *amae*, has at least one serious drawback. Because such a relationship is as binding psychologically upon the protector as on the protected, the executives of Japanese organizations sometimes insist upon unmerited advancement for their protégés—or worse yet, upon unwarranted consideration for a protégé's ill-advised policy proposals. As a result, most Japanese institutions are saddled with people whose rank outstrips their competence and spend a certain amount of time spinning their wheels in discussion of obviously impractical schemes.

Even so, no organization that hopes to function effectively in Japan or in cooperation with Japanese can safely ignore the claims of *amae*. Even if it means carrying a certain amount of deadwood, honoring the obligations that a Japanese executive feels toward his protégés is one of the costs of doing business in Japan—a cost perhaps no more irrational at bottom than giving a U.S. executive a carpeted corner office when he could operate equally well and far less expensively out of a windowless cubicle.

More important, catering to the *amae* syndrome has positive advantages: when a Japanese is convinced that he is "loved"—or more precisely, that he occupies a secure and respected role in the group to which he pays allegiance—he can operate with a degree of dedication and single-minded efficiency uncommon among Westerners. Unlike successful Americans who must always worry, at least subconsciously, about the possibility that their careers may be blighted by palace coups or the changing whims of top management, a successful Japanese can afford to focus almost exclusively upon advancing the fortunes of his organization. He has, in short, fewer monkeys on his back than his American counterpart—or at least, very different ones.

One monkey that *does* perch on the back of nearly all Japanese is a deeply ingrained feeling that individual gratification is possible only in a group context—a feeling which, like the taste for dependence, clearly stems from childhood experiences. The best explanation for this that I have ever heard was offered by Yoshiya Ariyoshi, a truly wise man who was once chairman of Japan's biggest shipping line and who at his death at age eighty was still active in his company's affairs. "The very start of life is different for Americans and Japanese," Mr. Ariyoshi told me. "In America, as I understand it, children are encouraged to assert their separate identity. Here in Japan, the first thing you learn is to harmonize with the group. In exchange for this conformity, people will be kind and considerate toward you. It's not necessary for you to ask for anything; your wishes will be granted without your asking. In childish terms, if you are good and don't make strident demands, people will spoil you."

At first blush, the inculcation of conformism may seem incompatible with the permissive approach to child rearing favored in Japan. But in fact, it is not. Permissiveness as practiced by Japanese mothers is akin to jujitsu in the sense that it turns the natural emotional responses of children into devices for their control.

At the core of Japanese behavior patterns is the notion of reciprocity—the idea that people are not good or bad in any absolute sense but good or bad in light of their relationships with others. For Japanese, the supreme source of guilt is not violating an immutable set of moral principles such as the Ten Commandments but the sense that they have hurt someone else by failing to behave as that person expected.

It is this psychic attitude that a Japanese mother instills in her children as they emerge from babyhood—and that simultaneously becomes her supreme weapon over them. When her children misbehave or disappoint her in any way, the typical Japanese mother does not get angry and shout. She forgives—and by making her children feel guilty about letting her down gains the psychological upper hand.

In this highly indirect process of character formation, moral and religious instruction in the Western sense usually play at best a secondary role. A Japanese home may well contain both Buddhist and Shinto shrines—generally tactfully separated from each other—and in conservative households the tradition of reporting major events to departed members of the family may still be observed. (I recall vividly the stunned silence that fell over the Americans present when the son of a deceased Japanese statesman greeted a tribute to his father's accomplishments with the matter-of-fact comment "I'll tell my father of your very kind remarks the next time I talk to him.") But in the great majority of cases such observances are essentially ritualistic, reflecting an attachment to form rather than any deeply felt religious sentiment. As a people, Japanese find the concepts of sin and reward or punishment in an afterlife so alien that they generally do not inflict them on their children. In a poll taken in 1979, only 19 percent of all Japanese between the ages of sixteen and nineteen professed any religion at all. That was the lowest percentage reported for any major nation in the non-Communist world—and even so may well have been deceptively high as far as educated Japanese are concerned. During his years as rector of Tokyo's Sophia University, recalls Father Joseph Pitau, 98 percent of the entering freshmen at that Jesuit-sponsored institution said that they had no religion.

What Japanese mothers inculcate in their children, then, is not the fear of God, or even any notion of a set of moral imperatives based on an ethical system of universal validity. Instead, what the great majority of Japanese children are taught is a code of behavior acceptable to the Japanese tribe and its component groups. This, of course, is not too different from the real underpinnings of the moral instruction that a fair number of contemporary Western children receive, and in their adult lives it serves most Japanese well enough—provided they are operating in situations familiar to the

Japanese tribe and for which it has developed consensual responses. The trouble comes when Japanese find themselves confronting unfamiliar problems for which there are no agreed-upon "Japanese" solutions; then they can be handicapped by their lack of a set of principles that are independent of time, place and cultural context. It is precisely this, I believe, that accounts for the insensitivity and seeming amorality which Japanese sometimes display when they are called upon to function in a strange environment.

To a Westerner, the great pressure that is put upon Japanese children to learn to "fit in" would seem to make growing up Japanese a highly constraining experience. And in fact, it does produce a certain amount of youthful rebellion in Japan—particularly, as we shall see, among teen-agers, upon whom Japanese educators make demands that would strike any Columbia Teachers College graduate as cruel and unusual. But even teen-age rebellion is still the exception rather than the rule in Japan. A government survey conducted in December 1980 showed that more than 70 percent of the senior high school students polled felt their parents treated them with warmth and a genuine effort at understanding. More remarkable yet, 35 percent of the teen-age boys polled and 51 percent of the girls confessed that they wanted "to go on being a child."

Most Japanese, in short, survive their upbringing reasonably successfully. Relatively few Japanese resort to psychiatry, with the result that psychiatrists are a rare breed in Japan. And in percentage terms, the number of people who are institutionalized or regularly treated for mental disorders is far smaller in Japan than it is in the United States.

A Western psychiatrist, however, might well argue that the psychic health of Japanese is more apparent than real—that it is, in fact, a matter of definition. And there are eminent Japanese who would agree, at least in part, with that proposition. For example, Dr. Takeo Doi, perhaps the best known of contemporary Japanese psychiatrists, argues that the dependency syndrome characteristic of Japanese results in behavior patterns less desirable than those produced by Western-style individualism and so should be overcome.

Doi's voice, of course, is a somewhat esoteric one, but many Japanese far less scholarly than he are ambivalent about the obvious contrast between their value system and those prevailing in the West. Half a century ago, a pioneering Japanese psychiatrist named Heisaku Kosawa tried to persuade Sigmund Freud that Japanese society operated on a maternal principle rather than on the paternal one that Freud had concluded was latent in the Western mind. Not surprisingly, the sage of Vienna displayed scant interest in this challenge to the universality of his analysis, and partly for that reason, Kosawa's ideas for decades went largely unheeded in Japan. Indeed, even today they tend to make Japanese uneasy. Yet the fact remains that the parent most commonly subject to bitter caricature in Japan is not the heavy father but *Mamagon*, the domineering, dragonlike mother.

The clear reason for this is that as Japanese reach adulthood, many of them come to recognize how they have been programmed by their mothers and to resent both the means and the results of that programming. But much as they may rail at Mama, very few Japanese ever succeed in escaping her psychological clutches. Just as the dependency syndrome continues to grip the great majority of Japanese throughout their lives, so does the responsiveness to guilt feelings that they acquired at Mama's knee.

Guilt, in fact, is the single most potent lever in personal relationships in Japan—a state of affairs that has some peculiar ramifications. One of the reasons Japanese find suicide less shocking than most Western peoples, for example, is that in their scheme of things suicide can be the ultimate form of imposing guilt on others; it was, I suppose, at least partly a desire to impose guilt on the Japanese soldiers who laughed at his nationalistic exhortations that led novelist Yukio Mishima to commit hara-kiri.* On a very different plane, I have also heard it argued by Japanese that relations between their country and the United States are still heavily colored by Japan's national sense of guilt over the unexpectedly benevolent treatment it received from the United States following World War II.

That, of course, is sociological speculation which cannot be conclusively proved or disproved. But what is undeniably true is that Japan's most effective leaders and managers very often operate on the guilt principle. Like Mama, they are externally modest and self-effacing people who don't order others around arbitrarily and who shoulder heavy burdens—often unnecessarily heavy ones—without complaining or asking for assistance. The spontaneous sense of guilt that this creates in their co-workers gives such

---

* *Though I have used it because it is familiar to Americans, the term "hara-kiri" is considered somewhat vulgar in Japan. A more elegant and generally preferred word for ritual self-disembowelment is* seppuku.

managers enormous leverage and induces their subordinates to try to work off that guilt by anticipating the boss's still unarticulated needs and wishes.

The other side of this coin, however, is that self-assertion comes close to being the ultimate no-no in Japan. To proclaim openly your right to special rewards for a job extraordinarily well done or to individual credit for what was nominally a group effort frees your colleagues of any sense of guilt toward you and hence is destructive to your prestige and influence. So strong is this feeling that one of Japan's most innovative industrialists, a man who has won widespread admiration and acceptance in Western business circles, has been repeatedly denied any real leadership role in Japan's domestic business establishment on the ground that he is, as we would say in English, "too pushy."

It would be both condescending and naive to suggest that Japanese are blind prisoners of the attitudes I have been describing; those with experience of the world outside Japan are under no illusion that Westerners share their taste for self-effacement, dependency relationships and strength through guilt inducement. Nonetheless, the more an American can adapt to these patterns, the more successful he is apt to be in his dealings with Japanese—particularly in continuing relationships.

The most dramatic evidence in support of that statement I know of was recounted to me some fifteen years ago by an American mining operator. He had made a contract to supply iron ore to a Japanese company with which he had been doing business for some time—and suddenly discovered that because of changing terms of trade, he stood to lose his shirt on the deal. An old-fashioned free enterpriser, he stoically told himself that a contract was a contract and unprotestingly continued to ship the ore. Then, to his astonishment, his Japanese customers informed him that they could not allow him to suffer losses on their account and unilaterally increased the agreed-upon price enough to assure him of a solid profit.

I certainly do not mean to suggest that all Japanese would deal so generously with Westerners under similar circumstances or that most Americans should attempt to negotiate with Japanese in totally Japanese terms of reference. But in their dealings with Japanese, Americans should at the very least refrain from the kind of table-pounding, confrontational tactics they might use with other Americans or Europeans. For when they are faced with overbearing foreigners with whom they have no common cultural bonds, Japanese sometimes react by convincing themselves that they are being persecuted by blackhearted villains. This inevitably fills them with resentment and feelings of aggression—and nothing in the group-oriented upbringing of the typical Japanese has equipped him to express aggressive feelings in a constructive fashion. So when he can contain his resentment no longer, he is apt to do what emotionally overloaded people in any society tend to do: explode into destructive, even violent, behavior.

The one thing that can be said with utter certitude about almost any aspect of contemporary Japanese society is that it is in evolution—and that is very clearly the case with family life and relationships in Japan.

Among young Japanese men, for example, a somewhat more Western concept of a father's role has begun to be visible. Though they are still in the minority, an increasing number of young husbands are devoting more time and attention to their personal lives. (As recently as 1971, only one-fifth of all Japanese workers actually took the paid vacation time to which they were entitled.) And at least some of these nonworkaholics are spending a significant part of their free time in family activities such as weekend barbecues, visits to parks and playgrounds and summer excursions to the mountains or the seashore with the kids. If this is the wave of the future—and it seems likely that it will prove to be so—the balance between the paternal and maternal influences on the Japanese psyche will presumably alter in the decades ahead.

At the same time, because the number of working couples has sharply increased in recent years, a greater number of Japanese children are being sent to day-care centers at a very early age instead of being brought up entirely by Mama. This is still far from a universal practice: as of 1980, only about a fifth of all Japanese children aged six or younger were attending such centers. But it is a rapidly spreading one: in the last twenty years, the number of day-care centers, the majority of which are operated by local governments and nearly all of which receive some government support, has more than doubled and now stands well above 20,000. And shipping the little ones off to a day-care center has long since become sufficiently commonplace to inspire passionate—and conflicting—predictions about its eventual impact on Japanese society.

My own view is that exposure to day-care centers may have less spectacular effects on Japanese children than either its foes or its advocates suggest—that it may, in fact, simply reinforce the group consciousness they have traditionally acquired at home. Indeed, nonworking Japanese mothers who entrust their children to day-care centers by choice rather than necessity frequently offer the explanation that they want to see their children "socialized" at an early age. Perhaps the only irrefutable comment I have heard on the subject is that of Yoriko Kawaguchi, who worries a bit about sending her children to a day-care center but consoles herself with the thought "You never really know in advance how these things will work out anyway."

Indeed you don't—and in any case, for at least a generation to come the great majority of Japanese are going to go on behaving as they learned to do at Mama's knee.

4

The Education Race

For some years now, the ritual has been unvarying. Every Sunday afternoon, hundreds of teen-agers all over Tokyo offer their parents carefully fabricated excuses for abandoning their homework and then sneak away to Yoyogi Park, on the west side of the Japanese capital. When they arrive at the park, many of the youngsters are lugging enormous transistor radios, and every one of them carries a large paper shopping bag. Concealing themselves behind clumps of bushes, they proceed to change from their street clothes into the contents of the shopping bags—fanciful costumes that mark them as members of the Harajuku Bamboo Shoot Tribe. (The name, which has no particular significance, was borrowed from a popular boutique in the Harajuku district of Tokyo.)

Watching the members of the tribe emerge from their impromptu dressing rooms is like watching so many butterflies emerge from cocoons. Boys and girls alike are heavily made up, and their outfits, each different from any other, range from filmy shocking pink pajama suits to somber heavily brocaded robes reminiscent of Chinese opera. Once in costume, the members of the tribe head out into the broad, tree-lined avenue that bisects Yoyogi Park and, gathering around their radios, begin to perform a remarkable variety of dance steps ranging from aimless shuffles to a complex athletic maneuver which I seem to recall was known in the 1940s—at least, in the Edgewood Club in New Haven, Connecticut—as Finnegan's Stomp.

Clearly, what these young people are expressing is a sense of alienation, a discontent with the grinding educational burden imposed on teen-aged Japanese and perhaps with the conformity of

Japanese life in general. There is, however, one curious fact about their behavior: they do not dance individually, but in circular groups of a dozen to twenty. Frequently, all the members of a circle wear tags that say things like "The Pure Heart Group of the Harajuku Bamboo Shoot Tribe." And at the center of each circle, there is a leader, generally male and generally equipped with a police whistle which he uses to signal changes in the step.

What takes place in Yoyogi Park is, in other words, a highly conformist display of nonconformity—which to a Westerner seems something of a contradiction in terms. "But not to the Japanese," I was told by a longtime American resident of Tokyo who, along with thousands of other Tokyoites, turned out one Sunday to gape at the weekly spectacle. "If this country ever develops an anarchist movement, it will be the best-organized damn anarchist movement in the world."

The inculcation of what the unkind might call the Japanese herd instinct begins, as we have already seen, at home. But it is powerfully reinforced by the peculiar nature of the Japanese educational system.

On one occasion, I set out to explain the workings of that system to my father, a kindly but somewhat strong-minded gentleman who spent his entire working life as a high school teacher. When I had finished, he snorted at me: "Good God, it sounds as though they've somehow managed to marry the nuttier notions of John Dewey with the pressure-cooker techniques of the worst kind of cram school."

Up to a point, that's a reasonably accurate description of how Japanese educators operate. And there are other aspects of Japan's educational life which most Americans, no matter what their philosophy of education, would find deplorable. As industrial nations go, for example, Japan is relatively niggardly in what it spends on its schools: only 5.3 percent of the Japanese Gross National Product is devoted to public education, as compared with 7.8 percent in Canada, 6.2 percent in Great Britain and 6 percent in the United States. As one consequence of this, the number of pupils per teacher in Japan's primary and secondary schools is larger than in any other developed nation.

Perhaps most disturbing of all to the American way of thinking is the fact that the Japanese public education system is highly politicized. The majority of the country's elementary- and secondary-school teachers belong to a union that maintains close ties to the

Socialist and Communist Parties and that has more than once called its members out on strike over essentially ideological issues.

But all that being said, one further—and somewhat paradoxical—point has to be made: judged in purely pragmatic terms, the Japanese educational system may well be the most effective in the world. Certainly it is considerably more effective than our own; in functional terms, the average Japanese is clearly better educated than the average American.

This is a point most Japanese are much too tactful to dwell upon. Only one of the scores of Japanese industrialists I know has ever been blunt enough to tell me openly that the workers in his U.S. factories were more poorly educated than those in his Japanese factories. But that is nonetheless what most Japanese businessmen who are familiar with the American scene believe. In a survey which Tokyo's Nikko Research Center conducted among Japanese companies with U.S. operations, 65 percent of the respondents said that productivity in their American plants was lower than in their Japanese plants. And without exception they blamed that fact in large part on the inferior education and job skills of American workers.

That is a put-down which any loyal American will find hard to accept, and it is tempting to dismiss it as simply a product of Japanese chauvinism. But unhappily, the facts don't permit that. Estimates of the number of functional illiterates in the United States, for example, run as high as 20 percent of the population. Among Japanese—whose language, remember, is far harder to read and write than English—the estimated illiteracy rate is less than 1 percent.

The humiliating comparisons don't end there, either. In 1970, a U.N.-sponsored group administered a series of identical science tests to ten- and fourteen-year-old children in nineteen countries. In both age groups, the Japanese youngsters tested scored higher overall than children of any other nationality. American youngsters, sad to relate, ranked fifteenth in overall score—and there is no reason to believe those relative rankings have changed significantly since 1970.

For Americans who would like to console themselves with the thought that our individualistic society breeds an ingenuity and originality of thought more useful than anything that can be learned from a textbook, there is yet another sobering message in the results of the 1970 tests. What accounted for the supremacy of the Japanese youngsters was not simply rote memorization of information, in which they ranked high but not at the very top. The thing that boosted them into first place was their superior understanding and application of the information they possessed. In the sciences at least, it would seem that Japanese schools are not content simply to cram more information into youngsters' heads than American schools do; they also teach their students to think more clearly.

It is a good deal easier to figure out why the Japanese educational system works as well as it does than it is to explain why the American system so often falters: Japanese schools are more consistent than American schools in what they teach and how they teach it.

Superficially, there are many resemblances between the Japanese and American systems. As a result of "reforms" imposed by U.S. authorities during the Occupation, pre-university education in Japan follows the American "6-3-3-" pattern: 6 years of elementary education, 3 years of junior high and 3 years of senior high. As in the United States, public elementary and secondary schools fall under the purview of local boards of education, which do not always adopt the same solutions to administrative and other problems. And Japanese parents who don't want to entrust their kids to the public schools have pretty much the same options as their American counterparts: private schools abound, particularly at the senior high school level, and there are also a considerable number of parochial schools, both Buddhist and Christian.

The truth is, however, that much of this diversity is more apparent than real. Though each local school board in Japan decides which particular textbooks will be used in its area, it must make its choices from a relatively limited list of books approved by the central Ministry of Education. Even more important, the Ministry of Education specifies exactly what subjects are to be taught in all elementary and junior high schools and distributes a very detailed curriculum for each course. And while individual teachers are given considerable flexibility in how they choose to teach a particular course, they are permitted none at all as to what material the children must master.

Japan being Japan, however, some of the most powerful forces for uniformity in education are not matters of government decree but flow naturally out of the culture—specifically, a deeply ingrained reluctance to publicly stigmatize or embarrass anyone. There is, for example, no "tracking" in elementary and secondary schools in Japan; in every classroom, the slow learners are mixed right in with the gifted. And throughout the nine years that Japanese children are legally required to attend school—in other words, in elementary and junior high schools—automatic promotion from grade to grade, regardless of a child's academic performance, is the unchallenged rule.

Educational conservatives in the United States, of course, insist that automatic promotion and lack of tracking are fatal to quality education—a fact that I once pointed out to Atsushi Kayashima, a young Japanese scholar who has made a special study of the American educational system and its impact on Japan. "Well," he answered, "you have to remember that our two countries are very different. Because Japan is a very homogeneous country, it is vital for Japanese children to learn a sense of community and family-ness. If you were to separate them in school according to ability—or any other criterion, for that matter—it might give some of them the feeling that they were different from the rest." And to a Japanese—even to Kayashima, who stoutly insists that he would like to see more "individual autonomy" in Japanese education—the deliberate encouragement of any sense of difference in a child is an almost unthinkably antisocial act.

Implicit in Kayashima's comment, too, is the assumption of Japanese public-school teachers that their role extends well beyond the mere imparting of information—an assumption that is shared by the rest of Japanese society. Despite the radicalism of their union and the knee-jerk Marxism that many of them personally espouse, Japanese elementary- and secondary-school teachers are by and large dedicated and conscientious people with a deep concern for the general welfare of their pupils. And in return for that dedication, teachers in Japan are accorded considerable public esteem.

When an adult Japanese refers to someone as his *sensei* (teacher), it implies a special sense of obligation and an enduring deference to the *sensei*'s judgment in personal matters as well as professional ones. The seeds of this attitude are sown in Japanese children in their earliest years in school; from the first grade on, every Japanese schoolchild gets instruction in "ethics"—which generally means in such Confucian values as reverence for parents and respect for teachers. And Japan's teachers capitalize fully on the leverage this gives them. They impose high standards of classroom behavior on their charges: the sight of American kids chewing gum within the precincts of a junior high school sent one Japanese teacher of my acquaintance into near shock. In enforcing these standards, however, Japanese teachers are generally able to rely primarily on moral suasion or mild verbal chastisement; actual punishment, such as ordering a child to leave the classroom for the rest of the period, is the ultimate weapon reserved for truly egregious offenders.

While they appear to ride with a light rein, however, Japanese teachers actually exercise a far more pervasive influence over their pupils than American public-school teachers do. In a 1973 study of Japanese teachers who had been given a chance to observe American schools in action, a constantly recurring theme is the astonishment of the Japanese at what one of them described as the lack of interest of their American counterparts in giving "life guidance to students with special problems." As Japanese teachers see it, their concern extends to the totality of their students' lives. If a Japanese youngster suddenly slumps academically, is caught smoking a cigarette or otherwise appears to be sliding into delinquency, his teacher will almost automatically call on the student's parents to find out what is troubling the child and to devise means of straightening him out.

In short, as Atsushi Kayashima puts it, "school and society are homogenized in Japan," and teachers play a major role in "the socialization process." In plain English, what this means is that Japanese teachers lose no opportunity to impress upon their charges, directly or indirectly, the overriding importance of the individual's responsibility to the group. There are, for example, no janitors in Japanese schools. Instead, the children themselves do the cleaning under the supervision of their teachers—a fact first reported to me with some incredulity by an American woman married to a Japanese editor. "Believe me," she added, "under this system, you don't get anybody running around spraying graffiti on the walls." In similar vein, Atsushi Kayashima recalls that in his elementary school each class had its own little garden in the school yard, "and if one child failed to cultivate his plant properly, the rest of us had to stay on until he finished his task."

Here again, there is a great difference between what a casual Western observer may think he perceives in Japan and what is actually going on; aspects of Japanese education that most Americans would regard as "progressive" do not truly conform to John Dewey's prescription that schooling should be "child-centered." Like the permissiveness of the Japanese mama toward her babies, the almost boundless concern of the Japanese schoolteacher for his students is ultimately a form of social jujitsu.

Americans who cling to our national heritage of rugged individualism like to argue that group-oriented societies stifle competitiveness. But however plausible that proposition, the Japanese educational system must be considered the exception which proves the rule. For despite the social molding process to which they are subjected, the academic competition among Japanese elementary- and secondary-school students is almost savage in its intensity—so much so that it makes the battle for grades that is waged in even the most competitive of U.S. schools look like a game of patty-cake.

The reason for this is a very pragmatic one: every Japanese youngster knows that the status he ultimately achieves in life will be heavily—often, in fact, almost entirely—determined by what university he manages to get into.

I have used the masculine pronoun in this context quite deliberately. A Japanese girl who goes to a "good" university certainly improves her career prospects, but relatively few girls see the need for such effort: fewer than 25 percent of the students attending four-year universities in Japan are women. Proportionally, the number of male and female high school graduates who go on to college is roughly the same—about a third in each case—but the great majority of the women content themselves with two-year junior colleges, where they often specialize in "women's subjects" such as home economics that are calculated to enhance their marriageability. Despite all the subtle changes going on in sex roles in Japan—a subject I shall deal with later—the prevailing Japanese attitude on women's education remains that expressed to me by a good friend in Tokyo, a man who proudly trots his teen-age daughter out to recite poetry or tinkle away on the piano whenever the family has guests. Much as he clearly cherishes this child, her father offhandedly remarked to me one day: "Of course, as a girl, it doesn't matter quite so much what school she attends."

For a normally ambitious Japanese male, however, winning admission to a four-year university matters desperately. It is not just the exception for a Japanese without a university degree to achieve success; it is a rarity. Even a man like former Prime Minister Kakuei Tanaka, who has managed to acquire great wealth and power without benefit of a college education, bears a certain social stigma simply for that reason. "When you drop out in Japan," notes Atsushi Kayashima, "you drop out for good."

Just graduating from university, however, is not an automatic ticket to the top; it's also of crucial importance which university you attend. Like their American counterparts, Japanese universities have been turning out such masses of graduates that industry can no longer find completely "suitable" jobs for all of them; between

1964 and 1974, the average starting salary of a Japanese university graduate actually declined compared with that of a high school graduate.

Reinforcing this problem of oversupply are the prevailing recruiting practices in Japan. Each year, most major Japanese corporations and government agencies stage competitive examinations to determine who shall be included in their limited annual "intake" of new college graduates. In many cases admission to those exams is by invitation only, and the most prestigious corporations and semi-public institutions extend such invitations only to graduates of a select list of universities.

That select list differs somewhat from company to company. But of Japan's 420 universities—which, incidentally, is a greater number than all the Western European nations put together can boast of having—about a dozen are generally considered to be in a class by themselves. And in sharp contrast with the situation in the United States, all of these are state-supported institutions rather than private ones.

At the very top of the heap is Todai—the acronym for Tokyo University—which in Japan carries the prestige of Harvard, Yale and M.I.T. all rolled into one. When a Japanese admits to you that he is a graduate of Todai, he generally does so, in my experience, in a flat, noncommittal tone, as if fearful that you will think he is putting on airs. And the admission is, in fact, inevitably a kind of boast. Half of Japan's post-war prime ministers have been Todai products, as are four out of five of the country's ranking bureaucrats and whole battalions of top corporate executives. In fact, even the more "revolutionary" forces in Japanese society tend to be spearheaded by Todai graduates: a number of Communist Party leaders went there, as did Yoriko Kawaguchi, a quietly brilliant government economist who, to the private discomfiture of many Japanese males, has successfully demonstrated that a wife and mother can also be an effective operator in the corridors of power.

In short, if you are a Japanese parent and want your child to be a winner in life, you do everything possible to ensure that he or she gets into Todai—or failing that, another top state institution such as Kyoto University. The trouble is, though, that all 81 of Japan's state-supported universities can accommodate only 20 percent of the students who win university admission each year. This means that the other 80 percent are relegated to the far more numerous private universities—and for these youngsters, career prospects are, generally speaking, substantially less bright. For although a number of private universities, such as Keio and Waseda, enjoy good reputations, the great majority are regarded as second- and third-rate.

Broadly speaking, that's an accurate assessment. Because they are not heavily endowed and receive far less government financial support than state universities, the private institutions mostly have poorer facilities than the "national" ones and are obliged to charge far higher fees—in some cases, five times as high. By American standards, this still makes them a bargain: their tuition charges average a third or less of those now prevailing at private universities in the United States. Still, the fact that they are so much more expensive than Japan's state-supported universities tends to scare off students with limited financial resources, however brilliant they may be—which means that the private universities wind up with a disproportionate number of students from higher-income families. And while in theory admission to all Japanese universities is on the basis of competitive entrance exams, there is a kind of backdoor route into some private universities which maintain their own elementary and secondary schools. A moderately intelligent child whose parents are prosperous enough to start him right off in the Keio Kindergarten, for example, stands a considerably better chance of ultimately winning admission to Keio University than a youngster of equal ability who has gone to public schools.

By contrast, Japan's state universities are meritocracies of a pure, if somewhat brutal, sort. Family connections, outstanding high school grades, glowing letters of recommendation—none of these are of any real help to a youngster seeking admission to Tokyo University. The only thing that matters at Todai is how the applicant does on the entrance exams. A wealthy industrialist's son who turns in a poor performance on the exams has no hope; a provincial postal clerk's son who does brilliantly will be accepted—and thus at one stroke win admission to Japan's elite.

Obviously, the process by which a poor but brilliant boy becomes a fully-fledged member of the Japanese establishment is somewhat more complex than that—but not necessarily much. One prominent Japanese whom I have come to know well—and whose story I must disguise slightly—is the son of a high school teacher in an impoverished rural area of what is known as *ura* (back) Japan. Partly perhaps because of his home environment, my friend studied inordinately hard, got into Tokyo University and upon graduation joined a prestigious government ministry. Sent off to the United States by the ministry for graduate study, he acquired a Ph.D. in political science and, even more important, the ability to mingle easily with foreigners. Upon his return to Japan, one of his superiors drew him to the attention of an industrialist who had large foreign interests, two daughters—and no son. In due course, my friend made an arranged marriage with one of the daughters, left government service and, with his father-in-law's financial backing, became a respected and highly successful publisher. "You know," he told me once, "I lead a very comfortable and rewarding life—and I think I've earned it. But sometimes it unsettles me a little to realize that everything I have is basically the product of a single roll of the dice—that one set of exams I took all those years ago."

With stakes like that involved, it's hardly surprising that Japanese children find themselves in a pressure cooker from the moment they start kindergarten. Even as small kids they attend school longer than Americans do: the standard public-school week is 5½ days, and the school year runs 240 days, vs. 180 in the United States. And the level of academic achievement required of children in Japan is substantially higher than in the average U.S. public school.

Purely in terms of subject matter, what young Japanese are exposed to is not too different from the curriculum in U.S. schools that follow traditional educational patterns. In the elementary grades, the courses required by Japan's Ministry of Education include arithmetic, general science, social studies, the Japanese language, music, art and physical education. (Foreign-language instruction, most commonly in English, begins only in junior high.) But the degree of mastery which Japanese children must achieve in any particular area of study is significantly greater than that customarily required of Americans of comparable age. During their junior high school years, for example, Japanese children not only make a rather detailed and sophisticated study of the long history of their own country but are also expected to acquire an understanding of matters as esoteric (at least for Japanese) as the historic interaction of the Christian and Islamic worlds and the rise of European imperialism.

To make sure that their charges do in fact cover all this ground, Japanese teachers dispense homework liberally: a minimum of one to two hours a day is required of primary-school students, and in junior high the minimum expected increases to 2½ hours a day. And even that is only part of the academic burden borne by most Japanese children. For here there enters upon the scene once again that awesome creature, the Japanese mother—this time in her guise of *kyoikumama* (education mama). One of the most widely denounced and bitterly caricatured figures in Japanese society, the true education mama sets her children's academic success above everything else in life. By the time they are in second or third grade it is a virtual certainty that she will have hustled them into supplementing their regular schooling with three or four sessions a week at a *juku*—a kind of private tutoring school which concentrates on teaching you how to beat the system educationally. Unlike tutoring in the United States, which is normally designed to help a laggard student pull up his grades, the instruction at *juku* is aimed at kids who are already doing well: its purpose is to produce not competence but preeminence.

The point of all this is that the *kyoikumama* knows that the battle of Tokyo University begins in kindergarten; if a child does exceptionally well in primary school, he can reasonably expect to get into a "good" junior high—which means one that gets a lot of its graduates into "good" senior highs. And a good senior high school, of course, is one that gets an uncommonly high percentage of its graduates into "good" universities.

This pattern, to be sure, is not totally unknown in the United States, but there are limits to how far most American parents are prepared to deform their lives—and their children's lives—for educational reasons. Not so in Japan, however. A Japanese businessman with school-age children may even reject a promotion if it would require him to move his family into a less desirable school district. And less dramatic but nonetheless painful sacrifices "for the good of the children" are commonplace. On one occasion a well-to-do Japanese friend mournfully confessed to me that he and his wife had not visited their beloved weekend home in the mountains north of Tokyo for nearly a year. The reason, he explained, was that their eldest son was trying to get into a particularly desirable private high school and, to help make sure that he did so, was attending classes of one kind or another seven days a week.

As this suggests, the hardships that academic competition inflicts on Japanese parents pale alongside those it imposes on their children. Not all Japanese youngsters, of course, are caught up in the higher-education race: roughly 90 percent of Japan's young people complete high school, even though that isn't compulsory, but only a little over 40 percent of senior high school graduates bother to take college-entrance exams. That 40 percent, however, constitutes the potential officer material of Japanese society, and the rigor of the regimen its members must follow is in many ways comparable to the one I recall suffering through in a U.S. Army Officer Candidate School.

One reason for this lies in the nature of the university examinations themselves. For applicants to the elite national universities, these take place in two stages. The first stage—a one-day affair essentially designed to eliminate the obviously unqualified—is a standard exam given at the same time all over Japan. The second stage, which involves examinations prepared by the particular university a student hopes to attend, lasts two or three days and may cover as many as eight different subject areas. Traditionally, these exams put almost exclusive emphasis on "objective questions"—which is to say the straight regurgitation of memorized facts. In recent years, however, there has been an increasing shift to essay questions, although of a rather limited character. In history, for example, students might be asked to analyze at length the origins, structure and characteristics of the Kamakura shogunate, the military government established in Japan in the late twelfth century. But such a question is not to be interpreted as an invitation to a display of original or independent thought. "Nobody wants your opinions," says a recent graduate of one of Japan's newer and avowedly more progressive universities. "They want to see if you know all the relevant facts and understand them correctly."

In the end, then, success on the university entrance exams still rests above all on rote memorization, and as a result, senior high school students in Japan spend interminable hours filling their heads with everything from railway routes to points of English grammar so obscure as to be unknown to most Ph.D.s in linguistics in the United States. Once on a Tokyo subway I spotted a teen-ager methodically working his way through a dictionary, obviously trying to memorize it entry by entry. When I expressed amazement at this spectacle, a Japanese traveling companion assured me that it was nothing particularly unusual among university-bound youngsters.

All this makes it predictable enough that, according to a government poll taken in 1980, high school seniors have the highest "worry level" of any segment of the Japanese population. The February–March period when university entrance tests are given is universally known as "examination hell," and a common Japanese saying has it that any youngster who gets more than four hours' sleep a night in the months preceding examination hell is doomed to failure. And many, in fact, do fail: only two out of every three applicants actually win university admission the first time they take the entrance exams. The remainder are relegated to obscurity or else become *ronin* (wandering warriors) who doggedly take the exams for two or three years in a row before finally attaining their goal or resigning themselves to defeat.

Inevitably, even among a people notable for uncomplaining acceptance of their lot, there are some who find the psychic stresses imposed by this kind of educational competition intolerable. According to Tokyo police statistics, it is the *kyoikumama* who is responsible for the majority of teen-age runaways in Japan. And nervous breakdowns, even suicides, are by no means unheard of among youngsters who fail their university exams or fear that they are going to.

Most disturbing of all to older Japanese is the increasing tendency of Japanese teen-agers to resort to violence. During the 1970s, when overall crime rates in Japan were actually dropping, the juvenile crime rate steadily increased until in 1981 it stood at the highest level since the end of World War II. By that point, in fact, fourteen- to sixteen-year-olds had actually outstripped adults as the nation's most frequent lawbreakers.

It is important to keep all this in perspective. By American standards, even juvenile crime rates in Japan are almost incredibly low: there are probably more acts of youthful violence committed in New York City alone each year than in all of Japan. But precisely because Japan *is* such an orderly society, even a marginal increase in antisocial behavior is seen as cause for alarm. And while the causes of adolescent alienation in any country tend to be complex, it seems reasonably clear that one contributing factor to it in Japan is the heavy emotional burden imposed on young people by the school system. Certainly it is hard to find any other explanation for the fact that at one Japanese high school in the summer of 1981, rioting students forcibly obliged one teacher after another to kneel in front of his classes. What was involved here was clearly not just the random cruelty of youthful hoodlums; these kids obviously saw their teachers as oppressive figures whose malign influence could be destroyed only by public humiliation.

Infrequent as they are by American lights, incidents such as this one invariably produce a rash of anguished reappraisals of the Japanese educational system in the nation's weightier magazines. Criticism of the educational system is, in fact, widespread among Japanese intelluctuals, whose basic complaint is one eloquently voiced by former Minister of Education Michio Nagai. The central problem with Japanese education, Nagai charges, is that it focuses on meeting "the practical needs of society rather than [on] a long-term contribution to the formation of culture through the detached pursuit of truth."

That charge, together with outrage at the inhumanity of the "examination hell," has sparked endless talk of educational reform in Japan and even some limited stabs at it. But no Japanese whom I know seriously believes that basic changes in the system will actually come about anytime soon. For unlike Japanese intellectuals, the great majority of Japan's people are pragmatists, and in pragmatic terms, the Japanese educational system has served the country well: whatever its side effects, it has produced a labor force that combines intelligence and work discipline to a degree unmatched anywhere else in the world and a managerial class equally outstanding for its ability to marry team play with individual initiative. And to a people whose national goals are still so heavily economic, that seems just what the doctor ordered.

Curiously, despite all its demonstrable effectiveness, there is at least one respect in which Japanese education is less efficient—or at least less demanding—than American education. When they get to college, the great majority of young Americans find themselves working harder and coping with heavier pressures than they did in high school. But for Japanese, admission to university is a kind of liberation. Once the dreaded entrance exams are behind them, it is commonplace for Japanese youngsters to suffer a psychological letdown and slack off in their study habits.

One reason for this is that most Japanese universities are not very stimulating or rewarding places intellectually. For the most part, students are herded into large lecture courses; classes of five hundred or more are far from uncommon. Opportunities for a youngster to pursue individual interests are minimal: within each "faculty"— such as humanities, engineering or economics—courses of study are rigidly prescribed, and because every faculty zealously guards its autonomy, interdisciplinary studies are almost impossible. To top it all off, the inadequate salaries paid Japanese university professors force the majority of them to moonlight—with the result that the tiresome business of actually teaching undergraduates often gets short shrift.

Even an inspired teacher, however, would have difficulty counteracting the most powerful psychological force working upon Japanese undergraduates: their keen awareness that the years they spend at university will be the only time in their lives that they are likely to experience genuine personal freedom.

Behind that awareness lies the fact that the great majority of Japanese universities are in one way extraordinarily permissive: once you get into one, it takes real effort to get kicked out. With relatively few exceptions, in fact, Japanese university authorities do not regard a student's failure to attend classes or even to pass courses as a ground for dismissal.

To Westerners, that sounds like a very odd way to run an academic institution. But in the Japanese context, it has a certain logic: after all, simply by emerging successfully from the examination hell, every Japanese university student has already demonstrated that he has "the right stuff." And in Japan, it is having the right stuff that matters above all.

In a highly perceptive essay on the interaction of business and education in Japan, Ryushu Iwata, a leading student of Japanese management, points out that in its recruiting practices Japanese industry puts a much lower premium on specialized skills and acquired abilities than Western industry does. This fact, according to Iwata, has basically deformed the nature of university education in Japan. To be sure, Japanese universities do turn out economists, engineers, physicists and so on; in per capita terms, in fact, Japan now graduates considerably more than twice as many engineers each year as does the United States. But at bottom, since a Japanese corporation generally hires young people not for a specific job but rather as "labor power in the abstract," it is only marginally interested in an applicant's college major or grades.

Instead, what Japanese corporations basically look for in a prospective employee is what Iwata has christened "latent ability"—the potential for acquiring competence in a wide variety of activities. And by common consent, the way the latent ability of a young Japanese is measured is by how he does on his college entrance exams and, to a somewhat lesser extent, on the corporate or government exams he takes once he has finished university.

The upshot of all this is that between the time they enter university and the time they graduate, most Japanese youngsters face no test of their abilities that can have serious practical consequences for them. After being stretched tauter and tauter on a kind of educational rack throughout his pre-university years, a university freshman in Japan abruptly and incredibly finds himself under no immediate pressure at all—free, if he chooses, to neglect his studies in favor of hobbies, sports, student politics or personal gratification. Under these circumstances, it's scarcely surprising that many students, particularly in their first two years of university, are students in name only.

But from the start there is a bittersweet and evanescent quality to this freedom. For in their hearts, most Japanese undergraduates recognize that once they leave university they will again be subjected to all the constraints and molding processes of Japanese society. Just how heavily this realization weighs upon them first became clear to me during the tidal wave of student rebellion that hit Japan in 1968 and 1969—a time of troubles when undergraduate strikes and violence seriously disrupted the life of fifty Japanese universities, some of which were forced to close down completely for as much as a year. This national upheaval was the culmination of a decade of intermittent student unrest and rioting whose precise causes are still a matter of debate. Sometimes the students were roused to rebellion by purely intramural matters, such as increased tuition fees, and sometimes their wrath seemingly reflected tensions in Japanese society at large: the deep-seated opposition of a substantial number of Japanese to the security treaty with the United States, unhappiness over U.S. control of Okinawa, unease over the Vietnam War and disgust at the seizure of agricultural land for construction of Tokyo's Narita Airport. But genuine as student concern over such specific issues may have been, I am convinced that underlying these ostensible causes for protest there was often a far more powerful private apprehension. On one occasion in 1969, my old friend Bernad Krisher, then *Newsweek*'s Tokyo bureau chief, arranged a meeting for me with a dozen striking students drawn from several different universities. When I questioned the members of this group about the reasons for their disaffection, most of the answers I got were so vague or parochial as to be meaningless. Finally, though, one uncommonly handsome and self-possessed boy, the son of a wealthy businessman, spoke up. "Look," he said, "the real point is that we don't want to become just interchangeable parts in this society."

Yet that is precisely what Japan's university students know they will become. And their discomfort with that knowledge, I believe, helps explain the fact that Marxism and other, far more esoteric revolutionary "isms" flourish so abundantly on Japanese campuses. By espousing these anti-establishment causes, Japan's future leaders are voicing one last protest against their destiny.

In this, moreover, they are mightily encouraged by the intellectual climate created by their teachers. American businessmen who inveigh against "fuzzy-minded professors" simply don't know how lucky they are, comparatively speaking. As a class, Japanese university professors are overwhelmingly *kakushin-teki*—a word that literally means "progressive" but is actually a euphemism for leftist. Embittered by the low financial value placed on their services and their almost total lack of political influence or effectiveness, most Japanese academics are openly hostile to the existing order in Japan. Even the most brilliant of them, in fact, tend to live in a kind of ideological cloud-cuckooland: one internationally known social scientist of whom I am personally very fond has been assuring me for years that Japan is in imminent danger of succumbing once again to right-wing nationalism—even though his dire predictions continue to remain unfulfilled and the only evidence he can cite in support of them is patently tortured and trivial.

At times in the past, the interaction of professorial "progressiveness" and student weltschmerz has had disastrous consequences for Japan's universities. The great riots of 1968–69 produced scenes eerily reminiscent of medieval warfare; one that lingers ineradicably in my memory is the spectacle of an army of students brandishing shields and staves like so many feudal levies as they prepared to do battle with mobile police whose acrylic helmets gave them the ominous facelessness of the Teutonic knights in *Alexander Nevsky*. In the end, only the arrest of some twenty thousand people, most of them students, put a stop to this kind of episode and restored peace to Japan's campuses.

Even today, however, the spirit which produced the explosion of the late '60s is not entirely dead in Japanese universities. In the '70s, university students played a major role in organizing a paramilitary campaign to close Narita Airport—a campaign so effective that in its early months of operation Narita resembled a besieged Special Forces camp in Vietnam, with heavily armed troops patrolling its perimeter and snipers poised at every vantage point. And from time to time there is still one of those inexplicable outbursts of savagery in which the members of some arcane student revolutionary sect bludgeon to death "deviationists" from their cause or members of an equally arcane rival sect.

But these are clearly aberrations. Whatever his frustrations, today's typical university student in Japan is not about to engage in violent protest of any kind. Rather, as one veteran of the '69 riots told me a bit contemptuously, "students nowadays indulge in radical talk for four years and then, as soon as they graduate, get their hair cut, put on three-piece suits and join a corporation."

The conventional wisdom has it that this docility stems from the same source often alleged to account for that of present-day U.S. college students: the intensified competition for desirable jobs produced by a reduced rate of economic growth and a great multiplication in the number of people who boast university degrees.

That, no doubt, is part of the story. But it is also true that a rapid transition from college radical to pillar of the establishment has been a traditional pattern in Japan. Perhaps the most striking case in point is that of a charismatic young man who as one of the leaders of a radical student federation played a significant role in organizing the riots that forced cancellation of a state visit to Japan by Dwight Eisenhower in 1960. Ten or a dozen years later, this erstwhile revolutionary won brief attention in the U.S. press by publicly expressing regret for his part in the Eisenhower affair. By then, he was a rising star in Japan's retailing industry, solidly ensconced in the executive suite.

The fact that most of their graduates become useful and valuable members of the community is not in itself, of course, any justification for the way Japanese universities operate. And a great many Japanese do feel serious concern about their university system and believe it needs major overhauling. Some, like Ryushu Iwata, argue that what is needed is a reversal of priorities—that instead of serving primarily as instruments for the selection and classification of future managers, Japan's universities should concentrate on the traditional academic functions of education and research. Almost everyone agrees that much more money ought to be spent on the universities, particularly the badly underfinanced private ones whose scientific facilities, for the most part, range from inadequate to nonexistent.

All this having been said, however, it would be a mistake to conclude that the years a young Japanese spends at university are wasted or useless ones. Most Japanese university students do eventually settle down and hit the books—particularly in the latter part of their college career, when the postgraduation corporate or government exams begin to loom larger. And most of them do profit intellectually from the experience, even if not as much as they might in a more academically encouraging environment.

My own view is that there could be serious social risks involved in tampering too heavily with the present university setup in Japan—particularly if such tampering were to impose heavier demands upon students. For I strongly suspect that the surcease from the pressure that the university years provide is critical to the psychological development and stability of young Japanese. In a sense, a university education in Japan is what the U.S. Army calls "temporary duty, rest and recreation"—the kind of leave given to soldiers who have spent a long time in a combat zone and who are slated to go right back into combat after they've had the chance to blow off some steam.

In contrast with the present-day United States, the formal education of an upwardly mobile Japanese is likely to end when he has acquired the equivalent of a B.A. Graduate schools in Japan are in general small and not very good. To some extent, this reflects the fact that since Japanese industry prefers to do its own R&D, Japanese universities play a far smaller role in the national research effort than do their American counterparts. At the same time, the "latent ability" syndrome of Japanese business reduces the incentive of a would-be leader of industry to bother with getting an advanced degree. (Curiously for such an economically oriented society, Japan has as yet no real equivalent of the Harvard Business School—although my friend Jiro Tokuyama recently succeeded in establishing something similar to Harvard's intensive postgraduate refresher program for established executives.)

As a result of all this, Japanese who feel the need of graduate study are much more apt to go abroad for it than Americans are. And this is true not only of fledgling academics but, in a remarkable tribute to the tolerance of the Japanese taxpayer, of fledgling bureaucrats as well: in some of the most prestigious government agencies, such as the Foreign Office and the Ministry of International Trade and Industry, it is standard practice for young career officers to be sent to American or European universities to get advanced degrees at government expense. In fact, when I stop to think about it, it occurs to me that virtually every Japanese bureaucrat I know who is obviously marked for higher things has studied abroad.

Here, admittedly, we are talking about a small elite; but as I have implied, graduate study of any kind is much more of an elitist phenomenon in Japan than it is in the United States. On the other hand, what Americans have come to call "continuing education" is a mass phenomenon in Japan, and one that has proliferated rapidly in recent years—particularly among relatively well-off women whose children have reached the age at which they no longer need constant attention. A host of institutions ranging from newspapers to women's clubs offer courses aimed at this segment of the population, and while much of the fare offered runs to things like flower-arranging or Chinese cooking, some of it is solid stuff such as courses in the Japanese classics or modern European literature.

Undoubtedly, however, the subject most widely taught outside Japan's formal educational system is the English language. Literally millions of Japanese are studying English at any given time, and one of the perennial hazards of a foreigner's existence in Japan is being cornered by a total stranger who proceeds to practice English on you willy-nilly.

What makes this a particularly trying experience is that the English most Japanese learn is excruciatingly bad. In part, this is a result of the fact that the instruction they get is often amateur and inept. In the private language schools and institutes that abound throughout Japan, the teachers tend to be resident Americans, Englishmen or other native speakers who are paid handsome fees for their presumed expertise, but who in fact often have only the dimmest understanding of the principles of English grammar and syntax and no previous experience whatsoever in teaching. (Perhaps the apogee of this kind of thing was the emergence in Tokyo a couple of years ago of late-night "English conversation bars" featuring topless instructors.) Alternatively—and this holds true for Japan's public high schools as well as for the private language schools—the teachers are Japanese who generally have a nitpicking knowledge of the grammatical technicalities of English but couldn't speak the language to save their lives.

Teaching as bad as this, as cultural anthropologist Masao Kunihiro has pointed out, "only reinforces the innate reticence of the Japanese and fortifies their attitude that there is 'safety in silence.'" But there is more behind the execrable English spoken by so many Japanese, I believe, than just bad teaching. You can't learn to speak a language really well unless you also acquire an understanding of the thought processes and value systems of the people who created that language. And so great is the basic insularity and introversion of Japanese culture that it is almost impossible for a secretary in Osaka or a bank clerk in Sapporo to develop any real comprehension of the psychology of the English-speaking peoples.

How true this is is suggested by the fact that whenever you meet a Japanese who speaks genuinely fluent English, you almost invariably find you are talking to somebody who has lived for a time in an English-speaking country. And while that may suggest that the struggles of the secretary in Osaka are sadly futile, it is a ground for hope overall. Precisely because so many more of them have lived or studied abroad, there is a far greater number of Japanese in the twenty-to-fifty age group who speak fluent English than in the age group from fifty up. The prospect is, then, that among the next generation of political and economic leaders in Japan the ability to speak good English will be relatively common—and since the ability to speak good Japanese isn't likely to be cultivated by many American leaders, that's a consummation devoutly to be wished.

A word of warning is very much in order here, however. Unconsciously, most Americans tend to judge the intelligence and reliability of Japanese by the fluency of their English—and that's a fundamental error. A Japanese may discuss a deal with a potential U.S. partner in flawless American English and even in purely American terms of reference. But unless he has a death wish, when he discusses that same deal with his Japanese colleagues, he's going to do so in Japanese terms of reference. So if the American really wants the deal to go through, he had better take the trouble to find out how his proposal can be tailored to Japanese patterns of thought and behavior. In short, language skills alone are simply not enough to bridge the cultural gap.

By the same token, it is foolish to assume that just because a Japanese doesn't speak good English he is a bumbling country cousin. Two of my good Japanese friends—one a businessman and one a bureaucrat—both handle the American language awkwardly. The bureaucrat habitually adds an "oo" to any English word that ends in a consonant sound: "train" becomes "trainoo" in his mouth, and "house" becomes "houseoo." As for the businessman, he talks English as if it were Japanese, spitting out staccato bursts of mispronounced words with only the vaguest detectable grammatical connection to each other. Both men sound remarkably like World War II Hollywood caricatures of Japanese Army officers. Both are, in fact, brilliant and highly effective executives who combine extraordinary knowledge of the U.S. economy with impressive understanding of the motivations of U.S. businessmen and government officials.

It is probably superfluous to add that both are also graduates of Tokyo University.

5

A Woman's Place

She was a rather plain person with no great style, and I had a resigned feeling that as a luncheon companion she was going to be less than stimulating. So she proved—until I got her talking about herself, at which point an unexpected degree of self-confidence and decisiveness entered her voice. Her husband, she confided, was a doctor, and she had worked as a secretary for three years to help put him through medical school. "Three months might have been bearable," she said, "but three years of that was just awful." Then, with a slight giggle, she added: "Still, it had its advantages. The fact that I was the one earning the money gave me greater power. So when my husband finally graduated, I told him: 'Now it's my turn to take three years for myself.'"

What had she done with her three years? I asked. "Oh," she said, "I spent them at a school for simultaneous interpreters." Now she was working as a free lance, mostly interpreting at international conferences, and had all the business she could handle. The free-lance status was important to her, she explained, because it meant she could accommodate her schedule to that of her two-and-a-half-year-old daughter.

To keep the conversation going, I fed her another question: who took care of the baby when Mama was off interpreting? "We have plenty of built-in baby-sitters," she told me. "My mother-in-law lives with us, and my own parents live next door. Six hours a day, though, my daughter goes to nursery school, because my husband and I are afraid that if she spent too much time with her grandparents, she'd get spoiled."

"Your husband sounds like a very modern man," I remarked.

"Oh, I guess so," my companion said. Then, with a faint but unmistakable note of bitterness, she added: "But you know how it is with doctors; he works long hours, and he's always on call—which means that I have to do all the housework."

In Manhattan, Chicago or San Francisco, such a dinner conversation would be banal to the point of stupefaction. What made this one far from banal was that it took place in Tokyo and that my luncheon partner was, in all superficial respects, a conventional young middle-class Japanese wife. Her calm assumption of equality with her husband was part of my introduction to what I believe is one of the most significant—and most underreported—social trends in contemporary Japan. What is going on among educated women in today's Japan is a kind of underground revolution—a quiet but inexorable process which sooner or later seems certain to alter profoundly the sexual balance of power in the land of Madame Butterfly.

In the aspects of Japanese life that we have considered so far, we have seen women primarily in a manipulative role—and often in one of de facto dominance. But with relatively few exceptions, that is the situation only within the home or family circle. When women seek to operate outside that context in Japan, they encounter male chauvinism of the most deeply ingrained sort. Throughout the modern history of Japan, the great majority of Japanese men have regarded women who are not exclusively family-oriented either as sex objects or as fodder for economic exploitation—or both.

It is no accident that until the advent of the Sony and the Toyota, the first word that sprang into the minds of most Westerners when Japan was mentioned was almost certainly "geisha." To be sure, the common Western conception of the geisha's function in Japanese society has always been erroneous, and it is even more so today than it was before World War II. For one thing, true geisha—those who have gone through years of laborious training in classical Japanese music and dancing—are a relatively rare breed in contemporary Japan: in 1976, Liza Crihfield, a Japanese-speaking American anthropologist who actually served as a geisha herself for some time, estimated that there were a mere seventy-five thousand true geisha in all Japan. And in contrast with prewar Japan, where women were often forced into the so-called *mizushobai* (floating world) by poverty, today's geisha all enter the profession by choice—their most common motive, according to Crihfield, being "love of traditional Japanese arts."

As entertainers everywhere tend to do, geisha lead "liberated" personal lives: some become the mistress, or "second wife," of a particularly wealthy politician or businessman, and nearly all have lovers or a regular patron. But they do not dispense their favors indiscriminately, and any foreigner who goes to a geisha party with the expectation of coming away with a bed partner for the night is almost surely doomed to disappointment. (Geisha, in fact, don't particularly enjoy parties at which Westerners are present; most foreigners find classical Japanese music and dance an impenetrable bore and don't speak the language well enough to follow the rapid, sophisticated repartee for which geisha are famous.)

Yet talented as they may be, geisha clearly perform an essentially sexual function: their primary job is to make men feel warm, witty and virile. And this is even more openly true of Japan's bar hostesses, who probably number half a million or more and who have in a sense usurped from geisha the day-to-day job of giving Japanese males that unbuttoned feeling. Where geisha invariably appear in kimono, bar hostesses wear Western clothes—sometimes expensive designer dresses—and in general more closely approximate Western standards of beauty. Though somewhat more accessible sexually than geisha, they are not prostitutes either—or even necessarily "pushovers." But their stock in trade is feeding sexual fantasies: in countless clublike establishments throughout Japan, they dance cheek to cheek with their clients, nuzzle them, pat knees—and turn aside with giggles or pretended shock the customary (and generally purely ritualistic) proposals for more basic intimacies.

Many explanations have been offered for the fact that so many political and business relationships in Japan are cemented at geisha parties or in between bouts of badinage with bar hostesses. Some sociologists argue that Japanese men are inherently awkward socially and require this kind of lubricant to become comfortable enough with each other to establish mutual trust and fellowship. An even less flattering view is that the typical Japanese male simply can't relax in the presence of "good" women, who subconsciously remind him of the indirect constraints imposed on him in childhood by his mother. Whatever its psychiatric implications, however, the function played by geisha and bar hostesses clearly reflects a conviction still held by most Japanese men: the only proper role for a woman, other than that of family manager, is one in which she bolsters up men.

That being so, it's scarcely surprising that Japanese women who pursue power, prestige or material success in their own right have always faced a rocky road. In Japan's political establishment, for example, women still play only the most peripheral part. As of 1981, women occupied only 26 of the 761 seats in Japan's parliament. Only two women have ever served as cabinet ministers, and none has done so since the early '60s. In fact, with the death in 1981 of the aged Fusae Ichikawa, the den mother of Japanese feminism and a much-respected member of the upper house of parliament, Japan was left without a single female politician who possessed clout of significant order.

On the economic front, things are in some ways even worse. More and more Japanese women hold jobs every year; some 48 percent of all females over fifteen now work, and they account for better than a third of the total labor force. But as in the United States, the salary of the average woman is less than 60 percent of that earned by the average man. Most major Japanese industrial and financial institutions, in fact, still refuse to hire women for anything but menial or clerical jobs, on the ground that it is not worth investing time and training in someone who is going to leave you as soon as she gets married and has her first child.

This is not a wholly disingenuous argument. Most of Japan's vast army of young unmarried "office ladies" are indeed simply filling in the years before they start a family; typically, they live with their parents, spend part of their salary on household goods they will need after they are married and blow the rest on chic clothes and foreign travel—a fact that has won them (and their young male counterparts) the somewhat invidious nickname of *dokushin kizoku*, or "unmarried aristocrats." But while this is the general pattern, it is by no means a universal one. Yet many Japanese companies use it as an excuse for discriminating against highly qualified young women who do want to pursue careers in the same way men do. Some Japanese companies, in fact, deliberately ease out women who are still on the job at twenty-seven or twenty-eight—partly by not promoting them as they would men with comparable experience and qualifications. Others simply decline to hire women for career-track jobs in the first place. Though it is rarely stated publicly any longer, the attitude of many male Japanese executives remains that reported to me by a Tokyo woman whose brother occupies a senior position in one of Japan's top economic-research organizations. "My brother says women economists are no good," this woman informed me in carefully neutral tones. "So his company just doesn't bother to interview them."

Any liberated young American woman surveying this situation would surely conclude that what Japan needs is a good, strong women's movement. But there's not much to be expected on that count. A Western-style women's movement does exist in Japan, but it is tiny, fragmented and too often slavishly imitative of the more extreme aspects of the women's movement in the United States. The result is that it carries no weight with Japan's political leaders and very little with the kind of young women who in other countries would be its natural recruits. "Of course, I approve of the basic aims of the liberation movement," one Tokyo career girl told me. "But they have been so noisy and foolish in their tactics that I think they have actually hurt the cause of equality."

On the surface, then, the prospects for female emancipation in Japan would appear to be, if not hopeless, at least extremely dim. But when you probe deeper, a very different picture emerges. A great many Japanese women—almost certainly, in fact, the majority of them—still derive their basic satisfaction in life from the power that they wield in the family. But for a growing minority, that is no longer enough. Among younger women who have been to college or university, aspirations for significant achievement outside the home are increasingly common. Of all the university-educated women under thirty I have talked with in Japan in recent years, I found only one who expressed no resentment at the discrimination against women in the business world—and even she proclaimed that she did not intend to let having children put a permanent end to her career.

Paradoxically, the root cause of this very contemporary phenomenon lies in events that occurred more than thirty years ago, during the U.S. Occupation. Probably the single most enduring reform imposed upon Japan by the Occupation authorities was their insistence that the Japanese Constitution guarantee women equal rights with men. In their eagerness to learn from their conquerors, the Japanese of the MacArthur era were for a time almost uncritically receptive of American ideas, and one result of this was the emergence in the early postwar period of a small but critical leavening of remarkable women.

One of these is a human typhoon named Taeko Matsuda, whose father, a former social worker, eventually became a major figure in Japan's ruling Liberal Democratic Party. Now fifty, Taeko was sent to study at U.C.L.A. shortly after World War II and, while in the States, married an American Nisei. When she returned to Japan and tried to buy an American-style house, she was outraged at the astronomical prices she encountered. Her solution was characteristic of the woman: though she had no architectural or business training, she started her own construction company, which, over the next dozen years, built and sold thousands of homes. In her off hours, she also bore and raised three children—to whom, she says, she has been "a marvelous mother."

Today, from an office decorated with a Picasso, a Dubuffet and sleek leather-and-aluminum furniture, Taeko operates a foundation which doubles as a kind of consumerist group for homeowners and a building-industry research group. She also dispenses, at the drop of a hat, no-holds-barred guidance and opinions on almost any subject you care to bring up. I have myself been the recipient of her advice on child rearing ("It's not the quantity of attention that counts, it's the quality") and have heard her tell an aspiring Japanese politician to his face that the reason he hadn't risen higher was that he was "too arrogant."

When it comes to the role of women in present-day Japanese society, Taeko is no less blunt. "Japanese women who feel they can't combine marriage and a career are simply weak or uninterested," she says. "Of course, you have to choose your husband carefully, but if you do that, there's no problem." Then, softening a bit, she adds: "I feel sorry for Japanese men; they're in a weak position now. Whereas women have so many choices open to them, they don't know what to do."

At first blush, Mayumi Moriyama appears far more the traditional Japanese woman than Taeko Matsuda. Mrs. Moriyama dresses in restrained tailored clothes, and the furniture in the office she occupies as a member of the House of Councillors—the upper chamber of the Diet, as Japan's parliament is called—is covered with lace doilies adorned with large pink and baby-blue rosettes. But it takes only a few minutes' conversation to discover that beneath a vivacious manner lies a steely determination.

It could scarcely be otherwise, for Mrs. Moriyama's entire career has been one of painfully achieved firsts for her sex. A seventeen-year-old when World War II ended, she succeeded, through extraordinary effort, in becoming one of the first women ever admitted to Tokyo University (which became coeducational only at the insistence of the Occupation authorities). After her graduation from Todai, she became the first woman to pass Japan's civil service entrance exams and was accepted as a junior official in the Ministry of Labor. In the ministry, despite the fact that she was married and the mother of three children, she advanced steadily to the upper levels of the bureaucracy, racking up another series of firsts for women in the process. And in 1980, after Liberal Democratic leaders persuaded her to enter politics, she became the first woman ever elected to the Diet simultaneously with her husband.

Though she clearly enjoys her new role as a politician, Mrs. Moriyama equally clearly has her reservations about the current political scene in Japan. Playing the devil's advocate, I asked her whether the fact that there were no women in Prime Minister Zenko Suzuki's Cabinet meant that there were no women qualified to handle ministerial responsibilities. "Of course there are women qualified to be ministers," she said in unruffled tones, "but Mr. Suzuki didn't think of us." Quietly, but very firmly, she added: "He should have. The male politicians neglect us. We must make them pay attention."

Loyal as Mrs. Moriyama is to her party, the Liberal Democratic leadership might be well advised to handle her with care. An expert on the economic lot of Japanese women—she was for a time director of the Women's Affairs Bureau of the Labor Ministry—she believes that the only important legal protection her countrywomen now lack is a law ordaining equal opportunity in employment. What would she do if such a bill were introduced in the Diet and the LDP's leaders opposed it? I asked. "If I thought it was a workable bill, I would vote for it," she said. "When I was running for the Diet, I told people I would speak for women—and that won me lots of women's votes, including the votes of women who don't normally support the LDP."

For all her pragmatism and air of moderation, in short, Mayumi Moriyama is a dedicated feminist. Though she disapproves of the tactics and many of the ideas of the women's movement in Japan, she is quick to add: "But it does help attract people's attention to the women's struggle." And looking back over her own career, she says a bit ruefully: "I always thought I had to work harder than my male colleagues for the sake of the women who would come after me."

Undeniably, the example of people like Taeko Matsuda and Mayumi Moriyama has served to pave the way for younger women. Without their pioneering efforts—and those of a number of other women their age—the resistance to equal opportunity for women in Japan today would be even greater than it is.

But there is another, equally important reason for the emergence

of more and more career-minded women in Japan—a process sometimes described as "Americanization," but which in fact simply
reflects inexorable social and economic trends in all advanced industrial societies. Today's Japanese women are better educated than
their mothers (in prewar years, the majority of Japanese girls
completed only the equivalent of the first year of a U.S. high school;
now 95 percent finish high school, and a third go on to get college
or university degrees). Female life expectancy in Japan is also much
greater than it used to be (seventy-eight today vs. fifty in 1945).
Finally, the widespread switch to nuclear family patterns and the
proliferation of household appliances has vastly reduced the amount
of time the average Japanese woman must spend on housework.

All these developments mean that a much higher percentage of
Japan's women now have both the ability and the freedom to do
something besides take care of home and family. And their desire
to do so has been heightened by the ever-growing appetite of
Japanese for material possessions. As in the United States, it is
increasingly difficult for a Japanese family with only one wage earner
to support the kind of middle-class life-style that numbers among
the "necessities" expensive housing, money-eating automobiles,
color TV sets and vacation travel. As a result 65 percent of the
female labor force in Japan now consists of married women.

In Japan as in most places, the great majority of working women
still occupy routine, lower-level jobs. But there are more and more
exceptions to that rule. Some of the most prestigious government
agencies now routinely include at least a few women in each year's
intake of recent university graduates destined to become career
officials. And a growing number of women in their thirties and
forties now hold influential positions in the media, retailing and the
service industries. Since the latter two areas are among the fastest-
growing sectors of the Japanese economy, it seems likely that they
may turn out to be a kind of backdoor route through which women
eventually gain access to the upper levels of Japanese business.

Just as important as the nature of the jobs some younger women
hold is the fact that a number of them manage their personal lives
in ways which would have been almost inconceivable in the Japan
of twenty years ago. A notable case in point is Yoriko Kawaguchi,
who, as I mentioned earlier, is one of Tokyo University's more
remarkable contributions to the Japanese elite. When I met her in
November 1980, Yoriko was director of the Office of International
Research and Development Cooperation and as such one of the only

four women division chiefs in the vast and powerful Ministry of International Trade and Industry (MITI). Her credentials for that job included a postgraduate degree in economics from Yale and, as one elderly male journalist informed me with a mixture of respect and incredulity, the authorship of a MITI white paper on international trade policy which marked her as a real comer in the eyes of those who keep book on the Japanese bureaucracy.

A trim, composed person in her late thirties, Yoriko has been married for more than a dozen years now to a fellow MITI official. ("I was too busy to date men outside the ministry," she explains.) By happy coincidence, both Kawaguchis hold the same rank at MITI, and both lead the harried lives characteristic of Japanese bureaucrats. They leave home each morning at eight thirty and seldom get home much before eight at night. Fairly often, Yoriko admits, she goes out after work for a drink and some socializing with her male colleagues, and then it can be midnight before she gets home.

Her long hours at work mean that Yoriko has relatively little time to spend with her children, a boy of five and a girl of three. Of necessity, both children attend a public day-care center and are cared for by maids much of the rest of the time. This is a state of affairs that would appall a traditional Japanese mother, but Yoriko accepts it as part of the price she must pay for her quiet but unshakable commitment to the principle of equality between the sexes. Fortunately, her husband apparently accepts that principle too, and like increasing numbers of younger Japanese men, he helps with the children and the housework—domestic responsibilities of a kind that Japanese males traditionally regarded as beneath their dignity.

Since she has no children, Ryo Ochiai has found it somewhat easier than Yoriko Kawaguchi to combine marriage and a career. Even so, life with her businessman husband has had its ups and downs. "Years ago," says Ryo, "my husband used to say that I was sacrificing him for my work. But now he's not so traditional; he even helps me with the dishwashing."

That Mr. Ochiai has had his consciousness raised is scarcely surprising. A tiny, birdlike woman who giggles a lot, Ryo Ochiai is nonetheless a person of tremendous decisiveness and force. A doctor's daughter, she joined Sony Corporation twenty-two years ago, immediately after graduating from university. Now, in her mid-forties, she is Sony's highest-ranking woman employee, with responsibility for planning the "software" aspects of Sony's line of household appliances.

In part, Ryo's rise to executive status reflects the fact that Sony is, by Japanese standards, a very progressive corporation. But there are limits even to Sony's enlightenment. It was only in 1980 that the company began to pay women and men the same wages for the same work. And Sony still hires ten male university graduates for each female graduate it employs. "Being a woman means you have to work three times as effectively as a man," says Ryo Ochiai.

Somewhat bitterly, Ryo blames the entrenchment of male supremacy in Japan primarily on women. "It's traditional-minded mothers who treat their sons like kings who are the real problem," she says. Ultimately, she believes, the solution lies in changing the Japanese educational system, right down to primary-school level, so that it does not reflect sexual stereotypes.

But that's for the long run. In the shorter run, Ryo is working on the construction of a kind of "Old Girl net." At Sony itself, she and other relatively senior women keep a sharp eye out for opportunities for employment or advancement for younger women. And together with 150 other women from both government and private business, she belongs to something called The Association of Home Economists and Consumer Affairs Professionals. "Eventually," she says, "I expect women will have a position of enough strength in business that we'll have to be listened to."

One Japanese woman who is already widely listened to—and widely discussed—is vivacious, fast-talking Mitsuko Shimomura, who until her recent return to the home office helped cover the United States for the great Tokyo daily *Asahi* and its weekly magazine, *Shukan Asahi*. Sooner or later in almost every conversation about Mitsuko with other Japanese, wondering mention is made of the fact that when she moved to New York, her husband, an executive in a paper-manufacturing company, remained at home in Tokyo. Mitsuko herself says that if she had had children, she might not have felt free to accept the New York assignment. But as things are, she emphasizes, her husband urged her to do so. "He said that two or three years wasn't a long part of the time we will be living together," she recalls.

When she took the New York assignment, Mitsuko became the first woman ever sent abroad as a permanent correspondent by a Japanese newspaper. It was a distinction she clearly relished—and understandably so; when she first went on the job market in Tokyo, no Japanese daily employed women in anything more than a clerical capacity. To break into journalism at all, Mitsuko was obliged to become a part-time employee of an English-language magazine which *Asahi* published for tourists.

By her own admission, Mitsuko has at times resorted to irksome expedients to achieve her career goals. As a very young woman, she dutifully studied most of the classic Japanese "bridal subjects," such as flower arrangement and the tea ceremony; that helped reconcile her very traditional family to the fact that she chose to major in the unfeminine field of economics at Keio University and subsequently went on to get her M.A. in the same field at New York University. Similarly, in her first job, she uncomplainingly made tea for her male colleagues. "Nobody forced me to," she says, "but if I hadn't, they wouldn't have liked it. Then my editor began to give me more and more responsibility, and after a while I didn't have to make tea anymore."

Eventually, Mitsuko was transferred to the staff of the *Asahi* weekly magazine, and there, with the oil crisis of 1973, she got her first big break. On a flying trip to the Persian Gulf, she succeeded in getting interviews with the rulers of eight of the Arab oil sheikdoms. That led to the first of her seven books and a long string of interviews with world figures that have established her as "the Oriana Fallaci of Japan."

A supreme realist, Mitsuko freely admits that "most men think my success is explained precisely by the fact that I'm a woman—and it's partly true. When I do interviews with business leaders, for example, I get more attention for it than a man would." At bottom, though, Mitsuko's success rests on her own talent, shrewdness and hard work, and she is keenly aware of that fact. "I did my work well enough so that after a while the men began to think, 'Well, she can do it after all.' And then I got the power; then they gave me the space with which to influence both men and women."

If you mention the kind of women I have been discussing to male Japanese—or male foreign residents of Japan—the reaction you almost invariably get is "Yes, but those women are only a tiny elite. Most Japanese women have no such ambitions. And even if they did, men in this country are so set in their ways that they will never accept women as their equals."

Most of the reams of statistics available in survey-loving Japan appear to support these contentions. As we have seen, most Japanese women still lead restricted lives, particularly during the years when they have small children, and the great majority of them accept that as inevitable, if not desirable. It's also true that the majority of Japanese males still strongly oppose any notion of greater freedom for women; a number of male writers on family subjects have roundly denounced women who put their children in day-care centers, and one of them, an academic named Jun Eto, has even accused such women of saddling their children with all sorts of problems ranging from slow speech development to the inability to fold origami paper properly.

But in this case, as in so many others, the statistics almost certainly fail to reflect social dynamics. Anyone who argues that relations between the sexes in Japan are going to remain essentially frozen in their present patterns overlooks, I am convinced, several key considerations.

One of these is that fundamental characteristic of the Japanese, extraordinary receptivity to foreign ideas and fashions. The fact that the cause of women's rights has made such rapid progress in the West—and particularly in the United States—has already had impact in Japan and will almost surely have even more in the future. "In a sense," Yoriko Kawaguchi told me, "it's à la mode that women should advance."

Perhaps even more important—and highly deceptive to foreign observers—is the fact that in their struggle for equality the majority of Japan's feminists have scrupulously avoided confrontation tactics. "If you want to change the social structure in Western culture," Mitsuko Shimomura explains, "you first have to fight—to challenge the system. But in our culture, once you start to fight, that's the end. In Japan, the process is conducted underground, so to speak. You have to try to do everything without big friction and change the consensus in quiet, even tricky ways."

To Westerners, the notion of trying to change the behavior patterns of an entire nation by indirect suasion sounds like a surefire recipe for indefinite survival of the status quo. But for Japanese, with their powerful group orientation and historic tendency to reshape their society by consensual means, indirect suasion can be a potent instrument indeed.

What is going on in Japan now, I believe, is a subtle but inexorable consensus-changing process concerning sexual roles. "Most Japanese men really don't like the idea of equality for women," Mitsuko Shimomura admits. "They have even stronger feelings about it than American men. But when it comes to formal discussion, they can't say so anymore because it's becoming socially accepted. Television and the newspapers are spreading the idea, and the government has contributed to the process too."

The role of the Japanese Government in promoting women's rights is an especially important, if ambivalent, one. It's abundantly clear that most of the elderly men who run the Japanese political establishment find the concept of sexual equality about as welcome as smallpox and will do whatever they safely can to delay its advent. But out of concern for Japan's cherished international image if nothing else, they have already been obliged to give considerable ground. In 1980 when a U.N.-sponsored women's conference in Copenhagen adopted a convention aimed at eliminating discrimination against women everywhere in the world, the Japanese Government at first declined to sign it. But under pressure from the press and women's groups which argued that no "modern nation" could take such a benighted stance, that decision was finally reversed. "If the women's groups keep up their pressure, I think the various relevant provisions of Japanese law will eventually be brought up to the standards specified by the convention," says Sadako Ogata, a professor of international relations at Sophia University and the first woman ever to achieve ministerial rank in the Japanese diplomatic service. "To what extent those provisions will actually be put into practice, however, I don't know."

There is also something of a feminist lobby inside the government itself. "Women in politics and the bureaucracy," says Mitsuko Shimomura, "work very hard in secret ways to promote our cause." They also work hard in some not-so-secret ways. During a trip I made to Japan in late 1980, the Women's Bureau of the Ministry of Labor was busily plastering the country with pamphlets and posters reminding everyone that 1980 marked the halfway point of the International Women's Decade and proclaiming the importance of equal rights. In Japan, where bureaucratic pronouncements are taken considerably more earnestly than in the United States, this sort of thing has impact.

Curiously, not too many Japanese men, so far as I can detect, fully comprehend what is happening to them. Perhaps because of the very obliqueness of the tactics involved, they frequently seem unaware that more and more educated women of this generation are devoting to the cause of female emancipation the same combination of guile and strength that originally served to make Japanese women dominant within the family. And few Japanese men seem to have paid much attention to some statistics that I *do* regard as significant, primarily because they reflect the opinions of all segments of Japan's female population and not just those of the educated minority. As recently as the early 1970s, polls showed that 80 percent of Japanese women believed that a husband should work and a wife should take care of the home; by 1976, however, only 49 percent still held to that belief, and by 1979 the figure had dropped to only 36 percent. Even more to the point, a survey taken in October 1979 showed that 60 percent of Japan's female population had come to believe that women who had the desire and ability should be allowed to enter fields of work previously considered reserved for men.

It would be a grave mistake to interpret what is going on in Japan purely in American terms of reference. Just as the tactics adopted by most Japanese feminists differ from those used by their American counterparts, so the end results of the women's revolution in Japan will surely be somewhat different than in the United States. "The weight of trying to reconcile individual achievement and the family will always be heavy here because of our group-oriented value system," says Sadako Ogata. Among other things, I suspect that a double standard concerning marital infidelity will persist considerably longer in Japan than in the United States, that far fewer women will be content to go childless in Japan than in the United States and that a modified form of arranged marriage will continue to be relatively common in Japan for a long time to come. But that Japanese women will in the end achieve a status comparable, in terms of their own culture, to that occupied by American women seems to me inevitable.

The key question, in fact, seems to me not whether the Japanese women's revolution will triumph, but how soon. On that score, even the participants differ. Most Japanese women agree with Sadako Ogata, who believes the process will be a slow and gradual one. But when I suggested to Mitsuko Shimomura that it might take twenty more years before Japan knows something like the degree of sexual equality that now exists in the United States, she stared at me in astonishment. "Much less," she shot back confidently. "It's happening very fast now."

Prudence tells me that Sadako Ogata's prognosis is the safer one—and if I were Jimmy the Greek, that's probably where I would feel obliged to put my money. But the truth is that it simply is not possible to predict with any assurance how fast this particular social revolution will unfold in Japan. Despite all the deeply entrenched resistance to the concept of female equality, there are strong economic forces working in its favor—the most important being the growing shortage of new entrants into the labor force brought about by Japan's low birthrate. Already, in fact, this situation has resulted in one development that would have been inconceivable in Japan only a decade ago: an increasing influx of women into the highly technical field of computer programming.

Perhaps more important yet is the fact that in the age of mass communications, what start out as minority views often snowball—a phenomenon that could prove of particular significance in Japan. Because it is consensus rather than immutable principles that rules Japanese life, the Japanese have in the past repeatedly done relatively quick flip-flops on the very basic issues. And given the instant dissemination of ideas and information characteristic of our day, it is entirely conceivable that the amount of time it takes the Japanese to accomplish the consensus-changing process may prove even shorter in the future than it was in the past.

All in all, then, I believe that a shrewd businessman in Japan these days would make a special point of recruiting female university and college graduates. For despite the increased opportunities now open to them, they still constitute an underexploited pool of talent—and tapping that pool intelligently today could do a company a lot of good, both operationally and in public relations terms, a few years from now.

6

"My Home"

My friend Wataru Hiraizumi, who is not only a prominent politician but the fortunate possessor of one of the largest and most elegant private homes in Tokyo, was holding forth one evening in his leather-lined study on the psychic differences between Japanese and Americans. "I'll tell you one really important one that's often overlooked," he said finally. "Where a young American will dream of making lots of money, a young Japanese dreams of acquiring space—just plain room."

Like many useful insights, Hiraizumi's aphorism contains an element of hyperbole. It seems reasonably clear that there are plenty of young Japanese who yearn for both space and money. Nonetheless, I know of no country other than Japan where the dream of acquiring a modest house with a tiny garden is so pervasive and powerful that it has been elevated to the status of an "ism." "My home-ism" the Japanese call this national preoccupation, and its allure, sadly, stems in large part from the fact that the great majority of Japanese live in conditions so cramped that most Americans would find them intolerable.

To great extent, this is a self-inflicted wound. It's undeniably true that Japan suffers from a shortage of easily usable living space. The country is only about the size of Montana to begin with, and nearly three-quarters of its land area is mountainous. Beyond that, the bulk of such flat land as does exist in Japan is occupied by farms, roads, industrial sites, golf courses, tennis courts and other nonresidential facilities. The result is that in terms of space actually devoted to housing, the entire Japanese people—all 118 million of them—are jammed into an area significantly smaller than the state of Connecticut.

In earlier eras, this huddling together of the Japanese in the flatter parts of their country made good sense; the mountainous areas were both inaccessible and particularly vulnerable to the ravages of typhoons and earthquakes. But today, modern transportation and building techniques have radically altered this situation—at least potentially. Herman Kahn and Thomas Pepper of the Hudson Institute have estimated that it would be economically and technically feasible to double or triple the amount of usable land in Japan by the year 2000 through the exploitation of hillside locations and sites in relatively remote areas. But in this respect, the usually adaptable Japanese have so far shown scant flexibility. Instead of heading for the high ground and its open reaches, they continue to cling doggedly to the crowded plain.

There is a good deal more to this, however, than simply an atavistic aversion to mountain living. Wataru Hiraizumi, for example, was elected to parliament from the district where his family originated, a rural area considerably north of Tokyo, and he still spends nearly every weekend there cultivating his constituents. I'm confident, however, that he would never consider living full time "in the provinces"—and neither would any other Japanese with ambitions to go far in the world.

The reason for this is that all the meaningful action in Japan takes place in an area which bears a remarkable resemblance to our own "BosWash corridor": the so-called Tokaido megalopolis. The vast human beehive runs along the south coast of Japan's main island of Honshu from Tokyo to Kobe and in addition to those two great cities includes such other major centers as Yokohama, Osaka, Kyoto and Nagoya. Considerably smaller in area than the BosWash corridor—it is only 300 miles long vs. 450 for BosWash—the Tokaido megalopolis is a monument to unplanned urban sprawl, and riding through it on one of Japan's famed "bullet trains" is reminiscent of riding the Metroliner through the grim landscapes of northeastern New Jersey. At intervals, traces of the old Japan are visible: graceful tiled-roofed houses surrounded by ancient trees seemingly shaped by some divine landscape architect, straw-hatted farmers working in their rice fields, a distant vista of forested mountains. But the dominant impression is one of industrial society at its worst: factories built without the slightest concession to architectural aesthetics, warehouses that look like Quonset huts afflicted with gigantism, enormous boxlike concrete apartment buildings and interminable clusters of shabby-looking Mom-and-Pop shops, auto-repair establishments and other small enterprises.

Even before World War II, what is now the Tokaido megalopolis was already the heart of Japan, psychically as well as physically. But today it comes dangerously close to being all of Japan that matters. Not only are the central government and all its major agencies located there, but so are the headquarters of nearly every large industrial and financial institution, two-thirds of Japan's universities (including virtually all the "good" ones), all of the major publishing and communications groups and an overwhelming concentration of the people and institutions that shape Japan's cultural life. Unlike the United States, Japan simply doesn't have an alternative capital of pop culture like Los Angeles, a "provincial" industrial complex comparable to Detroit or widely dispersed centers of economic and financial power such as Chicago, Houston and Dallas. With far more justification than New Yorkers, the residents of the Tokaido megalopolis—and most particularly of Tokyo itself—can make the scornful boast "Everywhere else is Bridgeport."

Under any circumstances, the extraordinary concentration of opportunity and amenities in the Tokaido megalopolis would surely have given it a magnetic appeal to venturesome souls in other parts of Japan. But that magnetic effect was vastly enhanced by the great shift of population that took place in Japan in the decades following World War II. In 1945, about 45 percent of the Japanese population was rural and about 55 percent urban. Since then, for reasons similar to those that produced the same effect in the United States a generation or so earlier, the farm population of Japan has dwindled until today only 13 percent of Japanese are country-dwellers. And inevitably, in their search for new sources of livelihood and a more comfortable existence, huge numbers of those Japanese who left the farm gravitated to the megalopolis. Between 1965 and 1975 alone, its population increased by some 10 million. By 1980, it was home to more than 50 million people—or some 42 percent of all Japanese.

The fact that this enormous ingathering was bound to have unhealthy social and economic consequences was perceived quite early on by many thoughtful Japanese. Among them was a remarkable man named Kakuei Tanaka, who in 1972 touched up a scheme he had had prepared for him by the Ministry of International Trade and Industry and published it in book form under the rather grandiloquent title *A Plan for Remodeling the Japanese Archipelago*. The book, which proposed a massive national program to lure people back into the outlying areas of Japan through wholesale decentralization of industry, immediately captured the public imagination, and in late 1972, when Tanaka was elected Prime Minister, it seemed a foregone conclusion that his highly imaginative scheme would become national policy.

Ironically, however, Tanaka's political triumph quickly backfired. Assuming that his book could now be taken as a kind of official blueprint, speculators began feverishly buying up land in areas of the country that seemed to be earmarked for development. This produced a wild inflation of real estate prices and also, since a number of the speculators were political insiders, considerable public disillusionment with the Tanaka plan.

Compounding this problem was the character of Tanaka himself. A self-made multimillionaire whose brusque, hard-driving style early on won him the nickname "the computerized bulldozer," he is a man of undeniable talent and vision. Yet when I met him briefly in the Prime Minister's office in 1973 I recall being struck by the fact that he somehow possessed the excessively well-barbered, quietly sinister aura of a Mafia boss. More concretely, he appears to hold the old-fashioned belief that provided a statesman serves his country well, it is perfectly reasonable for him to enrich himself and his friends in the process. As we shall see, the Japanese are somewhat more tolerant of what they call "money politics" than contemporary Americans are, but even by Japanese standards Tanaka went too far. In December 1974, after a series of press revelations concerning his freewheeling use of political contributions and questionable real estate dealings, he was obliged to resign as Prime Minister. And with his downfall, any hope for fullscale adoption of his great decentralization plan disappeared.

Despite this historic missed opportunity, some of the things Tanaka urged have actually come to pass. High-speed rail transportation is now being extended into areas of Japan that previously lacked it, tax incentives and other inducements have led to a certain amount of industrial decentralization and in the last few years a number of Japan's provincial cities have grown at a faster rate than Tokyo or Osaka. But relatively speaking, all this is small beer; to ease significantly the overcrowding in the Tokaido megalopolis, the Japanese Government would have to devote a major share of its resources to creating jobs in provincial cities and seeing to it that those cities offered cultural, academic and entertainment facilities of a much higher order than they now do. So far, there is no sign of a political will to do this. That, in turn, seems to mean that for the foreseeable future the great majority of Japanese will continue to dream of space—but actually live in what a sharp-tongued Common Market official named Sir Roy Denman a few years ago scornfully labeled their "rabbit hutches."

Invidious as it is, the phrase "rabbit hutch" is an accurate enough description of the typical Japanese dwelling to have achieved a certain bitter currency among Japanese themselves. One night a few years ago I had dinner at a Tokyo restaurant with a Japanese couple whom I had originally met in New York. When we had finished eating, the husband, a government official whom I shall call Chitoshi, somewhat startled me by suggesting: "Just for educational purposes, why don't you come along home for a brandy and let us show you our rabbit hutch." The remark was accompanied by a giggle, but like so many Japanese giggles, this one was totally mirthless.

When we got to Chitoshi's apartment, I could see why. By Japanese standards, it was luxurious—a condominium in one of the modern Western-style apartment buildings to which Japanese somewhat mysteriously apply the English word "mansion." Expensively decorated with furniture Chitoshi and his wife had brought back from the United States, it was thoroughly tasteful and blessedly quiet. It also had the advantage of being located only about half an hour's commute from the ministry where Chitoshi worked. But it consisted in its entirety of a windowless kitchen and eating space, a living room about 8 by 15 feet and a smallish bedroom and bath—in all perhaps 500 square feet of space. For this, sometime in 1980, Chitoshi had paid $250,000. In Manhattan at that time, the same amount of money would easily have bought him an apartment twice as big and just as centrally located.

Yet Chitoshi, as I have said, is privileged compared with most residents of the Japanese megalopolis and particularly in comparison with other residents of Tokyo, where the overcrowding is at its most acute. Partly because of sheer population pressure, but also because of successive waves of real estate speculation by large corporations, residential land prices in Japan long ago went through the roof; between 1955 and 1972, in fact, they increased six times as fast as the disposable income of the average city worker. And while their rate of increase has slowed down in recent years, both land and construction costs are now at such astronomical levels that the average skilled worker or ordinary *sarariman* (salaryman), as

Japanese call white-collar employees, simply cannot dream of acquiring the kind of living space that an American of comparable means would regard as minimally adequate. In the Tokyo area, for example, a house consisting of four or five rooms with a total area of 600 or 700 square feet—the equivalent of two or three modest-sized rooms in an American development house—sold in 1980 for five or six times the annual income of a highly paid industrial worker. And the alternative was even worse: the rent on a tiny two-room apartment in the remotest reaches of the city might well amount to a third or more of the joint income of a young working couple.

To ease this situation, many Japanese companies and government agencies help their employees with their housing problems. Close to 7 percent of Japan's people live in dwellings owned by their employers. And many Japanese who own their own homes—which is to say, as in the United States, roughly 60 percent of all Japanese families—are able to do so only because they have received financial assistance from their employer in the form of low-cost loans or discount land prices. (Nissan Motors, for example, has a subsidiary which specializes in buying residential real estate and reselling it to Nissan workers at prices significantly lower than those generally prevailing in the free market.)

The majority of Japanese, though, don't get this kind of help, and even those who do have to make every yen they spend on housing stretch as far as possible. Since housing costs in Japan, as everywhere else, tend to be lower the farther away you get from a central city, ordinary Japanese have a strong incentive to undertake the longest commute that flesh and blood can bear—and what flesh and blood can bear in Japan is quite extraordinary. For someone who works in Tokyo, a daily commute of two and a half to three hours is in no way remarkable. A few years ago, in fact, U.S. journalist John Saar discovered a technical writer named Ichiro Morinaga who had been commuting a mind-boggling five hours a day for eighteen years, riding nine different trains and two buses in the process.

Mr. Morinaga's long trek might be more comprehensible if what awaited him at the end of it were a spacious establishment in bucolic surroundings. But not so: what he was going home to all those years was a small wooden house on a tiny plot of ground. And the same—or worse—is true of nearly all of Tokyo's other long-distance commuters. For many, the payoff for all those interminable hours on jam-packed trains and buses is merely an affordable little flat in an unheated wooden apartment building. (Central heating is still uncommon in Japan—a country whose climate range is similar to that of the East Coast of the United States—and 80 percent of the country's housing units, including a high percentage of its apartment buildings, are still of wooden construction.) But increasingly often, particularly in the Tokyo area, the commuter's destination is likely to be a *danchi*, one of the huge concrete apartment blocks that the government-run Japan Housing Corporation has been busily throwing up since the early 1970s.

Danchi, I suppose, are a necessary evil. Without them and the government investment in the public welfare that they represent, Japan's current housing situation would be catastrophic instead of merely deplorable. But to paraphrase Lloyd George, they fall far short of being homes fit for heroes—even the purely pacific heroes of Japan's great economic victories. Grimly uniform in both exterior design and interior layout, *danchi* also tend to be inhabited by people of depressingly uniform background. There are *danchi* in which virtually all the mothers have only high school educations and the rare woman who possesses a college degree seeks to conceal the fact lest she be accused of putting on airs. There are also *danchi* whose residents all work for the government, and in such situations, one *danchi*-dweller explained to me, "everybody knows everybody else's salary, and if your husband has some special piece of good fortune you don't dare mention it for fear the other women will be jealous."

Heightening the oppressive intimacy of *danchi* living is the small size of the apartments, generally categorized by Japanese as 2DK and 3DK. A 3DK apartment consists of three rooms of perhaps 9 by 12 feet each, a kitchen with eating area and a bath. A 2DK, of course, has one room less; in terms of usable space, in fact, the typical 2DK is less than half the size of the tiny Connecticut weekend cottage which my wife and I consider really habitable only in seasons when we can spend most of our time outdoors and where we and our children keep only a very small fraction of our possessions. Yet many a young Japanese bureaucrat or junior executive manages to cram a family the size of mine plus all of its worldly goods into a 2DK—and feels himself, relatively speaking, not too badly off.

The most visible impact of the fact that all but a few Japanese must live in such extremely close quarters is to be found in the aesthetic aspects of family life. Americans who envisage Japanese homes as possessing the elegant austerity of a set from *Shogun*—a work that has a good deal less relevance to life in contemporary Japan than *Gone with the Wind* does to life in today's Atlanta—are laboring under a grave misapprehension. By that I in no way mean to imply that the extraordinary and uniquely harmonious aesthetic that characterized the Japan of centuries past has totally vanished. But in the urban Japan of today, it survives mainly in public or semipublic places: temples, palaces, traditional restaurants with gardens painstakingly planned to exemplify Alexander Pope's assertion that "all nature is but art unknown to thee." Essentially, moreover, these are oases of tranquillity and beauty in a world otherwise dominated by frantic bustle and relentless utilitarianism. For me, the aesthetic quintessence of late-twentieth-century Japan can be found in the magnificent garden maintained by the International House of Japan in the Roppongi district of Tokyo. Strolling along the shaded paths that wind amidst its flowering shrubs, ponds full of golden carp and artfully untended-looking specimen trees, it is possible to cherish the illusion that you are wandering in the wildwood—until you look up and spy the enormous boxlike concrete building that has recently been erected on the adjoining property.

But while such islands of repose, however circumscribed, do alleviate the grimness of Japan's cityscapes, anything but the most token concession to aesthetics is a rarity these days in the residences of ordinary Japanese city-dwellers. Today's typical Japanese house or apartment is, to be blunt about it, an unholy mess.

That, let me hasten to say, is not simply my subjective appraisal. In the late 1970s, a survey team headed by cultural anthropologist Yasuyuki Kurita made a scientific study of the contents of 140 homes and apartments of various types in the Tokaido megalopolis. Particularly in apartments of the 2DK size and smaller, Kurita and his colleagues reported, every available inch of wall space was taken up with wardrobes, bureaus and other large pieces of furniture. And that was just the beginning of the clutter. To create additional storage space, the tops of wardrobes, kitchen cabinets and sewing machines were almost invariably covered with piles of boxes. (In only one of the 140 households surveyed was there a sewing machine that could be used without the prior removal of other objects from its surface.) More often than not, both living rooms and bathrooms were littered with children's toys. And the typical home was, to use Kurita's word, "inundated" with anywhere up to thirty purely decorative objects, often displayed in similar fashion from family to family. The tops of TV sets and pianos, for example, appear to be generally regarded as suitable resting places for stuffed animals and

French dolls—perhaps, Kurita somewhat bemusedly speculates, because TVs and pianos were so adorned by department-store window dressers when they were first introduced to the Japanese market.

Quite clearly, the prime decorating problem of the contemporary Japanese housewife is how to jam all her possessions into space that might reasonably hold half of them—and one of the chief sources of that problem is the avidity with which Japanese have been acquiring appliances in the last couple of decades. As of 1981, there were 1,422 color TV sets in use in Japan for every one of the country's residents—man, woman and child. And more than 95 percent of all Japanese households now also boast an electric refrigerator, an electric washing machine, a vacuum cleaner and an automatic rice cooker. (That last item embitters me somewhat, since twenty years ago when I proposed to an American company with a uniquely suitable material that it go into partnership with a Japanese firm to produce electric rice cookers, I was dismissed as a wild-eyed dreamer.) What's more, the list of "necessary" appliances is steadily lengthening; recently, sales of air conditioners and electronic ovens have been growing so fast that it is presumably only a matter of time until these too become standard equipment in most Japanese households.

To some degree, all this reflects the national addiction to gadgetry that manifests itself almost anywhere you turn in Japan. Taxi riders in Tokyo, for example, never have to open or shut a cab door; that onerous task is performed for them by the cab driver, who operates his rear doors with an automatic control device. At restaurants and department stores, newly arrived patrons are frequently welcomed by kimono-clad robots who bow and utter the appropriate honorific phrases in mellifluous recorded tones. And in Japanese homes, this taste for gimmicks expresses itself in everything from table thermoses and elaborate space-age cigarette lighters to devices I have never encountered anywhere else in the world. My friend Chitoshi, for example, is inordinately proud of his "bilingual TV," with which, on certain channels, he can choose between English and Japanese sound for the same program. According to Chitoshi, this helps him keep his English up to snuff, and I have never had the heart to suggest that he might accomplish that just about as well—and at far less cost—by buying a good set of English-conversation records.

To be fair, however, the chief reason for the multiplication of appliances in the Japanese home is not just a passion for mechanical gimmicks, but the near-disappearance of a servant class in Japan. Thirty years or so ago, every middle-class Japanese family enjoyed the services of at least one live-in maid, but today, because of high wages and the exorbitant cost of a house or apartment big enough to include a maid's room, only extremely well-to-do Japanese can afford servants. To compensate, the ordinary Japanese housewife has, naturally enough, turned to labor-saving devices. And she has turned to them so enthusiastically that domestic chores nowadays often occupy only a secondary role in her life. Whereas the average housewife in prewar Japan spent no less than ten hours a day on homemaking, by the early 1970s the typical working wife with children spent only 3.7 hours a day at it—which was actually half an hour a day less than similarly situated American women. And even stay-at-home mothers in Japan put in only a bit over six hours a day. That, as it happens, is almost exactly the same amount of time that they devote each day to social and recreational activities and only two hours a day more than the typical Japanese adult devotes to watching television.

As the shift in housework patterns suggests, it's not just the way Japanese decorate and equip their homes that has changed significantly in the last few decades; it's also the way they live and behave at home. And to the dismay of traditionalists, most of these changes have been in the direction of Westernization. Most white-collar homes now include at least one Western-style room, with upholstered furniture instead of pillows scattered about the floor, permanent plaster walls instead of sliding paper ones and carpeting instead of the rice-straw mats known as *tatami*. Sleeping habits seem to be undergoing a similar metamorphosis: the majority of Japanese still sleep on the floor, using as bedding a small hard pillow, a folding mattress and a heavy quilt or two—all of which are kept in a closet during the day. But Western beds are steadily gaining ground; more than a quarter of all Japanese now use them. And so far as clothing is concerned, Westernization is virtually complete: when a Japanese man gets home from work and settles down in front of the TV set to relax, he may well shuck his Western suit and slip into a gray or black kimono. But his wife and daughters almost certainly will not follow his example; beautiful as it can be, the female kimono is both expensive and time-consuming to put on, so most Japanese women now wear it only on ceremonial occasions such as weddings and graduation parties. Normally, both for work and for play, they prefer what are still called "foreign clothes."

Perhaps the most radical single change in the Japanese life-style, however, has been in the kind of meals that are served in the average home. These would surely startle any American whose notion of Japanese cuisine has been formed by the traditional dishes served in most Japanese restaurants in the United States. Partly because of the large number of working wives who cannot afford to lavish large amounts of time on cooking, convenience foods are nearly as prevalent in Japan as in the United States. Nowadays, preparing the bean soup that many Japanese fancy for breakfast is apt to mean dumping a dried soup mix into hot water. And the same holds true for the noodle dishes of which Japanese are so fond; in 1980, well over 4 billion packages of dried "instant noodles" were sold in Japan—which works out to about 40 packages per person per year.

Along with the switch to convenience foods, moreover, have come major changes in the composition of the Japanese diet. At breakfast time, a good many Japanese now prefer dry cereal or toast and eggs to the traditional soup and rice. Rice consumption in Japan, in fact, has fallen by a third in the last twenty years and is still declining. Meantime, bread, which is cheaper than rice and which most Japanese children get in their school lunches, has steadily increased in popularity.

As this suggests, the general trend in Japanese eating habits is toward Western-style foods and greater variety. Historically, the staples of the Japanese diet were rice, vegetables and fish, but these are now supplemented by growing quantities of eggs, milk, dairy products and meat. Poultry sales in Japan, for example, have grown by 1,000 percent since the early '60s. And whenever schoolchildren are polled about what foods they prefer, hamburger regularly tops the list.

The increasingly Western tastes of Japanese children—spaghetti is another of their big favorites—have been an indirect boon to restaurateurs. Many Japanese men still have a craving for old-fashioned Japanese food, but working mothers understandably are often reluctant to prepare one meal for the kids and another for Daddy. The result has been the emergence of a whole class of restaurants that specialize in *o-fukuro no aji*—food like Mama used to make. Such establishments find their clientele primarily among urban salarymen who stop off after work for a few drinks and a plate of boiled fish in soy sauce or bean curd specialities—dishes which despite their simple ingredients are complicated to make and cannot simply be popped into the microwave to heat up.

Like the growing diversity of the Japanese diet, the frequency with which many daddies dine away from home obviously reflects Japan's new prosperity, but there are still some severe economic constraints on what the ordinary Japanese can eat and drink. Because of government protection of domestic tangerine growers, orange juice is prohibitively expensive; the last glass of it I had in Tokyo cost me $4. And the protection given to Japanese cattle raisers keeps the price of beef at what can only be called scandalous levels. A few years ago when the cost of steak in Tokyo hit nearly nine times what it was in New York, a college classmate of mine who has lived in Japan for twenty years and prospered mightily was so outraged that he threatened to abandon his business and move back to the United States.

Despite such anomalies, however, contemporary Japanese eat well by world standards: their average protein intake is roughly equivalent to that of the average American, and since they derive a smaller percentage of their calories from fats and carbohydrates than we do, their diet is nutritionally better balanced than our own. This, of course, represents an enormous improvement over the dietary situation in prewar Japan—and it is that improvement which, at least in large part, accounts for the striking change in the physical appearance of the Japanese people in the last few decades.

When I first landed in Japan in 1945, the overwhelming majority of Japanese were extremely short and squat. Such a high percentage of the women had heavy and unattractive legs—known in Japanese male slang as *daikon,* or radish, legs—that the rationale behind the floor-length kimono suddenly became blindingly clear. Today, however, the younger people one sees on the streets of Tokyo, while still in general considerably shorter than the average American, tend to be quite "Western" in their physical proportions, and girls with *daikon* legs are far scarcer than they used to be.

The statistics, moreover, bear out this impressionistic view. Between 1958 and 1978, the average height of Japanese fourteen-year-olds increased by $3\frac{1}{2}$ inches, while their weight increased by only a bit over 12 pounds. And happily, virtually all of the height increase has been concentrated in the area where it was most needed—at least, from an aesthetic point of view. As far as the length of their torsos (and their chest measurements) are concerned, today's Japanese teen-agers are just about identical to those of twenty years ago. The big difference is that today's youngsters have much longer legs.

By no means all Japanese, however, view the physical changes wrought by their new diet as an unalloyed blessing. The overall statistics, some doctors point out, conceal the fact that there are now a fair number of Japanese children who are seriously overweight—a problem that didn't exist in prewar Japan. And even what Westerners regard as the greater physical attractiveness of the younger generation of Japanese evokes mixed feelings in Japan itself. "Today," a Japanese Government information bulletin notes, "the physique of Japanese youths makes their elders wonder if they belong to the same race. . . . We may expect many tall, slim beauties among Japanese women in the future. The same physical transformation, however, will make men appear weak and less masculine." In an even more pessimistic vein, Japan's Bureau of Statistics reported a few years ago that for all their increased size, contemporary Japanese children are inferior to prewar kids both in strength and in their ability to do physical exercises.

Unless a foreigner stays in Japan a long time and becomes unusually intimate with his Japanese colleagues, he is not apt to see at first hand the kind of home and life-style we have been discussing. An upper-level Japanese businessman or bureaucrat who will pick up mind-boggling tabs for Western associates at a restaurant or geisha house will rarely invite those same associates to his home—and less exalted Japanese are even more unlikely to do so. This is partly because Japanese don't entertain much at home anyway, but also because most of them are uneasy about having their privacy invaded by foreigners and believe that foreigners, in turn, are uneasy with Japanese food and customs. Even a Japanese who has worked in Europe or America and become accustomed to entertaining Western friends in his apartment in Düsseldorf or Manhattan will rarely continue to do so once he has returned to Japan. His explanation, if he offers any, will be that his quarters are too small to entertain in, and that will almost surely be true. What he won't say—but what is probably the most powerful factor in his thinking—is that he would be embarrassed to have foreign acquaintances see how humble his dwelling place is compared with that of a person of comparable status in the West.

There is, moreover, something other than purely personal embarrassment involved here. In the last decade or so, Japanese have become more and more painfully aware that while their country is now a rich one, they as individuals remain relatively underprivileged—particularly where housing is concerned. One result of this is that for some years now, many Japanese intellectuals and other critics of the established order have argued that their country should deemphasize economic growth and concentrate upon "social spending" designed to improve the quality of life for ordinary Japanese. More recently, this same theme has been picked up by Europeans and Americans who are outraged by Japan's seemingly irresistible invasion of their markets and, purely in self-defense, would like to see the energies of the Japanese redirected to focus primarily upon Japan's internal economy. In early 1982, for example, *The New York Times,* in an editorial titled "A Fatter Japan Is a Safer Japan," called upon the Japanese Government to consider running budget deficits to stimulate domestic demand and help satisfy some of Japan's more urgent social needs—most especially the need for better housing.

Unfortunately, all these suggestions overlook some basic realities. As it happens, the Japanese Government has actually been running budget deficits for a good many years now—deficits which in proportion to the country's Gross National Product have been far larger than those which have caused such alarm in the United States. But the proceeds of those deficits, so to speak, have not been spent primarily upon public annuities or housing. Instead, they have largely gone to finance such things as old-age pensions, defense costs, transportation facilities and an enormously expensive farm-subsidy program which keeps Japanese rice growers in business and Japan's rice prices artificially inflated.

As we shall see later on, the leaders of the perennially dominant Liberal Democratic Party have what they regard as compelling political reasons for pursuing this particular course. Nonetheless, in my view, their failure to launch a really massive assault on the problems of urban congestion and inadequate housing has unleashed profound social forces which the politicians only dimly understand and whose long-term impact could be very grave indeed.

Already, in fact, the constricting quality of the "rabbit hutches" in which most Japanese must live has had significant social and psychic effects upon them. The fact that the number of elderly Japanese who live with their children is steadily dwindling—by early 1982 the figure for Tokyo had dropped to only 40 percent—certainly reflects in part the desire of many younger Japanese to lead a "modern" home life. But no less certainly, the trend to nuclear families has been powerfully spurred by the enormous financial burden—and not infrequently the sheer financial impossibility—of maintaining a home large enough to accommodate three generations.

For Japanese in their late sixties and seventies, all of whom were brought up to regard the family as the ultimate source of emotional and financial security, the discovery that they must live apart from their children is a wrenching experience. And until recently, the choices open to them were dismal: either to spend their final days in unwelcome solitude or to take refuge in cheerless government nursing homes for the poor. Now, a small but growing minority of elderly Japanese are settling in American-style retirement communities, the first of which was built at Yayu no Sato, in central Japan, in the late '70s. But even though these communities have all the facilities of their U.S. counterparts and their residents are generally well off financially—a condominium at Yayu no Sato costs $100,000 and carries monthly maintenance fees of up to $250—many, if not most, of the people who live in them are quietly bitter about having to pass their old age in the company of strangers. It is, in fact, hard to imagine a more un-Japanese sentiment than that expressed a year or so ago by a Yayu no Sato resident named Emiko Hagiwara. "I have learned," Mrs. Hagiwara told *New York Times* reporter Susan Chira sadly, "that you really can't depend on anyone else."

It's difficult to say, however, who suffers more as a result of the cramped quality of today's Japanese homes: the oldsters who are crowded out of them or the younger people who are crowded into them. In the majority of urban households in Japan nowadays real privacy is simply impossible to come by, and this, inevitably, has added to the tensions inherent in the marital relationship. In some cases the lack of privacy so inhibits sexual activity that respectable married couples are driven to patronize one of Tokyo's numerous "love hotels" in order to escape the observant eyes of their own children. No less frustrating to some men, the old notion of home as a place where one could engage in serious study or reflection has become a complete anachronism in most instances. A few years ago in an article titled "Married Women: Weak Link in Japan's Family," Professor Shosaburo Kimura of Tokyo University bitterly complained that contemporary Japanese women simply "will not allow their husbands to have their own castle—a study—in their home."

Just how a couple with children could hope to carve a study out of a three- or four-room apartment Professor Kimura did not explain. But a year after his blast appeared, a bureaucrat named Haruo Kitamura tackled essentially the same problem in a considerably more balanced and wider-ranging article. As far as the study problem was concerned, Kitamura pointed out, an easy solution existed: there are now buildings in midtown Tokyo where anyone who can't stand the racket in the family living room can rent a private reading room by the month.

As Kitamura perceptively noted, however, the burgeoning rent-a-study business is only one sympton of a general Japanese trend: the increasing "externalization" of what used to be home-centered activities simply because those activities require more space and/or quiet than the ordinary urban household in Japan now affords. Because few homes have yards—or at least, yards of any size—small children must go to parks or commercial playgrounds for their outdoor play. Older youngsters, unless they are fortunate enough to have a room of their own, must do most of their studying in libraries or after-hours tutoring schools. For the adult who wishes to do some serious reading and cannot afford to rent a study, the only recourse is the public library or a company reading room. Lacking a parlor or guest room, most Japanese do not entertain friends at home as much as they did in prewar days, but instead generally meet them in restaurants or coffee shops. One of the few feasible home pastimes left, in fact, is the passive one of TV-watching; for those who wish to play games requiring concentration such as *go* or *shogi* (Japanese chess), the most practical course is to go out to one of the special game halls that have sprung up in major cities.

In short, where the life of a Japanese family in modest circumstances once centered almost entirely around the home, there is today growing reliance on outside facilities and, as a result, a greater tendency on the part of the various members of the family to go their separate ways. In the Japan of forty years ago, I very much doubt that a girl of thirteen or fourteen could have left home for three or four hours on a weekend afternoon without her parents' knowing exactly where she was. But as the young dancers in Yoyogi Park prove, that is often no longer the case.

It would be logical enough to assume that this fragmentation of the family is eroding the traditional group orientation of the Japanese, that it is inducing in younger Japanese a greater sense of individual choice—and with that, greater insistence on self-gratification as the primary goal of life. Many older Japanese, in fact, argue strongly that this is precisely what is happening, and there are some developments in contemporary Japan which would seem to bear out that argument. Probably the most talked-about book to appear in Japan in recent years is a novel entitled *Call Us Crystal* which was published in 1980 by a university senior named Yasuo Tanaka. The protagonists of *Call Us Crystal* are people of Tanaka's own age, and their most notable characteristic is an obsession with being seen at the "in" places and acquiring status-conferring possessions—Louis Vuitton handbags, Lee jeans, Lacoste polo shirts, Yves Saint Laurent suits and so on ad infinitum. In the course of his book, Tanaka drops the names of more than four hundred imported luxury items and chic restaurants and boutiques, all of which are carefully described, with no detectable irony, in a forty-one-page glossary.

The young people Tanaka writes about are, of course, members of a relatively small elite, and unquestionably he allows himself a certain amount of literary license. Nonetheless, there is statistical evidence suggesting that somewhat similar tendencies are characteristic of the majority of young people in today's Japan. A 1980 government poll of people between fifteen and nineteen revealed that only 28 percent of them are consciously working toward future goals; more than 50 percent said they were simply doing what they wanted to do now, without concern for the future. These figures were almost the exact reverse of those elicited by a similar poll twenty years earlier, and their message was reinforced by another set of statistics that emerged from the 1980 survey: more than 71 percent of the youngsters polled said they craved an "individual lifestyle," and only a little over 9 percent professed a desire to lead lives useful to society. By contrast, a poll taken a year later showed that among Japanese between forty and sixty, the number of people who wished to be of service to society substantially exceeded those who had no such interest.

Clearly, figures like these cannot simply be brushed aside. In some degree at least, they mirror changing social attitudes induced by the altered living patterns and economic circumstances of the Japanese people. At the same time, it would be dangerous, in my view, to put so much weight on them as to conclude that what might be described as the psychic Americanization of Japan is utterly inevitable. Even if the home is no longer as effective at instilling group orientation in young Japanese as it used to be, every other major institution in Japanese society from the educational system to the business establishment continues to promote a group-centred ethic—a fact which constitutes a powerful deterrent to the emergence of rampant individualism in Japan. If only as a practical matter, young Japanese are still under great pressure to heed the rule that used to prevail in the U.S. Congress: "If you want to get along, go along."

Whether individualism will in fact make serious inroads is a crucial question for Japan and one that I propose to examine more thoroughly when we come to consider scenarios for Japan's future development. Perhaps the commonest view of the matter held by thoughtful people in Japan itself, however, is that expressed by my Jesuit friend Father Joseph Pitau, whose intimate involvement with the younger generation of Japanese began nearly thirty years ago. "Young people in this country have changed significantly since I first taught high school here in 1954," Father Pitau told me in late 1980. "The kids back in those days had suffered when they were small and felt a compulsion to change Japan. But now the motivation to be a leader or start something new is extremely rare even in brilliant students. The prevalent ambition, in fact, is to become a salaryman and to achieve more balance between one's personal life and the demands of the job than has previously existed in Japan."

It was entirely obvious that Father Pitau deplored this cast of mind and that he attributed it at least in part to the changed atmosphere of the Japanese home. "So far," he said a bit grimly, "companies and government agencies have been able to take these youngsters and reshape them, giving them the traditional social formation in which loyalty to one's company or ministry is paramount. But already it's not so easy as it used to be to instill a spirit of service in young people in this country. And it could get harder and harder."

SECTION THREE

The Social Animal

7

Masses and Classes

Americans who have only a casual knowledge of the Japanese tend to think of them, half contemptuously, as forever bowing and scraping—and this is one instance in which an ethnic stereotype is reasonably accurate. As a people, the Japanese have a far more highly developed sense of hierarchy than Americans and manifest it far more openly. When three or four well-fed, wisecracking top executives of an American corporation board an aeroplane, it may take a bystander a bit of time to figure out which one of them is the boss. But when a group of executives from a Japanese firm board a plane, it's invariably immediately obvious who is top dog; he's the one who gets the window seat, whose briefcase is carried by someone else and whose bows to his colleagues follow their bows to him.

Even in situations in which the power relationships are less clear-cut, moreover, Japanese always retain a keen awareness of who owes deference to whom. No matter what dizzy heights of success a man may achieve in Japan, someone who graduated from the same university a couple of years ahead of him will forever remain in some meaningful way his senior.

What's important to bear in mind, however, is that hierarchical position in Japan is purely personal and that the national addiction to bowing and scraping in no sense implies that Japanese society is rigidly stratified or frozen. Just as many Americans do, Japanese like to think that they live in a classless society—or more accurately, a society almost totally composed of people of the same class. For close to twenty years now, opinion polls have consistently shown that 90 percent of all Japanese think of themselves as "middle-class." And in important respects, the Japanese are more entitled to cherish this illusion than we Americans are.

For one thing, wealth in Japan is considerably more evenly divided than it is in the United States. In Japan, the difference between the average income of the richest fifth of the population and the poorest fifth is only about 60 percent of what it is in the United States. To translate this into individual terms, the president of a privately owned company in Japan normally earns between four and six times as much as a blue-collar worker of the same age; in the United States, the president will generally make at least ten times as much as the worker.

Perhaps just as important, well-to-do Japanese do not insulate themselves from contact with the less prosperous to nearly the same extent as well-to-do Americans. In Japan there are no Grosse Pointes, Scarsdales or even any true equivalent of Manhattan's Sutton Place. In most Japanese neighborhoods, large homes and expensive condominiums exist side by side with tiny wooden houses, small shops and office buildings. Except in the sprawling *danchi* colonies, in short, Japanese of every income level and widely varying occupations live cheek by jowl and share a sense of local identity akin to that possessed by the inhabitants of a small village.

The fact that they do not physically segregate themselves reflects, among other things, the absence of any strong sense of class solidarity on the part of Japan's more prosperous and successful citizens. Instead, their loyalties and interests are primarily occupational and/or institutional. As one Western woman who lives in Tokyo put it: "There's really no point here in trying to mix businessmen, artists and intellectuals at a cocktail party the way you would in New York. All that happens is that the businessmen talk to the businessmen and the intellectuals to other intellectuals."

One striking manifestation of this social fragmentation is that there is no group in Japan really comparable to the Beautiful People of Western Europe and the United States. There are, to be sure, a certain number of Japanese, such as designer Hanae Mori and Sony's cosmopolitan boss Akio Morita, who enjoy Beautiful People status whenever they show up in New York or Paris. But although Yasuo Tanaka's young Crystal People may change this as they grow older, the sort of party religiously chronicled by New York's *Women's Wear Daily*—the enormously "in" affair where wealthy businessmen, entertainers, artists and out-and-out social butterflies meet to accord one another the ultimate seal of acceptance—is alien to present-day Japan. It is, in fact, so alien that not only is there no Japanese equivalent of *WWD*, there aren't even any society pages in ordinary Japanese newspapers.

This lack of a universally recognized social elite may well stem in part from the fact that inherited social status is a far rarer commodity in contemporary Japan than it is in Western Europe or even in the United States. There is, of course, one notable exception to that rule: anyone closely related to the Imperial Family occupies a special role in the public mind in Japan. Just how special that role is became fully apparent to me one day in the late '60s when a fun-loving young U.S. Congressman and his wife who were paying a visit to Tokyo invited me to go discotheque-hopping with them and "a Japanese princess." Since no one but a daughter of the Emperor now carries the title of princess in Japan, I assumed that my friends had gotten a bit mixed up and were probably referring to a member of one of the families that had belonged to the pseudo-European nobility which was created by the Emperor Meiji in the nineteenth century and abolished by the Americans following World War II. But when I arrived at the nightclub where we had agreed to meet, I discovered to my amazement that my "date" for the evening was in fact Emperor Hirohito's youngest daughter, Takako Shimazu.

Technically speaking, Takako had ceased to be a princess some years earlier when she married a commoner—a banker who happened to be off in Bangkok on business on this particular occasion. Nonetheless, wherever we went that night, she—and by association, the rest of our party—were literally treated like royalty. When we entered a bar, no matter how crowded, a table was instantly made available to us and all tables immediately adjacent to it magically emptied. And when we stepped onto a dance floor teeming with gyrating couples there was suddenly enough open space around us to accommodate even my clumsy attempts at the frug.

University unrest was at its height in Japan just then, and among the mod youngsters who had packed the discotheques we visited that night there were surely some who held extremely radical views. Yet no one showed Takako the slightest sign of disrespect; no one, in fact, was even rude enough to stare at her. Even in this frenetic and seemingly blasé environment, the Imperial mystique still held.

The Imperial Family apart, however, aristocratic ancestry no longer counts for a great deal in Japan. There are a fair number of Japanese families that can trace their pedigrees back for several centuries, but in most cases they derive relatively little social or practical advantage from that fact. In countries as diverse as Italy and the Soviet Union, I have often been pointedly told about a new acquaintance, "His mother was a Torlonia" or "She's descended from Prince So-and-so—you know, the one in *War and Peace*." And in our own country, of course, the mere possession of a surname like Roosevelt or Auchincloss automatically confers status on its bearer. But in all the time I have spent in Japan I can recall only a single occasion when one Japanese felt obliged to alert me to the ancestry of another—and it is by no means irrelevant, I believe, that in this case the once-powerful feudal family involved still possesses considerable wealth.

The fact is that in Japan as in most capitalist societies, a patrician pedigree unsupported by large amounts of money soon ceases to carry much weight. And this is a phenomenon of particular importance in Japan for the reason that "old money" is comparatively uncommon there nowadays. Though I know of no way to prove the point statistically, it is clearly true that both in absolute numbers and in percentage terms, there are far fewer families in Japan whose wealth dates back a century or more than there are in the United States. Indeed, I would guess that there are more such families in the state of Massachusetts alone than in all of Japan.

The chief credit—or blame—for this state of affairs rests, somewhat ironically, with that dedicated establishmentarian, Douglas MacArthur. To be sure, World War II impoverished many once-wealthy Japanese. But the coup de grâce to such great fortunes as survived the war was delivered during the U.S. Occupation when MacArthur decided that the best way to prevent the remilitarization of Japan was to destroy the great family-held economic combines known as the *zaibatsu* and, to achieve this, imposed a crippling levy upon capital.

Not everybody, of course, was caught in MacArthur's web. There are some old families that have managed to recoup their fortunes—generally by selling off inherited art treasures or urban landholdings. (They had no rural land to sell, since under another Occupation-era edict all large agricultural properties were seized on what amounted to confiscatory terms and then redistributed to the peasantry.) Such survival stories are the exception, however; the great bulk of the very wealthy in today's Japan are nouveaux riches—people who have made their pile themselves.

In terms of their contribution to society, it is debatable whether Japan's new rich constitute any great improvement over the prewar rich. A number of them, including former Prime Minister Kakuei Tanaka, have made their fortunes through somewhat unproductive activities, most notably real estate speculation. As recently as 1973, in fact, land speculation accounted for 98 of the 100 largest incomes reported to Japan's tax authorities. Still, as far as economic and social mobility goes, it has to be conceded that Japan is now very much an "equal-opportunity" society—even more so in many respects than the United States.

To say that Japan is an equal-opportunity society, however, is by no means the same as saying that it is an egalitarian society. The latter is a claim that many Japanese make, and in certain respects it has plausibility. Because it is genuinely risky to draw attention to oneself by unconventional behaviour in Japan, most Japanese prefer to be thought of as "just like everyone else" and are reluctant to be markedly different in any visible way from other Japanese in similar circumstances. A young woman who works for the Japanese Foreign Office, for example, confided in me that when she was sent on a mission to Southeast Asia in midwinter, she went to great lengths to avoid getting a tan for fear of arousing invidious comments from her peers when she returned to Tokyo. It is also true that some of the more obvious benchmarks of social class in the United States are largely missing in Japan. A Japanese factory worker's accent is not likely to differ markedly from that of a university-educated executive, and the chances are good that they will read the same newspaper; the New York City pattern in which the masses read the *Daily News* or the *Post* and the classes read *The New York Times* simply doesn't obtain in Tokyo.

Nonetheless, the periodic debate among Japanese intellectuals as to whether Japan really is or is not an essentially one-class society has always struck me as a fruitless exercise in semantics. Whatever sociological jargon you choose to employ, the fact is that there are notable differences in the way various groups in Japanese society live and behave and that those differences are closely linked to economic, educational and occupational status.

That same statement, of course, applies to the United States at least as well as it does in Japan, and in many respects the rewards of superior income, education and professional achievement in the two countries are similar. But there are also some interesting and important differences, particularly in terms of occupational status. One of these is that while civil servants in Japan are not, relatively speaking, as well paid as their American counterparts, they enjoy considerably more prestige. This is not to say that the bureaucracy is widely loved: the Japanese press enjoys nothing more than trumpeting to the world the occasional instance of official corruption, and Japanese businessmen constantly complain of the "arrogance" of the bureaucrats. (One of the few times I have seen one important Japanese publicly bait another came at a meeting where an obviously irate industrialist repeatedly paid a representative of the Ministry of Trade and Industry sardonic compliments on the "unfailing wisdom" of his pronouncements.)

Nonetheless, even a relatively obscure section chief in a Tokyo ministry enjoys more public respect than, say, a prefectural governor—and that despite the fact that the bureaucrat is merely an appointee while the governor is an elected official. To some extent, this reflects capital-city snobbery: by the same token, a white-collar worker in Tokyo considers himself superior to the mayor of a small provincial city, and privately if not publicly, the mayor would almost certainly agree. But there is considerably more to it than just that: in what may well be a distant echo of the status enjoyed by the mandarins of Imperial China, Japan's bureaucrats are universally considered to be in some sense "above" the rest of the populace.

The fact that mere membership in the bureaucracy automatically confers prestige upon someone reflects perhaps the most important single aspect of social status in Japan: far more than in the United States, it is acquired not by individual achievement but by group affiliation. A number of years ago, at a breakfast meeting with a representative group of "young" Tokyo businessmen, I was particularly impressed by a handsome, compact man in his late thirties who had parlayed some innovative ideas into a profitable business of his own. Apparently I concentrated my attention upon him somewhat too heavily. In any case, when the breakfast was over, one of the people who had helped to arrange it politely pointed out that there had been other, more important people present—namely, middle-level executives from some of Japan's biggest corporations. None of these cautious corporate types struck me as being nearly as imaginative as the entrepreneur, and certainly none of them had accomplished as much personally as he had. But in the Japanese scheme of things they carried more weight, because the great institutions to which they belonged shed a kind of glory upon them that the medium-sized company the young entrepreneur had created could not match.

There are, of course, Japanese who do achieve status and renown purely through individual performance. As in the United States, highly successful public personalities—entertainers, baseball players, writers and so on—can become superstars in their own right. But these are the exceptions to the rule, the rule being that the most important factor in establishing the social status of a Japanese is the prestige enjoyed by the organization of which he is a part.

This rub-off effect, moreover, operates at every level of Japanese society. One of the supreme rewards that can be offered an outstandingly successful Japanese executive is exemption from his company's mandatory retirement age; even though his job may become purely decorative, a man who has won that privilege is likely to go on showing up at the office for as long as he can totter around simply in order to escape the loss of identity he would suffer if he were to relinquish his corporate ties. And at the other end of the scale, lower-level employees facing imminent retirement have been known to beg desperately to retain at least a nominal connection with their firm so that they may have a better chance to make good marriages for their daughters. (Carrying this spirit to the extreme, the Kyoto Ceramic Company some years ago acquired a mass tomb for its workers and their families to ensure that they "won't feel lonely" after death.)

At first blush, all this may not sound as radically different from the situation in the United States as it really is. There are, after all, many Americans who derive much of their self-esteem from the fact that they work for a particularly powerful and respected institution and whose prestige with their neighbors rests more upon the nature of their employment than upon their personal qualities. But individual enterprise and the achievement of wealth or fame on independent terms continue to be highly honoured by Americans in fact as well as in our national mythology. By contrast, the great majority of Japanese find it almost impossible to conceive that an individual can achieve true stature and success except as part of a group. To put it more concretely, in most American communities a prosperous self-employed businessman—the owner of a flourishing hardware store or automobile agency, say—is normally considered a person of more substance than a salaried office manager in the local branch of a national corporation. In Japan, the exact reverse is true.

The extraordinary degree to which the position of a Japanese within a particular hierarchy determines his overall social status is perhaps best revealed by the compulsiveness with which Japanese exchange *meishi*, or calling cards. Except for salesmen, few Americans that I know habitually carry calling cards anymore, but virtually every Japanese above the blue-collar level does, and the trading of *meishi* is an absolutely indispensable part of any first business encounter in Japan. The reason is a simple one: until a Japanese finds out someone's group affiliation and specific position within that group it is almost impossible for him to be sure how much deference that person should be paid.

This is true in part because the kind of external caste marks that often make it relatively easy to determine an American's social status are not nearly so numerous or revealing in the case of the Japanese. Consider, for example, two good Japanese friends of mine—Chitoshi the bureaucrat and Isamu the salaryman. Chitoshi is a graduate of Tokyo University and a rising star at the prestigious Ministry of International Trade and Industry. With luck, he will one day be the top career official at MITI, and even if that glittering prize eludes him, he will certainly wind up with a lucrative job in the senior ranks of private industry. Isamu, on the other hand, attended a thoroughly undistinguished private university and now works as a combination interpreter and escort officer in a small company that specializes in making arrangements for foreign visitors to Japan. The most he can reasonably aspire to is eventually rising to a modestly paid supervisory role in his present firm.

Chitoshi, in short, is a certified member of the Japanese establishment, while Isamu is one of the spear-carriers of Japanese society. Yet in a casual meeting it would be difficult to put one's finger on any significant superficial differences between them. They have the same social mannerisms and speech patterns, much the same tastes in food and drink and the same reverential attitudes toward their work. Neither enjoys a fancy private office, affects to be a connoisseur of wine or the ballet or dresses with conspicuous elegance and expense. (Though a growing number of "upscale" Japanese men do dress with flair nowadays, the majority still favor conservative business suits—and the older and more powerful an executive is, the more likely this is to be the case.) Just about the only reason, in fact, that Chitoshi would command more attention from a stranger than Isamu is that he is older—a fact which automatically gives him added status in Japan.

Of course, as would be true in most countries, Chitoshi's superior professional status means that he can enjoy more of the good things of life than Isamu does. He drives a bigger and sportier car than Isamu, has an expense account which permits him to lunch at classy restaurants instead of the humbler places Isamu must patronize and has filled his apartment with expensive furniture and elaborate gadgets that Isamu could not possibly afford. And all this does, in a sense, give Chitoshi an edge, since competitiveness about such matters has intensified in Japan to a degree that some older Japanese find alarming. "Japanese are getting much too materialistic," lamented businesswoman Taeko Matsuda when I last talked to her. "I know a very distinguished journalist who tells me that his wife and children aren't at all impressed by his writing or his professional reputation. Instead, they keep telling him, 'Next door brings home more money' or 'Next door has gotten twin ovens; we must get them too.'"

But while it may provoke the envy of his neighbors, Chitoshi's relative affluence avails him relatively little if one goes by the standards that Westerners use to measure social class. It does not get him into the "better" cocktail parties and dinners, since there are virtually none to go to. His apartment, while more lavishly appointed and much closer to his office than Isamu's, does not afford him significantly more living space by American standards. And the degree to which he can transfer his personal status to his children is quite limited. Because Chitoshi is in a position to pay high tuition fees, his son, even though he is doing only passable work in high school, will probably be able to attend a university of some sort. But the boy has no chance whatever of getting into Tokyo University, whereas Isamu's ten-year-old, who has already shown himself to be extremely bright, may well do so—and thereby effectively overcome the financial advantages currently enjoyed by Chitoshi's boy.

Socially speaking, in short, money does talk in Japan, but by no means so authoritatively as it does in the United States. Indeed, the place where money and life-styles seem to me to interact most interestingly in Japan is not in general living standards but in recreation.

In Japan as in other countries, some of the most common forms of recreation appeal to people from every income and educational level. Here I am thinking not only of such top spectator sports as baseball and sumo wrestling but also of the closely interrelated and uniquely Japanese pastimes of festival-going and nature savoring. As a people, the Japanese are festival-crazy. The country has scores of these affairs each year—village festivals, shrine festivals, city neighborhood festivals—and even sophisticated young Japanese plunge into them with delight. Some festivals in these degenerate times have descended to such latter-day hoopla as marching bands and baton twirlers, but processions featuring traditional costumes, floats and images of local deities still abound. And while the central activity of a festival can be anything from a horse race to dancing in the streets, very often what is being celebrated involves some aspect of nature.

This last fact reflects the continuing influence of Shinto, with its reverence for natural phenomena: an oddly shaped rock, a particularly venerable tree or a local waterfall. Though Shinto as an actively held set of beliefs is moribund in today's Japan, it has undeniably had a profound effect on the way Japanese view the natural world. And its influence in that respect has been reinforced by Buddhism, which sees the entire universe—animal, vegetable and mineral—as one.

The most visible manifestation of this is the extraordinary Japanese passion for natural beauty. Japanese, as far as I know, is the only language that boasts special words for the acts of flower-viewing and moon-viewing. And Japan remains the only country I know of where hundreds of thousands of people will travel considerable distances to feast their eyes on a particular variety of plum tree that blossoms in winter.

In the West, this sort of behavior by Japanese is sometimes taken as evidence of a keen aesthetic sensibility—and so, in fact, it is. But it is also true that quite frequently Japanese use ostensibly aesthetic pursuits as the occasion for a good old-fashioned booze-up. In a book he wrote about Japan a few years ago, my former *Time* colleague William Forbis reported that at a "moon-viewing" party staged by prosperous Kyoto businessmen he found two of the celebrants lying on their backs on the pavement—a position which, they explained in cheerfully inebriated tones, gave them an ideal perspective on the moon's beauties. Similarly, back in the 1940s while riding horseback in the Chiba Peninsula, I came upon a scene that still haunts my memory. Gathered under a grove of ancient cherry trees to celebrate blossom time was the entire population of a farming village. At first sight, the tableau was a lovely one: artfully posed amid fallen blossoms so numerous that the ground appeared to be covered with pink snow were twenty or thirty women in magnificent kimono. On second look, however, the artistic effect was somewhat marred by the fact that all the males in sight were stretched out on their backs dead drunk, snoring stentoriously as vagrant cherry petals drifted into their open mouths.

In retrospect, it has occurred to me that my experience in Chiba was more than just an instance of the way in which the Japanese sometimes marry aestheticism and conviviality. It also served to illustrate in somewhat extreme fashion the fact that most forms of recreation in Japan that cut across class lines—spectator sports, nature-viewing and, of course, TV-watching—are essentially passive. By contrast, more active forms of recreation tend to be keyed to the income level and social status of the participants.

Gambling, for example, is a pastime dear to the hearts of many Japanese, but one that in most of its forms is also illegal. The commonest solution to this difficulty is to play *pachinko*—a modified version of something called the Corinthian game which is a kind of vertical pinball machine without flippers. There are currently more than 10,000 *pachinko* parlors in Japan, and all together they possess 1.6 million machines—or one for every 75 Japanese. In these garishly lighted establishments blank-faced addicts stand elbow to elbow striving endlessly to win small steel balls which can be exchanged for prizes ranging from cigarettes to cassettes. (These prizes in turn can be exchanged for cash in nearby shops which specialize in reselling them to *pachinko*-prize wholesalers.)

But popular as *pachinko* is—an estimated 14 million Japanese play it regularly—its devotees are chiefly blue-collar workers or males from the lower white-collar ranks. The more successful a Japanese is—or can reasonably expect to become—the more likely it is that he will choose to win or lose his money at mah-jong. So firmly entrenched a part of Japanese corporate life is the after-work mah-jong game that the practice has even come to the attention of some New York taxi drivers. The astute cabbies have learned that if they turn up in front of certain Japanese restaurants in Manhattan just as the mah-jong games are breaking up for the night they can confidently expect to pick up a lucrative fare to one of the residential suburbs favored by New York-based Japanese executives. And if his fare happens to have come away with a walletful of I.O.U.s—in a halfhearted bow to the legalities, no money actually changes hands at these hush-hush games—the driver can also hope for an uncommonly handsome tip.

Gambling, however, is by no means the only diversion in which Japanese tend to divide up according to income level. Assuming that he is still active enough to enjoy competitive athletics, a blue-collar worker is likely to have to resort to a company gymnasium or playing field—which generally limits him to team sports such as basketball or baseball. But these are not the games favored by management personnel—partly, no doubt, because of the age factor. Among senior Japanese executives, there is a certain vogue for sports drawn from the samurai tradition. The most luxurious Tokyo executive suite I have visited boasts a large photo of its occupant all decked out in the traditional garb of an ancient Japanese bowman plus a tasteful selection of the trophies he has won for his prowess at archery. Similarly, a considerable number of top Japanese still practice swordsmanship—not, as at least one unkind foreigner has alleged, because they dream of reviving "the way of the warrior," but because Japanese sword play is a demanding combination of mental and physical exercise with something of the cachet that polo, say, enjoys in some circles in the United States.

As most of the world knows by now, however, the quintessential executive game in Japan is golf. In this the Japanese merely reflect a phenomenon that is curiously widespread among the movers and shakers of East Asia: at one time or another during my journalistic career, I had to accommodate myself to the golfing schedules of Singapore's Prime Minister Lee Kuan-yew, Indonesia's President Suharto, President Ferdinand Marcos of the Philippines and Hong Kong's Sir Yue-kong Pao, the owner of a shipping fleet whose tonnage exceeds that of the entire Soviet merchant marine. But what distinguishes the Japanese from other Asian aficionados of golf—and even from the game's Scottish originators—is the single-minded quality of their mania. Your true Japanese linksman never misses any opportunity to improve his game. As a case in point, the roof of the downtown Tokyo office building with which I am most familiar is occupied by a driving range—a tiny one, to be sure, on which a net stops your ball after only a 10-yard flight, but still enough to ensure that no golf addict who works in the vicinity need miss his daily fix. More impressive yet is the fact that although the cost of membership in Japanese golf clubs ranges from inordinate to astronomical, golf courses proliferated so rapidly in Japan in the 1960s and '70s that they began to make significant inroads into the country's limited supply of level land—inroads so serious that in some cases local governments cracked down and prohibited the construction of any more greens and fairways.

The somewhat intemperate enthusiasm with which Japan's businessmen approach golf is also characteristic of the predominantly youthful devotees of two other relatively upscale sports: skiing and tennis. On winter weekends the trains leaving Tokyo for skiing areas are so chockablock full of bodies and equipment as to strike terror into the heart of anyone with even the faintest touch of claustrophobia. Apart from its inevitable toll of broken limbs, of course, skiing is a beneficial pastime in the Japanese context, since it is primarily confined to mountainous country, of which Japan has a superfluity. The growing passion for tennis, however, has created environmental problems similar to those posed by golf, albeit on a somewhat smaller scale. A few years ago, while driving with a friend through the countryside near Lake Yamanaka, a fashionable weekend retreat for prosperous Tokyoites, I was startled to see literally scores of tennis courts—far more than the permanent residents and cottagers of the region could conceivably make use of. "Oh, those," said my friend when I asked for an explanation. "Well there just aren't enough courts in Tokyo to accommodate all the tennis nuts. So on weekends quite a lot of people from Tokyo travel the seventy miles or so out here to play. Meantime, the farmers here have discovered that it's easier and more profitable to tend tennis courts than to tend crops. Some of them, in fact, have given up farming entirely—which has the local authorities all in a tizzy."

Despite the indefatigability with which Japanese pursue their tennis or golf, they are also addicted to the pastime that American teen-agers call "hanging out." One form of recreation that has great psychological importance to Japanese is simply being with other people—specifically, that is, with other Japanese. How strongly they feel this need is reflected by the clientele of the country's increasingly numerous "capsule hotels," in which the sleeping accommodations are almost literally capsules—plastic boxes so small that a guest can touch the ceiling and all four walls without moving from the center of the cubicle. Basically, the capsule hotels, with their very modest "room" rates, are intended to appeal to traveling businessmen on per diem, but in practice a fair number of their patrons have proved to be single men who have apartments of their own nearby but who nonetheless rent a cubicle—often on a regular basis—purely in order to savor the human contacts and conversation available in the hotel lounges.

Together with the physical difficulty of entertaining in the average Japanese home, this craving for the security and warmth of a surrounding crowd helps to explain the Japanese penchant for what to a foreigner often seems aimless milling about. For many Japanese, a perfectly satisfactory way to spend free time consists of wandering the city streets window-shopping, perhaps visiting one of the art exhibits regularly staged by department stores and generally absorbing the din and bustle.

More often than not, the highlight of such an excursion is eating out. Tokyo alone boasts some 100,000 eating places, a great many of them fronted by a glass showcase containing remarkably realistic plastic models of the delicacies to be had inside. The most heavily patronized eating establishments, naturally, are relatively unpretentious places: noodle shops, sushi shops, restaurants offering a variety of inexpensive Japanese dishes and the local outposts of such American fast-food empires as McDonald's and Kentucky Fried Chicken. (The fast-food industry in Japan, incidentally, now does a gross business equal in size to that of Japan's mighty auto industry.)

Some of these simpler places serve very good food indeed and are patronized by affluent as well as less affluent Japanese. But purely for the upscale citizen, Tokyo also offers an extraordinary variety of chic—and inordinately expensive—restaurants. Some of the pleasantest of these are traditional Japanese establishments in which kimono-clad waitresses serve customers the classic delicacies of old Japan as they gaze out on a miniature garden that magically creates the illusion of rural tranquillity in the midst of the city. But there are also elegant Chinese restaurants superior to any I know of in New York, fancy Swiss and Italian places and several excellent purveyors of France's haute cuisine, including one called Maxim's whose top chefs studied their craft at Maxim's in Paris.

At these establishments, as at Tokyo's geisha houses, many of the patrons are spending expense-account money. Characteristically, such "business" lunches or dinners are stag affairs—and geisha parties invariably are. In fact, the only geisha party I've ever attended at which there was a female guest was a luncheon that a major Japanese newspaper gave in honor of Katharine Graham of The Washington Post Company—and that was something less than a smashing success. The geisha, whose whole training had been in dealing with men, were clearly bemused at having to cope with a woman, and as we were leaving, Mrs. Graham made it plain that she had not been enchanted by the spectacle of a group of males being served by kneeling females.

For motives quite different from Mrs. Graham's, some Japanese women profess to welcome the fact that they are not obliged to participate in their husbands' business entertaining. "Wives here are happy with the way things are," I was told by Mrs. Mayumi Moriyama, a Liberal Democratic member of parliament. "It would be very troublesome to have to go out with your husband constantly—particularly in Tokyo, where travel times are so great. Sometimes I feel sorry for American women who have to go to so many boring affairs to help their husbands' careers."

There is a certain plausibility to that statement, and I have no doubt that Mrs. Moriyama made it sincerely. Still, I suspect that it was at least in part a rationalization and that a considerable number of Japanese women would like to share more fully in the perquisites enjoyed by their successful husbands. What lends at least implicit support to that suspicion is the fact that in recent years it has become considerably less more common for Japanese men to include their families in their weekend recreation.

For most Japanese, these family activities remain relatively simple: a barbecue, a visit to a nearby park with the kids, or, for the 55 percent of Japanese householders who now own cars, perhaps a drive in the country. But for the affluent, togetherness can involve much more ambitious undertakings: it is by no means unusual these days to find entire families lunching in style at the most chic Tokyo restaurants. At a particularly elaborate French establishment one Sunday noon a few years ago, I spotted just such a group: the father resplendent in a Pierre Cardin suit, Mama decked out in what even I could recognize as a designer dress and two small boys looking very British in blue blazers and grey flannel shorts. In a quiet sort of way, they seemed to be enjoying themselves; and I hope they were, because to judge from my own bill, theirs must have run well over $300.

So much for the egalitarian society.

8

Automatic Controls

One of the most revealing aspects of any society is the way in which its members choose to misbehave, and this, I think, is particularly true of Japan. The group constraints that bear upon Japanese when they earnestly seek to discharge their personal and social responsibilities are scarcely less operative when they feel driven to let off psychic steam. In contemporary Europe or America, the concessions the individual must make to public standards are so few that people are driven to more and more extreme deviations in order to proclaim their individuality; to achieve a real sense of rebelliousness in the West today requires considerable ingenuity. But in Japan, where the obligations owed society are so numerous and specific, it is in a real sense much easier to assert individuality. Just as recourse to alcohol and "loose women" used to satisfy the pent-up antisocial urges of most Western men in the Victorian and Edwardian eras, there are today tacitly acceptable forms of achieving psychic relief in Japan. Prominent among these is one of the most cherished diversions of the Japanese male: dropping in at his favorite hostess bar after work.

To call such establishments bars is to some extent misleading, for they are not simply drinking places; they are informal social organizations which in certain respects are the psychic equivalent of a London men's club. In fact, while they are legally open to the public, the "better" hostess bars, such as Tokyo's improbably named Le Rat Mort, effectively *are* private clubs; strangers are unwelcome, regular guests are billed monthly and a "member's" tab, so I am told, can depend as much upon how well the proprietress likes him as upon how many overpriced drinks he has actually bought.

The analogy with a London club cannot be pushed too far, however, since the goings-on at a hostess bar are emphatically free of any trace of upper-class English inhibition. Besides the ceaseless sexual badinage and knee-squeezing I referred to earlier, there is much drinking, loud jesting and noisy laughter. And from time to time, when the mood strikes, one of the guests will commandeer a microphone and belt out an off-key rendition of a popular song. (Solo singing in public, known as *karaoke*, became a national craze in Japan a few years back—so much so that it spawned tens of thousands of "*karaoke* bars" which provide frustrated crooners with microphones and loud recorded accompaniment.)

To many Westerners, all this appears somewhat childish and thoroughly boring. But an invitation to accompany a Japanese acquaintance to his hostess bar is not something to be lightly rejected. For one thing, bar friendships can help cement business relationships. Beyond that, the bar behavior of Japanese males offers interesting insights into some of the psychological differences between Japanese and Westerners.

The amount of laughter to be heard in a hostess bar, for example, is likely to strike a Westerner—even one who can understand Japanese—as somewhat mystifying. This is partly because Japanese laughter, like the famous Japanese smile, often reflects embarrassment rather than amusement. But even when a Japanese clearly does find something genuinely amusing, the humor will often be lost on an American or European. To some extent, I believe, this is because Japanese see incongruities in situations where Westerners don't and find even minor incongruities funnier than we do. In addition, as one longtime foreign observer of the Japanese scene has suggested to me, there is a strong analogy between some Japanese humor and the old story of the two American comedians who used the same joke-book and could send each other into stitches simply by saying "Number Twenty-four" or "Number Thirty-six." When two or more Japanese have shared an experience they found amusing, a code word evoking that experience will set them laughing forever afterwards, and this kind of in-group joking is a staple of Japanese wit.

What may also strike some Westerners as a bit odd is the fact that so much of what passes for humor in a hostess bar consists of sexual innuendo. Japanese attitudes toward sex have traditionally had a matter-of-fact, unromantic quality that has been matched in the West only since the general move to social permissiveness of the last couple of decades. Male philandering, whether with occasional partners or with a regular mistress, has always been taken as a matter of course in Japan—so much so that Japanese men tend to be puzzled and even a bit hurt if they present a Western guest with the opportunity for a sexual encounter and he fails to capitalize on it. And despite the fact that the Japanese Government somewhat mysteriously clings to its prohibition against frontal nudity in magazines, Japanese sex shops were famous long before such establishments became legally acceptable in countries like Denmark and West Germany.

Yet despite all this, an almost adolescent prurience is considerably more common in my experience among middle-aged Japanese men than among middle-aged Americans. It may, in fact, be precisely because of its easy availability that a good many Japanese males take what seems to me a rather mechanical, almost joyless approach to sex. Though I'm no expert on the subject, I find it hard to conceive that there could possibly be a live sex show more fundamentally anti-erotic than one that a solid Japanese family man eagerly hustled me into in Kyoto a few years ago under the impression he was offering me a rare treat. And in no country other than Japan have I ever had a male acquaintance casually remark that he hadn't been satisfied with the quality of his sexual performance of late and then inquire how I felt about my own.

Unless he is already reasonably familiar with Japan, however, an American guest at a hostess bar is apt to find Japanese attitudes toward sex more readily understandable than the Japanese attitude toward drinking. Though there are numerous exceptions, the typical Japanese just doesn't hold his liquor very well. A number of physiological theories, none of which I'm competent to pass judgment on, have been advanced to explain this phenomenon. Whatever the reason, however, it is an observable fact that quantities of alcohol much too small to have any visible effect on most Westerners will frequently cause a Japanese to turn brick red, speak in slurred tones and generally display the symptoms of drunkenness.

More often than not, however, Japanese refuse to be inhibited by this vulnerability. Though imported spirits are wickedly expensive in Japan—so expensive that a duty-free bottle of choice brandy or malt whiskey makes one of the most welcome gifts a visiting foreigner can offer Japanese friends—well-to-do Japanese slosh them down with remarkable abandon. And the less affluent are equally diligent in knocking back (in descending order of status) Japanese whiskey, beer and sake. The result is that at night the spectacle of well-dressed men reeling about the streets of Tokyo's entertainment district is a commonplace.

Such behavior, particularly on a repeated basis, would, of course, damage the reputation and career of any American executive. In Japan, however, public drunkenness does not carry any stigma. Instead, it is an accepted way to relieve personal and professional tensions, and the statement "I was drunk at the time" is universally taken as an adequate excuse for all sorts of breaches of the normal code of conduct, up to and including publicly insulting your boss.

For a Westerner dealing with Japanese, this is both good and bad news; no one will take any offense at what you say while drunk—but no one will feel any sympathy for you if you get angry at a grossly insulting remark from a drunken Japanese.

As I have suggested, the tolerance that Japanese display toward drunkenness and the raffish camaraderie of the hostess bars constitutes a tacit social convention; it is a product of an unspoken—and often unconscious—recognition that for sanity's sake, the individual must get surcease from the physical pressures of a rigidly structured environment. But the acceptable relief devices are themselves highly circumscribed; in most respects, Japanese society is far less permissive than American society about public displays of alienation. Such inherently antisocial manifestations as graffito "art", the pervasive smell of marijuana smoke in movie theaters and youngsters who defiantly stalk the streets inflicting their blaring "boxes" on the public at large are not features of the urban scene in Japan.

But perhaps because of the conformist face that Japanese society generally presents, Western admirers of Japan sometimes go a bit overboard in their panegyrics to its orderly and law-abiding nature. To suggest that antisocial behavior is virtually unknown in Japan is quite simply wrong. Japanese protest demonstrations, for example, periodically become so violent as to make the most extreme activities of anti-nuclear-power groups in the United States look like nothing more than high spirits; in 1979 alone, youthful radicals who were attempting to force the closure of Narita Airport organized some twenty-six bombings and armed assaults, in which eight people died and thirty-two were injured. What's more, Japan is home to virtually every kind of malefactor known to the United States—murderous motorcycle gangs, arsonists, kidnappers, embezzlers and even professional mobsters. In 1980, in fact, Japan's National Police Agency with its customary precision reported the existence of 2,507 underworld organizations with a total of 106,754 individual members.

Inevitably, some foreign crime writers have succumbed to the temptation to attribute a special exoticism to Japanese gangsters, who are known as *yakuza* and who have a penchant for getting themselves tattooed, which has rendered that particular form of bodily decoration even less classy in Japan than in the United States. In reality, however, the run-of-the-mill *yakuza* is no more romantic a figure than the average "soldier" in a Mafia family. Like mafiosi, *yakuza* have traditionally gone in heavily for gambling and protection rackets, but in recent years they have switched increasingly into drug-smuggling, which is now estimated to be a $4.5-billion-a-year business in Japan. This change in focus is at once a consequence and a partial cause of the fact that drug abuse is one of the two areas in which crime has lately been on the increase in Japan. In 1979, some 18,000 Japanese were arrested for using illegal drugs; this was 26 times the figure only a decade earlier, and Japanese police believe that the total number of drug addicts in the country may now run as high as "several hundreds of thousands."

Though this may sound to foreigners like another example of the "Americanization" of Japan, the patterns of drug abuse there actually differ considerably from those prevailing in the United States. Because Japanese only infrequently entertain at home, there is almost none of the chic social cocaine-sniffing popular in some circles in the United States, and "pot parties" are equally rare. Marijuana, in fact, plays a much smaller role in the Japanese drug scene than it does in the United States. Rigid surveillance makes drug production of any kind in Japan itself excessively risky, and because of its bulk, marijuana is awkward to smuggle into a small, well-policed country like Japan in commercially profitable quantities. As a result, the drug most readily available to Japanese adults is "speed," the bulk of which is originally synthesized in Taiwan or South Korea. Among the most frequent adult users of drugs are truck drivers and bored housewives, but more than half the drug-related arrests Japanese cops make nowadays involve persons under twenty-four. Many of these are high school students who, when they can't get classier drugs, resort to sniffing paint thinner or glue.

The growing abuse of drugs by youngsters, however, is only one aspect of a phenomenon that thoughtful Japanese find deeply disturbing: a recent upsurge in juvenile crime of all kinds. In 1979 alone, juvenile arrests jumped by a startling 48 percent, accounting for nearly 40 percent of the total number of criminal arrests made by the Japanese police. All told, more than 140,000 youngsters were taken into custody for offenses ranging from "sexual aberrations" and violence against teachers to homicide. Ominously, too, the average age of juvenile offenders was significantly lower than in earlier years. Unless this trend to juvenile lawlessness can be reversed, it clearly constitutes what a police white paper somewhat laconically described as "a pointer to future social problems."

All that being said, however, Japan remains by any standard a remarkably law-abiding society. In all of Japan in 1979 the number of crimes involving the use of handguns totaled only 171—a figure that would be incredibly low for some individual police precincts in the United States. And a comparative study of crime rates made in 1978 revealed that for every 100,000 inhabitants New York had 8 times as many rapes as Tokyo, 10 times as many murders—and 225 times as many armed robberies. More remarkable yet, the per capita incidence of violent crime, which has been sky-rocketing almost everywhere else in the industrialized world, has actually declined somewhat in Japan over the past twenty years.

Here again, the explanation for "the Japanese difference" is the very great degree to which the self-esteem of the ordinary Japanese depends upon his identification with the group. This makes social sanctions reflecting the withdrawal of group approval a far more powerful deterrent to crime in Japan than it is in contemporary Western societies —and also a far more effective means of rehabilitating those who do stray from the strait-and-narrow. In their criminal cases, Japanese prosecutors have an astonishingly high conviction rate: some 99 percent of those people who are brought to trial are found guilty. But even more astonishing to an American way of thinking, a considerable number of confessed criminals are never taken to court, and only about 4 percent of convicted criminals ever go to jail. The rest are let off with fines or suspended sentences and placed under the guidance of a nationwide network of volunteer parole officers. The prime objective of a Japanese prosecutor, in short, is not to send an offender to prison but to secure his confession, repentance and reform.

This, of course, bears close resemblance to what many American penologists regard as the ideal approach to criminal behavior. But any American who advocates such policies must somehow get around an ugly fact that Japanese penologists don't have to worry about. Where U.S. newspapers routinely carry indignant stories about paroled criminals who have gone out to mug, rob or murder again, Japanese papers seldom have occasion to do so. The reason:

any Japanese who has once suffered the psychic torments of social disapproval or rejection is unlikely to risk facing that experience again.

Repentant criminals are by no means the only people in Japan whose problems are often dealt with outside of court, for just as there are social arrangements for dealing with individual stress, there are similar arrangements for dealing with conflicts, real or potential, between the various members of Japanese society. Incredible as it may seem to anyone inured to the litigious nature of American society, Japanese generally take civil disputes to court only as a last, desperate resort. When they are confronted with a traffic collision, Japanese police will frequently work out a financial settlement between the two parties involved right on the spot. And even where the matter at issue is far more serious than mere auto repairs, resort to litigation is the exception. Between 1977 and 1982, for example, Japan Air Lines suffered two crashes in which 57 people were killed, the second involving a pilot who had previously been grounded for "psychosomatic disorders." Yet not a single damage suit was filed against JAL by relatives of the crash victims. Instead, the company worked out with the relatives of the dead a series of privately negotiated settlements which varied in size depending on the victim's age, salary and family obligations. So common is this kind of procedure that the number of civil lawsuits filed in Japan each year amounts to only a tiny fraction—probably no more than 5 percent—of the comparable figure for the United States.

Some American legal experts, who apparently find it inconceivable that anyone would voluntarily pass up an opportunity to plunge into adversary proceedings, argue that the reason Japanese don't sue one another more often is that it takes an inordinately long time to extract a verdict in a civil case from the Japanese courts—and the last half of that assertion, at least, is undeniably true. Japanese court dockets are, in fact, badly overcrowded: to get a decision in even a routine civil case takes an average of more than two years, and some particularly complex suits have dragged on for twenty years or more.

If this were the primary reason Japanese are reluctant to go to court, however, one would expect a great public clamor for legal reform. But such is not the case. What really discourages litigation in Japan is not defeatism, but rather the widespread and deeply held conviction that taking someone to court constitutes a breach of the community harmony to which Japanese attach such enormous value. When a Japanese does sue someone, he himself sees his action as evidence of a miscarriage of the social process—specifically, of the failure of the people he is suing to show a decent regard for his feelings and interests and for the accepted value system.

Whether both parties are prepared to show a regard for the properties is, in fact, a central question in any civil dispute in Japan. An essential element in an out-of-court settlement of such a dispute—an element that can be nearly as important as the financial terms arrived at—is often the public acceptance by one side or the other of moral responsibility for whatever went wrong. One of the longest and most notable lawsuits in postwar Japan was that brought on behalf of victims of the so-called "Minamata disease"—people who had contracted mercury poisoning as a result of the dumping of chemical wastes into the sea by the Chisso Corporation. In this instance, Chisso, which eventually lost the case, stoutly denied any responsibility. Had it been willing to accept blame and make a public apology early on, it is conceivable that the matter would never have gotten into the courts at all.

What Chisso would have been wise to remember is that in Japan nothing turns away wrath like a contrite apology. Some years ago when Japanese consumer groups loudly protested the sales practices of a company run by a friend of mine, my friend offered a public mea culpa and promised reform. In the United States, such action would constitute a semisuicidal invitation to a blizzard of lawsuits. In Japan, by contrast, it almost certainly served to reduce the number of claims against my friend's company and the size of the settlements it was obliged to make.

Inevitably, the disfavor with which lawsuits are regarded means that the legal profession in Japan is far less attractive than it is in the United States. Japanese lawyers do not enjoy the same social status as American lawyers, or anything like the same career opportunities. Unlike the U.S. Congress, where it is impossible to throw a stone without hitting a lawyer, relatively few lawyers sit in Japan's Diet—and even fewer head major Japanese corporations. "One of the problems with U.S. business," President Taiji Ubukata of Ishikawajima-Harima Heavy Industries told me disapprovingly a few years ago, "is that lawyers and accountants play too big a part in its management." Nor is this just one man's view: many a big Japanese company doesn't feel it either necessary or desirable even to have a corporation counsel on its staff.

Under these circumstances, it is hardly surprising that lawyers are a far scarcer breed in Japan than they are in the United States.

In fact, while there are more than 30,000 practicing lawyers on Manhattan Island alone (and roughly half a million in the United States as a whole), all of Japan struggles along with just a few over 10,000. And even at that, many members of the Japanese bar spend a high percentage of their time not on essentially domestic cases but on business dealings between Japanese and foreign concerns. Significantly, in fact, one of Tokyo's most successful law firms—Anderson, Mori and Rabinowitz—was founded by three Americans and, as of 1982, still included two of them among its top partners.

Japan's ever-increasing economic involvement with the outside world, however, has done more than simply provide additional employment for the country's lawyers; it has also served to modify the attitudes of Japanese businessmen and, to a lesser degree, Japanese bureaucrats toward law itself. More and more, Japan's movers and shakers have come to realize that in their operations abroad they have no choice but to play the Western legal game—and many of them now do so with considerable sophistication. One Manhattan lawyer who has dealt extensively with Japanese businessmen, in fact, finds them particularly satisfying clients. "They always know exactly what they want to accomplish in business terms—which is more than I can say for a lot of our American clients," he told me. "And they are very precise and patient in dealing with the legal details necessary to accomplish their business objectives. An American will often tell you, 'Oh, don't bother me with all that crap,' but the Japanese never do."

Nonetheless, for the majority of Japanese, Western legal concepts still remain essentially alien—chiefly because Japanese are far more relativistic than Westerners both in personal and in group dealings. To the Japanese way of thinking, the drawing-up of an elaborate written contract intended to bind two parties indefinitely to a given set of terms borders on the absurd and, in a sense, smacks of trickery. As Japanese see it, when circumstances change significantly, the relationship between two people—or two companies—should change accordingly. In particular, this applies in situations where rigid adherence to a particular set of terms would work irreparable hardship on one of the parties. For while Japanese are intense competitors, they find it very difficult to accept one of the logical consequences of competition: that it sometimes produces losers. "For us," my bureaucrat friend Chitoshi once explained to me, "the destruction of any institution, however much it may have brought its fate upon itself, is a tragedy—a cause for guilt and dismay."

Their distaste for elaborate written contracts, however, in no way means that the Japanese are shifty in their personal or business relationships. On the contrary, in my experience, they are uncommonly honorable and have if anything an exaggerated devotion to the letter of the law. I still recall with sneaking admiration a train conductor who, the day after U.S. forces first landed in Japan in 1945, stoutly insisted that I and two other U.S. soldiers must pay the regular fare to travel from Yokohama to Tokyo. The fact that we had no Japanese money—and did have both side arms and very short tempers—did not sway him. Regulations, he pointed out, were regulations. All that finally changed his mind was our assertion, totally fictitious, that as one of his first acts as Japan's new ruler, General MacArthur had decreed that Occupation personnel were entitled to free passage on public transportation.

But scrupulous as the Japanese are about observing legal niceties, the relativism of their society comes into play here as well. For the letter of the law in Japan can change drastically with little or no notice and no legislative action whatever. As I noted earlier, Japanese judges can and do take advantage of the imprecision of their language to radically reinterpret the meaning of legal statutes. What amounts to rewriting of the law through judicial interpretation is something that happens in the United States too, of course. But in Japan the practice is far more commonplace; it is, in fact, a key element in the way Japanese law evolves to meet changing conditions. And it is by no means unknown for a Japanese judge, by dint of semantic sleight-of-hand, to decree that a law means something close to the exact opposite of what its original framers clearly intended it to mean. As Takeyoshi Kawashima, a prominent Tokyo lawyer and legal scholar, once put it: "When laws are drafted in Japan, it is taken for granted that the meanings of the words of their provisions will not be clear-cut. . . . No debate in the Diet to clarify the meanings of provisions and no pledges extracted from government leaders are to be relied on. . . . Once a law is enacted it begins a life of its own and no one can foretell how its content will develop."

To most Americans, I believe, this would seem to introduce an unacceptable degree of unpredictability and judicial whim into the legal process. But to Japanese, with their profound distrust of neat constitutional compartmentalization and unalterable legal commitments, it seems nothing more than a bow to reality. For Japanese, the law is not, as it is for many American lawyers, an intellectual chess game, nor is the concept of justice a kind of Platonic ideal independent of the practical concerns of the moment. Indeed, the word Japanese most commonly use where Americans would use "justice" is *seigi*—a Chinese compound which means "right principle" and has no necessary reference to legal matters at all. For better or for worse, in short, Japanese come far closer than contemporary Americans to living by the precept of Henry Thoreau: "It is not desirable to cultivate a respect for law so much as a respect for right."

9

The Gaijin *Complex*

Once, at the height of the Korean War, I found myself unavoidably eavesdropping on an encounter in a Tokyo commuter train between a Japanese girl who erroneously assumed that she knew how to speak English and a young American lieutenant whose Japanese consisted of half a dozen mispronounced phrases that had made their way into G.I. slang. Because the girl had initiated the conversation, the American had jumped to the conclusion that she was sexually available and was politely but insistently trying to convey his readiness to strike a bargain. Meantime, the girl, who was actually a touchingly naive coed from a local university, was eagerly seeking to explain how much she and some of her fellow political science majors would welcome a chance to engage the lieutenant in a discussion of the foreign policies of the Truman Administration.

As it happened, I was obliged to get off the train before this dialogue reached what must have been a mutually frustrating denouement. But it has stuck in my mind ever since as a microcosmic example of a problem which in its ultimate implications is neither funny nor trivial. Complex as the social interaction is between Japanese themselves, the interaction between Japanese and foreigners is trickier still. And not infrequently the consequences of such encounters are both unexpected and disappointing—chiefly because Japanese and non-Japanese so often approach each other with radically different assumptions and some serious mutual misperceptions.

Even on a purely personal level, the psychic divide between Japanese and non-Japanese can be akin to a minefield; it often contains hidden charges whose presence becomes apparent only after they have exploded. In my own first encounters with Japanese during the Occupation, this was driven home to me in a way that I still find embarrassing to remember. Although I had not yet read the late Ruth Benedict's classic exploration of the Japanese psyche, *The Chrysanthemum and the Sword*, I was generally aware of the heavy obligations imposed on Japanese when they are recipients of *on*, the word normally used to describe a favor—but which also, revealingly, means "a debt." Somehow, however, it did not occur to me that the *on* concept would apply to what I had been brought up to regard as minimal and rather casual manifestations of civility. Accordingly, when one of my Japanese assistants lamented that his pregnant wife could not get as much milk as her doctor said she needed, I gave him an unopened bottle of calcium tablets that had been sent to me by my protective parents while I was serving in the South Pacific. About the same time, I briefly took in tow a small, obviously frightened Japanese girl who had become separated from her mother in a crowd. Neither of these acts cost me anything much in time, effort or money or seemed to me to call for more than a simple "Thank you." But the result in both cases was the same: in due course, I was presented with gifts far more expensive than either family involved could reasonably afford. In my American innocence, I had saddled these people with what they saw as debts of honor.

In the years since then, it has become almost second nature to me not to extend any significant courtesy to a Japanese without first reckoning what kind of obligation it is likely to impose upon him—and how prepared I am to hold up my end of a closer relationship with him. In dealing with highly traditional Japanese, for example, one small gift must be regarded as the inevitable forerunner of an endless exchange of gifts. And while the rules that govern gift-giving tend to be less scrupulously observed by younger and more cosmopolitan Japanese—I have a number of good Japanese friends with whom I have exchanged gifts only intermittently or not at all—the exchange of favors remains a more conscious and complex aspect of friendship in Japan than it is in the United States. This can easily lead to situations in which a Japanese comes to expect more of an American acquaintance than the American is prepared to give—with the result that the Japanese is confused and sometimes embittered by the American's sudden and, to the Japanese way of thinking, inexplicable evasion of the unspoken obligations of their relationship. On more than one occasion in my own experience Japanese friends have wanted me to do things that were either legally impossible or incompatible with American journalistic ethics, and I know that my failure to oblige them has put serious though unacknowledged strains on our friendship.

A rather similar phenomenon sometimes complicates and ultimately destroys romantic attachment between Japanese and foreigners. I know of a number of marriages between American men and Japanese women that have failed because each partner inadvertently aroused false expectations in the other. During the courtship phase of such relationships, the woman typically assumes that in an "American marriage" she will enjoy greater social freedom than she would in Japan while retaining all the matriarchal powers of the normal Japanese wife. Meantime, her demure, soft-spoken manner often leads her American suitor to conclude that she will make a more dutiful and obliging marital partner than most contemporary American women are prepared to be. The conflict that can result from these misapprehensions was vividly expressed to me once by a New York executive who had just broken up with a Japanese woman to whom he had been married for nearly ten years. "Everybody thinks I'm a son of a bitch and that Tomiko is a wronged woman," he complained. "To outsiders—even to you, I imagine—it looked as though her only purpose in life was to gratify my every whim. But believe me, all that Madame Butterfly stuff was just on the surface. Underneath she was like steel. She had rigid ideas on everything from how much of my salary we should bank to what religion the kids should be brought up in, and there was just no reasoning with her."

By American lights, moreover, it's not just Japanese women who often appear deceptively compliant but Japanese men as well—including Japanese businessmen and politicians. Because of their distaste for confrontation and their ingrained horror of openly embarrassing anyone, Japanese in general find it difficult to respond to any proposition, however outrageous, with an unqualified "no." Some Japanese who have dealt extensively with Westerners have learned to overcome this aversion, but even those who have made that breakthrough sometimes find such an alien form of behavior so uncomfortable that when they do say "no," they do it gracelessly and with unnecessary vehemence. It is this, I believe, that accounts, at least in part, for the fact that now and again Japanese Government spokesmen will denounce unwelcome foreign proposals as "hypocrisy" or "ridiculous nonsense"—phrases that few Western diplomats would employ except under extreme provocation.

Such outbursts, however, are very much the exception.

Characteristically, a Japanese faced with a proposal that he is not prepared to accept will seek to save face for his negotiating partner by resorting to vagueness—often the suggestion that the whole matter requires further study.

Sometimes such vagueness reflects nothing more than a polite way of saying that the proposition in question is a nonstarter; sometimes, it presages a genuine search for a compromise solution. The obvious danger, however, is that such calculated and artificial imprecision can mislead an unwary foreigner into concluding that he has received some form of commitment—an error in judgment classically exemplified in a 1970 summit meeting between President Richard Nixon and the late Prime Minister Eisaku Sato. At that meeting, Nixon for domestic political reasons put heavy pressure upon Sato to curtail Japan's proliferating textile exports to the United States. In response, Sato used a Japanese phrase which, loosely translated, means "I'll do my damnedest." All that Sato meant to convey was that he would look into the problem and see if there was some way he could alleviate it without too many ugly repercussions. To Nixon, however, it sounded as though Sato had promised to remedy the situation. And so, when Sato failed to take really effective action, Nixon bitterly concluded that he had been double-crossed.

This misunderstanding, which had all sorts of adverse consequences upon U.S.–Japanese relations, was as much Nixon's fault as Sato's. But as far as I know, that point was never made to Nixon. If it had been, I suspect his reaction would have been similar to that of Mark Twain's Nigger Jim when he was confronted with the proposition that a human being might speak in French rather than English: "If he's a man, why don't he talk like a man?"

It may still be possible for Presidents of the United States to operate successfully on the basis of that kind of cultural chauvinism—although I doubt it. But for less exalted Americans and Europeans who must deal on a day-to-day basis with the realities of a Japanese economic power, a conscious effort to master some of the principles of Japanese behavior and negotiating style would seem highly advisable—not out of any idealistic commitment to cultural egalitarianism but for the pragmatic reason advanced by former U.S. Ambassador to Japan James D. Hodgson. "It has been my experience," Hodgson once said, "that if you try to accommodate the Japanese in matters of style, they will usually try to accommodate you in matters of substance."

★

Sound as Ambassador Hodgson's advice is, the great majority of Westerners have as yet shown little disposition to go to the trouble of informing themselves about Japanese social patterns and thought processes. Partly for that reason and partly because of the limitations of the Japanese themselves, Japan remains a psychological outsider in the developed world. And for all the difficulties this can cause in personal relations between Japanese and non-Japanese, its most damaging consequences are not for individuals but for the Japanese people as a whole.

Internationally speaking, the Japanese undeniably suffer from what public relations men like to call an image problem. In diplomatic councils, Japan is seen more often than not as a kind of rich eunuch, and the pronouncements of its representatives commonly carry less weight than those of spokesmen for any number of impoverished, misruled and mischievous minor powers. And in large parts of the globe, the man in the street tends to regard Japanese as either figures of fun or ruthless predators—or a bit of both.

Most people in the United States would indignantly deny that they subscribe to such stereotypes about the Japanese, and it is quite true that for the past quarter century or so Americans in general have looked benignly on Japan and the Japanese. But in the last few years, as Japan's industrial power has burgeoned and our own economy has been increasingly plagued by seemingly intractable problems, there has been a significant erosion of American goodwill toward Japan. A poll taken in 1980 for a Washington research group called Potomac Associates showed that 84 percent of Americans looked favorably upon the Japanese and only 12 percent had negative feelings toward them. In a poll taken in early 1982, however, the "favorable" figure had fallen to 63 percent and the "negative" one had jumped to 29 percent.

Though these figures reflected a shift of opinion notable for both its magnitude and its rapidity, they were easy enough to shrug off if one wanted to do so; most U.S. politicians, after all, would be overjoyed if 63 percent of their constituents held them in reasonable esteem. But the trouble with such easy optimism is that it fails to take into account the intensity of emotion among those Americans who in recent years have come to feel hostile toward Japan. Shortly after the 1982 poll results were published, Congressman John Dingell of Michigan, whose constituents include a great many auto workers, publicly referred to the Japanese as "the little yellow people." And that bitter remark with its racist overtones clearly expressed the sentiments of many U.S. businessmen and laborers.

At a Teledyne plant in Milwaukee in the fall of 1981, workers tore down a Japanese flag that had been raised in honor of a group of visiting businessmen from Tokyo; in Ohio a few months later, the credit union at a titanium-processing plant barred loans for the purchase of imported cars; and at more than one U.S. auto factory in the early '80s, the company parking lot was formally or informally closed to Japanese cars. (Had they only been aware of it, most U.S. auto workers would probably have found it totally appropriate that the president of the Mitsubishi Motors Corporation at the time was a son of Japan's World War II Prime Minister, General Hideki Tojo.)

Admittedly, these were no more than straws in the wind. But they were ominous ones, if only because the U.S. political system rests so heavily on what New York lawyer Sherwin Goldman has christened "the pain principle." The pain principle stipulates that in American politics, the passionate protests of a minority whose interests are being hurt more often than not prevail over the opposed but less strongly held opinions of a majority with no great personal interest at stake. And in the case of Japanese–American relations, the operations of the pain principle are reinforced by the fact that Americans as a whole have little real comprehension of Japan and hence no solidly grounded fundamental commitment to a Japanese–American alliance. There is, in short, almost certainly a higher degree of potential volatility in American attitudes toward Japan than in our attitudes toward European allies.

This is a state of affairs that troubles thoughtful Japanese—and with very good reason. Quite apart from the critical importance of the American alliance to Japan in economic and strategic terms, the United States is virtually the only foreign country in which there is any significant degree of popular respect for the Japanese. Some time ago, I remarked to a senior official of the European Common Market that it seemed to me that broadly speaking, Western Europeans did not like the Japanese, had no desire to understand them and devoutly wished they would just go away. I intended the comment as a criticism both of the naked protectionism with which European governments seek to exclude Japanese products from their countries and of the cultural and ethnic arrogance that ordinary Europeans display toward Japanese. But the response I got was not in the least defensive. "That's very well put," the Common Market man said brightly. "Do you mind if I borrow it?"

If they felt any need to justify their contempt for the Japanese, Europeans could at least claim that Japan is geographically remote from their world and that Japanese are ethnically and culturally completely alien to them. None of these excuses, of course, are available to other Asians. Yet in Asia too the Japanese are suspect outsiders. The Chinese, with whom the Japanese feel more affinity than they do with any other foreign people, do not return this regard: they tend to consider the Japanese crude and unsophisticated and, in business and political dealings alike, try to browbeat them by playing on the complex mélange of cultural indebtedness, war guilt, romanticism and cupidity that constitutes the contemporary Japanese perspective on China. The South Koreans, while paying Japan the compliment of imitating its development strategies, nonetheless bitterly dislike the Japanese and are determined to make them atone indefinitely for the thirty-five years during which Korea was part of the Japanese Empire. As for Southeast Asians, they have their own unhappy memories of being bludgeoned into the Greater East Asia Co-Prosperity Sphere during World War II and in any case do not for the most part find the Japanese socially or culturally compatible. Exactly how alien the Japanese seem to many Southeast Asians was suggested in the early 1980s when the Tokyo government, after much soul-searching, decided to offer permanent residence in Japan to 3,000 Vietnamese "boat people." As it turned out, this came close to being an empty gesture; so little empathy do the Vietnamese feel for the Japanese that as of this writing the quota was still unfilled; the great majority of boat people preferred to gamble on the iffy prospect of eventual admission to the United States rather than accept an assured haven in Japan.

As I have suggested, there are obvious historical reasons why considerable numbers of people around the world regard Japan with distrust and even outright dislike. But I do not believe than Japan's image problem can be adequately explained purely in terms of the Japanese penchant for territorial aggression in the first half of this century or of the painful defeats that Japanese industry has inflicted on so many of its foreign competitors in more recent times. A significant part of the problem, it seems to me, stems from the fact that the Japanese not only operate on premises unfamiliar to most foreigners but fail to explain themselves or their premises effectively to the rest of the world.

Specifically, their distaste for confrontation, beneficial as it often is in their own society, serves the Japanese poorly in their dealings with foreigners. Their instinctive efforts to reconcile inherently contradictory viewpoints—or at least to achieve the appearance of such a reconciliation—not infrequently lead Japanese into courses of action that strike Westerners as two-faced and opportunistic.

Sometimes, this Western perception is an accurate one. Between their essentially relativistic view of morality and their profound sense of the vulnerability of their society, the Japanese as a people are somewhat less prone to stand on principle than Westerners. In their eagerness to retain their bureaus in Peking, for example, Japan's major newspapers have at times practiced a kind of self-censorship in their reporting on China that no respectable American publication would indulge in. Similarly, in its anxiety not to imperil its supplies of Middle Eastern oil, the Japanese Government has truckled to the Arab states in general and the Palestine Liberation Organization in particular with a shamelessness unmatched by even the most oil-hungry of the major Western European states.

Very often, however, what Westerners perceive as a lack of principle in Japanese behavior is not that at all but simply reflects a difference in managerial or negotiating styles. Thus, New York lawyer William Walker, who was deputy special trade representative to Tokyo during the Ford Administration, recalls: "Sometimes we'd get a proposal accepted by the Cabinet ministry principally involved only to discover that it was being blocked by another ministry with a lesser interest in the matter. Unhappily, it was generally impossible to find out just who it was in the second ministry who was holding things up, so you were always working partly in the dark and waiting for the famous consensus to emerge. Inevitably, this kind of situation—the fact that nobody seems to take personal responsibility—tends to create the appearance of bad faith even when that's not the reality."

Another cultural misunderstanding of similar nature occurs when foreigners make what the Japanese perceive as absurd or unjustified demands upon them. In such a situation, the immediate impulse of most Japanese is to cast about for some action they can take that will damage their own interests as little as possible and yet appear conciliatory. They do this on the assumption that whatever "concession" they make will be accepted by the foreigners as a gesture of goodwill and an effort to reach a solution that saves face all around. And they never cease to be astounded when the foreigners, who are interested not in saving face but in achieving concrete goals, denounce the Japanese gestures as meaningless or deceitful and interpret them as tacit admissions of guilt.

Over and over again in the past forty years I have seen such mutual misperceptions cloud personal and business relations between Japanese and Americans. And in the past fifteen years they have become increasingly dominant in relations between the Japanese and American Governments. Faced with ever-escalating American demands for changes in their national economic behavior, the Japanese have severely taxed their intricate decision-making process to come up with one concession after another. Yet as I write this, the U.S. trade deficit with Japan is running at the highest level in history, and more and more Americans, including many who should know better, angrily argue that responsibility for this state of affairs rests primarily if not entirely with the Japanese.

In a sense, that is scarcely surprising, since very few Americans have been adequately exposed to any intelligent arguments to the contrary. It would, of course, be foolish to suggest that the Japanese have been without sin in their economic dealings with the United States; they have, in fact, been guilty at one time or another of a wide variety of restrictive and predatory practices. But there is a very powerful case to be made that it is not Japan's sins but America's that are primarily responsible for the one-sided nature of the U.S.–Japanese trade. And in any event, it is somewhat difficult to see why it is more reprehensible for Japan to run consistently large trade surpluses with the United States than it is for the United States to run consistently large trade surpluses with the Common Market, as we have done for the past twenty-five years, or with Canada, as we have done since time immemorial. Yet powerful as some of these arguments are, the Japanese have been singularly hesitant and inept in bringing them to the attention of American politicians and the American public.

On a conscious level, the chief reason for this public relations failure probably lies in the fact that most of the elderly men who dominate Japanese politics are still afflicted with what some of their juniors call "the Occupation mentality": they feel an overwhelming sense of dependence upon the United States and hence believe that it would be grossly imprudent and ungrateful of them to give the Americans too much back talk. But consciously or unconsciously, Japan's leaders are also inhibited by an even more crippling affliction: the fact that they do not possess either the communications skills or the cast of mind that would enable them to conduct an effective public relations campaign in the United States.

Here again the villains of the piece are that ubiquitous Japanese duo, dread of confrontation and distaste for explicit statement. Between them, these two inhibitions make it extremely difficult for Japanese—even Japanese who have achieved considerable fluency in English—to engage in the kind of lucid, logically structured exposition that is basic to effective debate and persuasion in a Western context.

Sweeping as that generalization may sound, it is one whose validity was forcibly impressed upon me in the early 1970s when I was obliged to assemble a team of non-American columnists for the international edition of *Newsweek* magazine. In Western Europe I rapidly lined up several excellent people—writers whose English was sometimes flawed, but whose thoughts were expressed with a directness and clarity that overcame any shortcomings in syntax. In Japan, by contrast, it proved relatively easy to find people who could write grammatical English, but extraordinarily hard to find one who could or would write a column with a straightforward message. Instead, virtually all the Japanese journalists and academics whose work I considered approached the task of making a point somewhat the way my dog approaches his bed: they would circle compulsively around and around their central—but unstated—idea and then, just as they seemed about to settle down and spit it out, would abruptly veer away and wander off again at a tangent.

Ultimately, *Newsweek* did acquire an admirable Japanese columnist in the person of Jiro Tokuyama, a man who lived for fifteen years in the United States and has had three successive careers as a soldier, a civil servant and a think-tank official. In short, as a Tokyo newsman somewhat disapprovingly reminded me one day, Jiro Tokuyama is far from being a typical Japanese. To which I could only reply that this undoubtedly was the reason for his uncommon effectiveness in explaining Japan to foreigners.

The fact that my journalist friend found Jiro Tokuyama's cosmopolitanism cause for disparaging comment reflects one of the most curious aspects of the Japanese psyche: the very deep ambivalence most Japanese feel toward foreigners and foreign cultures.

On one level, as even a superficial look at Japan makes plain, the Japanese are quick to ape things foreign—and particularly things American. Indeed, so many of the externals of Japanese life have now become effectively Westernized that a casual visitor could be pardoned for concluding that the people of Japan are hell-bent on transforming themselves into ersatz Europeans or Americans. It is even tempting to speculate that in their fantasies the Japanese may already have done so: it is a curious fact that the people who appear in Japanese commercials, both live and animated, tend to have distinctly more Caucasian features than the general run of Japanese do.

Significantly, however, every Japanese friend whom I have ever asked to explain this phenomenon has flatly assured me that it does not exist and that the actors in TV commercials are, in fact, typically Japanese in appearance. Since this is manifestly not the case, it might seem that my friends were displaying some sort of chauvinistic touchiness, but I do not believe that to be so. Rather, it simply had not occurred to them that the actors in those TV commercials looked uncommonly like Europeans or Americans—like anything, in fact, except "modern" Japanese. My friends, in short, were indulging in an absolutely standard Japanese practice: the cultural domestication of what are seen as desirable foreign attributes and institutions.

Though there are increasingly numerous exceptions to the rule, it is still true that the majority of Japanese, particularly those who are middle-aged and older, become uneasy when they are obliged to deal directly with foreign cultures or practices. They are truly comfortable with Western concepts and life-styles only at one remove—which is to say when these things have been transplanted to Japan and somehow "Japanized." And when this process has been fully realized, the foreign origin of a borrowed custom, word or institution is almost completely forgotten. I doubt, for example, that one Japanese in a hundred ever stops to think that beer is not a native Japanese beverage, that the uniforms Japanese schoolboys wear were originally German in inspiration or that *pachinko*, the toothbrush and the seven-day week are all importations from the West. (Prior to the Meiji Restoration, Japanese used the Chinese lunar calendar, and for domestic purposes they still reckon years not from the birth of Christ but from the accession of the incumbent Emperor. Thus, to a Japanese, 1982 was "Showa 57" because it marked the fifty-seventh year since Hirohito succeeded to the throne and decided, somewhat ironically in light of subsequent events, that his reign should be officially known as the period of Showa, or "Bright Peace.")

But while it is relatively easy for the Japanese to dilute or disguise the foreign provenance of ideas, objects or customs, it is impossible for them to accomplish this with human beings. Physically, Caucasians, blacks, even most southeast Asians always remain conspicuously and intractably alien to a Japanese eye. For Americans who find it hard to tell Orientals apart, it may be comforting to know that not infrequently, the Japanese have difficulty in telling individual foreigners apart: at a large reception in Tokyo a few years ago, I was roundly snubbed by the very man who had invited me to the affair, simply because he found it impossible to distinguish me from the dozen or so other tall, graying Americans present. But what is of key importance about a foreigner in Japan is not so much his individual identity as the mere fact of his foreignness. In most American or Western European cities, a foreigner, no matter how visibly alien in color or clothing, can expect to walk the streets without attracting overt comment. But as any foreign resident of Japan can testify, it is commonplace in virtually every Japanese city except Tokyo for giggling bands of schoolchildren to alert one another to the presence of an outlander with pointed fingers and muted cries of *"Gaijin, gaijin"* ("Foreigner, foreigner").

There is, I believe, a message in this childish candor—and the message is that at bottom, the majority of Japanese don't feel comfortable with foreigners and don't really approve of them. The word *gaijin* literally means "outside person"; and outside is just where most Japanese wish non-Japanese would stay. In a Japanese Government survey taken in 1980, 64 percent of the people polled flatly declared that they did not wish to associate with foreigners and had no intention of doing so. And of the 25 percent of those polled who did express a desire to associate with *gaijin*, fewer than a sixth—which is to say only 4 percent of the total sample—were actually doing so.

Inevitably, of course, Japan's emergence as a major international economic power has meant that more and more Japanese are being thrust into contact with foreigners willy-nilly. The number of Japanese obliged to live abroad for business reasons is large and steadily growing; as of 1981, in fact, there were some 30,000 Japanese citizens living in New York City and its suburbs alone. And foreign travel has now become a commonplace even among Japanese of relatively modest income. Once, while visiting what is generally considered a rather backward area of rural Japan, I was startled to have a rice farmer casually inform me that he had visited mainland China and most of the nations of Southeast Asia on junkets sponsored by various agricultural organizations.

As a result of this increased exposure to the world outside Japan, the number of truly cosmopolitan Japanese is far larger now than it was a generation or so ago. It is not, however, as much larger as one might expect, for contrary to the conventional wisdom, travel is not necessarily broadening—particularly if you happen to be Japanese. Anyone who has witnessed a flock of a hundred or so

Japanese being shepherded through a European or American airport by a flag-waving guide with the command presence of an army top sergeant has been exposed to Japanese tourism in its most characteristic form. Such groups often confine their patronage to resorts and establishments that cater specially to Japanese—which means that the only locals their members have to deal with are shop clerks and waiters; and even then, Japanese-speaking clerks and waiters are preferred. "It is difficult," one Japanese acquaintance of mine matter-of-factly explained, "to eat while speaking English."

Not even prolonged foreign residence, in fact, automatically widens the horizon of a Japanese greatly. The American communities that sprang up in Western Europe following World War II have sometimes been described as "golden ghettos," but that term applies at least as well to such major Japanese expatriate communities as the ones in Düsseldorf and New York. A Japanese resident of New York can, if he so chooses, get his news from Japanese-language radio programs and the special New York edition of Tokyo's *Yomiuri Shimbun,* watch Japanese variety shows and samurai movies on cable TV, drink at predominantly Japanese bars, keep up with Japanese cultural developments through the lectures and exhibits at the Japan Society and send his children to a Japanese school. What's more, a considerable number of the Japanese in New York do in fact choose to live just that way. According to a pair of surveys conducted in 1981, a third of the Japanese residents of the New York area never read an American periodical, nearly 40 percent of the men—and presumably an even larger number of the women—had made no American friends at all and two-thirds admitted to taking no part whatsoever in community activities.

Deplorable as it may seem, however, such reluctance to step outside one's own culture makes considerably more sense in the Japanese context than in a Western one. The reason for this is that to become "too cosmopolitan" entails very real dangers for a Japanese. Even if they have attended the best preparatory schools in Britain or America, Japanese youngsters who have gotten any major part of their secondary education abroad have relatively little hope of getting into one of Japan's more prestigious universities; they simply cannot compete on equal terms with stay-at-homes whose entire education has been pointed toward the all-important university entrance exams—and while Kyoto University recently established a special entrance exam for youngsters brought up abroad, that is still very much the exception. Nor is it feasible for a youngster who received his secondary education overseas to circumvent the Japanese system entirely by attending an American or European university. After getting a B.A. and M.A. in the United States and completing most of the work for a doctorate at Stanford, one young Japanese I know resignedly returned to Tokyo to get another bachelor's degree at a private university there. His explanation: "If I want to have a career in Japan, I simply must have a Japanese degree. As long as I have only American degrees, no matter how many of them I get or how distinguished they may be, I'll never amount to anything in Japan."

In that, my young friend was almost certainly right. Because they have been tainted with Western individualism, Japanese who have received a large part of their education abroad tend to be regarded as unduly aggressive or abrasive and are often shunned as unreliable by potential employers. And by the same token, any ambitious Japanese businessman or bureaucrat, no matter how much he may enjoy living abroad, knows that for the sake of his career he must return to Japan the moment he is offered the opportunity to do so. For at the highest levels of Japanese industry and politics, an intimate acquaintance with foreign ways and extensive contacts with foreigners can actually be a handicap—so much so that one of Japan's most intelligent politicians, a man widely known and respected abroad, has frequently been written off as a potential Prime Minister precisely for that reason. "He's the foreigners' candidate," my bureaucrat friend Chitoshi once told me with a sardonic smile. "You don't get to be Prime Minister of Japan by speaking good English and getting on well with Americans."

There are, I believe, two major factors that serve to explain the limited tolerance Japanese have for foreigners. One of these is the strong exclusionary strain in the Japanese psyche, an attitude born of the historic scarcity of space, resources and opportunity in Japan. By the early 1600s, nearly four hundred years ago, Japan was already afflicted with a population density almost twice that of the present-day United States. (To look at this another way, if Japan today had the same population density as the United States, there would be only 8 million Japanese instead of 118 million.) This combination of large population and limited wealth inevitably produced keen competition for economic survival, and that, in turn, led the Japanese early on to bond into mutual-security groups whose members protected each other's interests against all outsiders, including other Japanese. Such mutual-support groups, whose coexistence rests on the unspoken rule "I won't break your rice

bowl if you don't break mine," still play a major role in Japanese
society, the most notable cases in point being the great industrial
confederations such as the Mitsui, Mitsubishi or Sumitomo
combines. And in a very real sense, the Japanese nation as a whole
constitutes a kind of supergroup, one which, like its component
elements, is heavily motivated by defensive considerations.

The fact that Japan is in this sense a closed society is something
a fair number of Japanese will admit; in fact, it was Jiro Tokuyama
who first brought this concept to my attention. But something
that few if any Japanese are prepared to admit is that along with
defensiveness, their exclusionary behavior also rests on a strongly
entrenched superiority complex.

What is involved here is more than simple racism—even though
the Japanese have their fair share of that. The central element in
the Japanese sense of superiority is, I think, tribal rather than purely
social. Convinced, accurately enough, of the uniqueness of their
culture, the Japanese also like to think that it is so subtle and
complex that no one who was not born Japanese and reared in
Japanese society can ever truly become part of it.

As a general thing, Japanese are prepared to treat foreigners with
great courtesy and often with genuine warmth—provided that they
are only visitors or, if resident in Japan, content to remain essentially
foreign in their attitudes and life-styles. But if a *gaijin* shows signs
of successfully mastering the nuances of Japanese culture and social
behavior, the instinctive Japanese response is to grow uneasy and
to seek to freeze him out by somehow reminding him of his ineradicable foreignness. Such behavior, of course, is characteristic of
bigots and chauvinists in any country, but in Japan it extends far
beyond such circles—a fact made plain a few years ago when the
magazine *Bungei Shunju* assembled a panel of intellectuals to discuss
former Ambassador Edwin O. Reischauer's book *The Japanese*.
During the course of the debate, one of the participants seized on
the book's word picture of the vast, antlike crowds that throng
Tokyo in the rush hour—a description very similar to some I have
heard from Japanese themselves—and with evident satisfaction
remarked that it "makes one realize that Reischauer is a foreigner
after all, for all his being born and raised in Japan and married to
a Japanese."

It is doubtful that this comment particularly disturbed Dr. Reischauer, who has never lost sight of his American identity. But the
attitude that it reflects has been a source of grief to some foreigners
who have fallen in love with Japan. As a number of serious students

of Japan have testified, the more eagerly and knowledgeably a foreigner seeks assimilation into Japanese society, the more firmly that society rejects him. This is not to say that it is impossible for foreigners to form close friendships with individual Japanese; they can, and on occasion, do. But the basic verdict on overall relations between Japanese and foreigners remains the one handed down by a highly gifted American scholar—a man who, after devoting most of his adult life to acquiring an intimate knowledge of Japan and things Japanese, has now somewhat bitterly turned to other pursuits. "There is no way," he says, "that a *gaijin* will ever win complete acceptance in Japan."

At first blush, this may not seem a particularly extraordinary statement; it might, in fact, be argued that one could say much the same of France or Britain. But there is a very real difference—which is that what is difficult in the older and more rigidified Western societies is impossible in Japan. There have, for example, been many foreign-born members of the British Parliament, including the House of Lords. For anyone of foreign birth to achieve comparable status in Japanese politics or society is quite simply inconceivable.

For the outsider, all this can be very uncomfortable. But offensive as foreigners may find them, the exclusionary attitudes of the Japanese are to some degree understandable and even defensible. Because they have borrowed so heavily from other cultures, the Japanese have throughout their modern history lived in fear of losing their own special identity. Admittedly, it is hard to specify precisely what constitutes that identity; Japanese themselves have debated the subject endlessly without, as far as I can see, ever having arrived at any generally accepted conclusions. Nonetheless, the homogeneity of the Japanese people and the fact that they feel, however inchoately, a great sense of commonality are among Japan's major strengths, and any dilution of those strengths would surely carry with it inherent dangers.

But there are also very real dangers inherent in the defensive mechanisms by means of which Japan has traditionally sought to maintain its special identity. Overinsistence on the unique nature of Japanese culture can lead to self-delusion: one of the reasons that Japan's World War II leaders never faced up to the rather obvious fact that the United States was reading their military and diplomatic codes lay in their unwarranted assumption that the Japanese language in itself constituted a code that very few *gaijin* were capable of penetrating. (In reality, the U.S. armed services turned out hundreds of people capable of reading Japanese messages and inter-rogating Japanese prisoners within two years after Pearl Harbor.) And there may well be the risk of similar self-delusion today in any assumption that a penchant for hard work and an extraordinary degree of personal thrift are intrinsic elements of the Japanese character rather than the products of specific—and potentially mutable—historical circumstances.

Even more serious in a day when Japan clearly cannot escape ever-growing international involvement are the dangers posed by instinctive exclusionism and distrust of cosmopolitanism. For as long as these remain the Japanese norm, Japan will continue to be handicapped in its political and economic dealings with the rest of the world. Americans and Europeans more often than not exaggerate the degree to which Japan is a closed society and are frequently illogical in their charges against the Japanese, as well as unreasonable in their demands upon them. But the broad perception that the Japanese as a people are psychically resistant to what they regard as foreign intrusions into their garden contains an undeniable germ of truth, and that fact has served both to envenom Western economic frictions with Japan and to lend them a dangerous political dimension.

Among the many things that could be done to defuse this situation, one obvious one is for Japanese industry to go multinational; by producing more of their goods abroad, Japanese companies could rely more heavily upon income from foreign investments and less upon enormous—and destabilizing—export sales. The Japanese themselves are keenly aware of this and have taken considerable strides in that direction: direct Japanese investment abroad, which amounted to barely $2 billion as late as 1968, had soared to more than $36 billion by 1980. This, however, has to be put in perspective: U.S. direct investment abroad as of 1980 was nearly ten times the Japanese figure, and even Britain, with an economy considerably smaller than Japan's, had roughly twice as much invested overseas.

Japanese industry, in short, is still far from being truly multinational, and it seems clear that it will be hobbled in its efforts to become so as long as most Japanese corporations continue to be as culturebound as they now are. Thus, the reluctance of Japanese management to deal with anything but cooperative Japanese-style trade unions has been a major inhibition to the establishment of U.S. plants by the Japanese steel and auto industries. Similarly, insistence upon staffing middle management posts in the United States exclusively with Japanese males has created legal problems for the U.S. subsidiaries of two big Japanese trading companies. Perhaps most crippling of all, however, is the fact that few if any Japanese companies are psychologically capable of granting foreigners, even foreigners fluent in Japanese, full-fledged membership in their top management councils. This inevitably makes it difficult for them to recruit outstanding local nationals to run their overseas operations—a practice which the best-run U.S. multinationals long ago concluded constitutes the only formula for successful long-term operation abroad.

Still, as deplorable as the consequences of Japan's *gaijin* complex may be and as deep as its roots run in Japanese history, it would be misguided to assume that it will always retain its present strength. There are, in fact, many signs that the younger generation of Japanese are more ready to accept foreigners and deal with them on easy terms than their elders. Despite the self-imposed blinkers worn by so many Japanese tourists and expatriates, there are now a significant number of young Japanese who not only have acquired firsthand familiarity with a foreign society but actively enjoyed that experience and, as a result, find the traditional restrictiveness of their own society a bit ridiculous and embarrassing. It is no longer particularly unusual to encounter youthful Japanese who recall with evident nostalgia life with an American Friends Service Committee "foster" family in New Jersey, the free and easy existence they knew as schoolchildren in Australia or the eye-opening quality of a year's service in a Philippine barrio as a member of Japan's version of the U.S. Peace Corps. And such statistics as are available on the subject suggest a heightened cosmopolitanism not only among young people who have actually lived abroad but among younger Japanese as a whole. In the 1980 government poll mentioned earlier in this chapter, only 11 percent of men over sixty expressed any desire to associate with foreigners, whereas 23 percent of those between thirty and thirty-nine did so. And among men under thirty the figure soared to 40 percent.

How soon these changing attitudes will have any real impact upon the policies pursued by the Japanese Government and Japanese industry, however, is difficult to predict. Japan is still, after all, a country whose major institutions are largely run by men of sixty or more, and that seems likely to continue to be true for some time to come. And by the time today's twenty-five-year-olds finally reach positions of influence, they may well have been at least partially remolded by the institutions they serve and display less enthusiasm for the prospect of an open society than they do at present.

In any case, how soon and how thoroughly Japan will conquer its *gaijin* complex is a matter over which foreigners seem unlikely to exercise decisive influence. So for the foreseeable future, any Westerner who becomes involved in extensive dealings with Japanese should bear in mind that he can hope to penetrate Japanese society only to a limited degree. Obviously, it is vitally important for anyone in such a position to learn everything he can about Japanese life and culture. But any attempt to command acceptance or to force the social pace by parading such knowledge is almost certain to prove counterproductive. In short, no matter how fascinated he may become with Japan, the prudent *gaijin* will resign himself to the fact that his role in the Japanese scheme of things will always remain somewhat akin to that of the "Shabbas goy"—the Gentile traditionally engaged by Orthodox Jews to perform chores which they themselves may not undertake on the Sabbath.

SECTION FOUR

Work and Power

10

The Information Society

There are a certain number of people—not all of them natives of Japan—who argue that the Japanese are quite literally smarter than the rest of us. Early in 1982, for example, British psychologist Richard Lynn reported that a study he had made of Japanese between the ages of six and sixteen showed that they performed significantly better on I.Q. tests than Americans of the same age; the average score of the Japanese youngsters Lynn studied was 111, whereas their American peers averaged only 100. More mortifying yet, Lynn estimated that only about 2 percent of all Americans had I.Q.s of 130 or more but that at least 10 percent of all Japanese did.

Given the notorious trickiness of all statistics concerning group intelligence, it would be ill advised to put too much weight on Dr. Lynn's findings. But even if one were to accept them as totally valid, it still seems unlikely that the high level of functional intelligence displayed by the great mass of Japanese stems primarily from inherently superior mental abilities. What appears more to the point is that the Japanese educational system trains people to get maximum mileage out of such native ability as they possess and that in an informal sense, education in Japan never ends. In all advanced societies today, the range of information available to anyone who wants it is mind-boggling. But it seems safe to say that in no other contemporary society do so many people eagerly subject themselves to such a ceaseless and diverse information bombardment as in Japan.

To begin with, books play a bigger role in the life of the average Japanese than they do in the life of the average American or European. Japanese publishers churn out some 35,000 new titles a year—which is almost as many in absolute terms as are published in the United States and in per capita terms amounts to nearly twice as many. As far as subject matter goes, the range in the two countries is more or less the same, but the Japanese have a much greater appetite for fiction: the great majority of the 30 best-selling books in Japan in any given year are novels, and Japanese publishers devote nearly twice as high a percentage of their lists to fiction as their American counterparts do.

This is very nice for novelists, since a really popular book will often sell a million copies or more in Japan, earning its author hundreds of thousands of dollars in royalties. And to feed a writer's ego, there are also grounds for believing that Japanese are more likely to actually read a book they have purchased than Americans are. Book clubs have never caught on in Japan, so personal libraries there are not sprinkled with unwanted volumes that people forgot to refuse or accepted only to fulfill a club requirement. Instead, Japanese buy nearly all their books in bookstores, the most ambitious of which are eight- and nine-story affairs carrying extensive stocks of foreign as well as Japanese books. And on an ordinary day a shop like Sanseido, in Tokyo's Kanda district, will be far more crowded than any Fifth Avenue bookstore in Manhattan.

Unhappily for the cause of international understanding, much of what the Japanese read remains inaccessible to most foreigners. For the majority of Westerners, serious Japanese fiction is at best an acquired taste. Though a few Japanese novelists such as Yasunari Kawabata, Kobo Abe and the late Yukio Mishima have won international reputations, Japanese fiction tends to be highly introspective and culturebound. Often, too, it is heavily dependent upon untranslatable Japanese wordplay, whose full flavor is next to impossible to convey in a foreign language. Similarly, much of the nonfiction published in Japanese is too parochial to travel well: though they may be big sellers in Japan, books about seventeenth-century Japanese statesmen or nineteenth-century Japanese philosophical currents aren't apt to find sizable markets abroad. As a result, relatively few translations of Japanese books are published in the West, and even fewer are widely read there. There are, in fact, a fair number of Japanese authors, ranging from the much-admired woman novelist Sawako Ariyoshi to all-purpose pundit Kenichi Takemura, whose books have sold millions of copies in Japan but whose very names are all but unknown outside Japan.

In sharp contrast, a remarkably high percentage of the books written elsewhere in the world are readily available in Japanese.

Year after year, the list of books most widely read in Japan includes such Western classics as *War and Peace,* Stendhal's *Le Rouge et le Noir,* De Maupassant's *Une Vie* and Pearl Buck's *The Good Earth.* One of the most intelligent appraisals I have ever heard of Ernest Hemingway's strengths and weaknesses as a writer came from a young Tokyo newspaperman who had read and reread all of Hemingway's work—in Japanese.

The Japanese appetite for Western thought and literature, however, extends far beyond the classics. Since they are even more obsessed with their national image than the members of most other societies, Japanese are particularly fascinated by anything foreigners write about Japan; such books, indeed, sometimes sell far better in Japan than in the author's homeland. (In a permutation on this, some Japanese artists and writers have achieved real renown at home only after winning favor with foreign critics. Here the most notable case in point is film director Akira Kurosawa, whose first ten or a dozen films began to be taken seriously by Japanese only after his *Rashomon* created a sensation at the Venice Film Festival of 1951.)

To suggest that narcissism is the predominant element underlying Japanese interest in contemporary foreign books, however, would be seriously misleading. Almost any significant or trendy new Western book, regardless of subject, rapidly finds a Japanese publisher. An important consequence of this vast traffic in translated books is that it is perfectly possible for a Japanese to keep abreast of current intellectual and artistic trends around the world even though he commands no foreign language. And this, in turn, can be deceptive for Westerners who deal with Japanese. In Europe or America, it is generally safe to assume that someone who speaks and reads no language but his own has at best a superficial acquaintance with foreign literatures and cultures. That, however, is never a safe assumption to make about a Japanese.

Besides manifesting such a lively interest in the life of the mind, Japanese are news addicts of the deepest dye. Some 93 percent of all Japanese regularly read newspapers, and per capita newspaper sales in Japan are far higher than in any other country in the world with the solitary exception of Sweden. In an era when the number of U.S. dailies is steadily contracting, the local and regional press in Japan continues to flourish. And so does an institution which, apart from *The Wall Street Journal,* does not really exist in the United States: the national daily press.

Japan's three top national dailies—*Asahi Shimbun, Yomiuri*

Shimbun and *Mainichi Shimbun*—are all behemoths by American standards. Where the New York *Daily News* prides itself on selling nearly 1.8 million copies a day, the morning edition of *Mainichi* alone has a circulation of 4.5 million, *Asahi* nearly 7.5 million and *Yomiuri* more than 8.7 million. And when their morning and evening editions are lumped together, both *Yomiuri* and *Asahi* sell more than 12 million copies a day. Even *Nihon Keizai Shimbun*—whose readership is limited by its heavy emphasis on economics, but which is perhaps the best edited of Japan's national dailies—can boast daily sales of more than 3 million copies.

To reach their vast audiences, the Big Three of Japanese daily journalism are printed in scores of plants scattered throughout Japan. Such decentralization of production is necessary in part because relatively few Japanese buy their daily newspaper at a newsstand; more than 90 percent insist on having it delivered at home—a fact that has led to increasingly savage competition among newspapers for the services of the dwindling number of people who are prepared to work the peculiar hours delivery boys must.

Thanks to their huge size, Japan's Big Three also have huge financial resources and, unlike most U.S. newspapers, are prepared to expend those resources freely on their news coverage. Each of them has anywhere from 8,000 to 10,000 employees and can deploy hundreds of reporters at a time, backing them up with all the tools of the modern journalist's trade from company-owned planes and helicopters to elaborate mobile communications centers. Because they are so heavily staffed, the Big Three can also afford to invest more reportorial time and effort in ensuring continuity of coverage than American papers generally can: typically, one particular reporter from each of the Big Three will begin to cultivate a special relationship with a promising young politician or bureaucrat at a much earlier stage than is customary in U.S. journalism. And a similar situation exists when it comes to covering the world overseas; only a handful of individual U.S. publications even approach the depth of foreign coverage that *Asahi* and *Yomiuri* regularly offer their readers. Taken together, in fact, the Japanese media blanket the world; there are more full-time Japanese correspondents in Paris alone than *Newsweek* has in all its foreign bureaus put together.

Given this unstinting approach to news gathering, it would be reasonable to expect Japan's dailies to be among the best newspapers in the world—and in many respects they are. They offer extremely wide-ranging and sophisticated coverage of the arts and cultural affairs and do not shrink from extensive regular analysis of relatively abstruse social, scientific and economic issues. Perhaps their outstanding strength is that they provide their readers with far more detailed and knowledgeable coverage of government policy while it is still evolving than even *The New York Times* or *The Washington Post* does in the United States. In short, while they are "mass" publications in terms of circulation, Japan's national dailies compare favorably in intellectual level with the "class" newspapers of Europe and America—which presumably is a consequence of the fact that the line between the highly educated elite and the mass of ordinary citizens is less sharply drawn in Japan than it is in the West.

All that being said, the overall quality of Japan's major newspapers nonetheless leaves something to be desired. Because they tend to mirror the attitudes of Japan's predominantly "progressive" intelligentsia, the Big Three are even more reflexively critical of the government of the day than the U.S. newspapers have become since Watergate. And in searching for cudgels with which to belabor the powers that be, Japanese editors and reporters do not hesitate to twist the facts to suit their opinions. Only rarely, for example, can the Big Three bring themselves to concede that far more Japanese approve of their country's mutual-security treaty with the United States than oppose it. In fact, in 1981 when then Prime Minister Zenko Suzuki visited Washington and agreed to a communiqué that referred to the Japanese–American relationship as an "alliance," there was a fire storm of denunciation in the Japanese press. Yet how else would one accurately describe an arrangement under which one country grants another military bases in return for a guarantee of protection against all outside attack?

No less deplorable than the biases of the major Japanese dailies is the fact that for all their vaunted watchdog role, they are remarkably unenterprising when it comes to investigative reporting. To some extent, this is because they are considerably quicker to bow to pressure than the best European and American papers. It is unusual to find serious criticism of a major advertiser in a Japanese newspaper; and out of a combination of journalistic expediency and ideological predisposition, all of the Big Three have on more than one occasion truckled to Peking. The classic example of this occurred in 1971 when an attempted coup against Mao Tse-tung ended in the mysterious death of his heir apparent, Lin Piao. Rather than risk having their correspondents expelled from China, all the major Japanese dailies simply suppressed the story until it had been so widely reported abroad that they could no longer do so.

Unlike the Peking regime, their own government can't—or at

least, doesn't—seek to manipulate Japan's newspapers through direct pressure. Nonetheless, the major national dailies almost never take the lead in exposing scandals within the government or even in the top circles of the ruling Liberal Democratic Party. The reason for this is that despite all their shrill criticism of the political establishment, Japanese journalists live in a curious kind of symbiosis with the officials and politicians whom they cover.

The source of this symbiosis lies in the fact that every Japanese Government office, including major prefectural and municipal ones, has its own "press club" to which all Japanese reporters regularly covering that office belong. (In yet another manifestation of the *gaijin* complex, these clubs, with very few exceptions, exclude foreign reporters.)

All told, there are some four hundred *kisha kurabu*, to use the "Japlish" term commonly applied to them, and each exerts great influence over the official or officials that it covers. During a visit that I made to Japan in the 1970s, for example, then Prime Minister Takeo Fukuda apologetically informed my magazine's Tokyo bureau that while he would be happy to talk to me informally, he could not give me an on-the-record interview because the *kisha kurabu* in the Prime Minister's office had established a quota on how many interviews he could grant to foreigners. And on far more significant matters the press clubs wield equally formidable powers: any Japanese bureaucrat with even a modicum of wisdom makes certain to keep his *kisha kurabu* fully informed of the latest wrinkles in his thinking concerning the major policy questions before his office as well as any changes in the circumstances bearing on those questions.

All this means that Japanese journalists can and do give their readers a remarkably intimate account of the processes of government and a great deal of forewarning of the probable nature of governmental decisions before they are actually taken. But in return for these useful insights the reader pays a price. In a very real sense, each *kisha kurabu* acts as a journalistic collective: when it has news to report, an informal directorate of the club's senior members decides what is important about this particular story and what is not—and all the club's members tailor their files to their papers accordingly.

Inevitably, this produces a distressing homogeneity in the tone of Japan's major national dailies. Though it would be an exaggeration to say that the Big Three are identical in political stance—*Asahi* is the most stridently "progressive" of the trio and *Mainichi* the most restrained—it is nonetheless true that if you have read a major domestic story in one of them, you have effectively read it in all three. What is even more damaging about the characteristically Japanese form of group journalism practiced by the *kisha kurabu* is that it discourages individual initiative on the part of reporters and, assuming that club members are favorably disposed toward the man they cover, facilitates a conspiracy of silence in his behalf. Since the editors of Japanese dailies do not pressure their reporters for scoops as relentlessly as U.s. editors do, this means that Japanese politicians and bureaucrats enjoy a degree of immunity from investigative reporting that their American counterparts cannot hope for.

Nothing in recent Japanese history better demonstrates this than the high-wire act performed so successfully for so long by former Prime Minister Kakuei Tanaka. Had Tanaka been operating on the American scene, everything about him would have set the antennae of the veriest cub reporter to quivering. Early on in his political career, Tanaka had been convicted of accepting bribes from coal-mining interests, and although that conviction was subsequently overturned, he was generally perceived as a wheeler-dealer. Throughout his years in government, he steadily increased the wealth he had amassed by means of construction and real estate operations, and his path to the premiership, which he assumed in 1972, was widely rumored to have been greased by vote-buying and what the Japanese euphemistically call "money politics." Significantly too, once he became Prime Minister, land speculation by political insiders soared to unusual heights.

Despite these highly suggestive circumstances, none of the major Japanese dailies ever bothered to take a really hard look at Tanaka's personal finances or his creative use of political contributions. In fact, the first publication to do so was a monthly magazine titled *Bungei Shunju,* whose reportorial resources are negligible compared with those of *Asahi* or *Mainichi.* Nonetheless, in November 1974, the editors of *Bungei Shunju* managed to put together a sixty-one-page report on Tanaka's financial dealings which, among other things, estimated that his election to the premiership had involved more than $15 million in payoffs and strongly suggested that there had been irregularities about the way he had acquired some of his vast real estate holdings.

So damning were the facts uncovered by *Bungei Shunju* that they quite quickly forced Tanaka to resign as Prime Minister. But even after the magazine's exposé appeared, the major Japanese dailies stubbornly ignored the story until the international edition of

Newsweek and other foreign publications that circulate in Japan picked it up and made further silence too difficult to explain.

As the Tanaka episode suggests, magazines in Japan have taken advantage of the shortcomings of the daily press to preempt in considerable degree the investigative reporting function. Partly for that reason, the best of Japan's magazines in recent years have acquired heightened influence and credibility.

Like the United States, Japan is metaphorically awash in magazines: nearly 3,000 of them were being published regularly at last count. Inevitably, many of these make little contribution to human understanding and may, in fact, set it back a bit. There are, for example, some 50 Japanese magazines that peddle lust and violence in comic-strip form, and at least three of these boast circulations of over a million. And as in the United States, special-interest periodicals abound; there is one for almost every conceivable human activity, including a number of women's magazines which range from "service books" to purveyors of scandal in the entertainment world.

Some gaps do exist in the Japanese periodical spectrum: newsletters have never achieved anything like the success in Japan that they enjoy in the United States. Senior Japanese executives, I am told, are not disposed to lay out large sums for information which they believe is mostly available in their daily papers or, if not, can generally be dug up free of charge by their diligent subordinates. And as in Britain, there are no true newsmagazines in Japan—presumably because the national newspapers there serve essentially the same functions that *Time* and *Newsweek* do in the United States.

To compensate, however, Japan does have roughly 70 general-interest weeklies, some of the biggest of which are owned by the national dailies and regularly carry stories of a kind that their parent publications do not deign to print. It was, in fact, a weekly owned by *Mainichi* that first broke the news of Lin Piao's death in Japan—though it did so by the curious expedient of publishing a translation of an American article on the subject.

To their credit, the best of the weeklies, while sometimes preoccupied with trivia, nonetheless offer their readers welcome candor and variety; they are more open about their political and economic biases than the national dailies and differ considerably from each other in their editorial stances. But while the weeklies as a result enjoy considerable popularity—the top half dozen or so have circulations of 500,000 or more—they do not play as big a role in shaping national opinion as monthly magazines do.

Japan's top monthlies are, in fact, remarkable animals with no exact parallel in American journalism. *Bungei Shunju*, which is both the biggest and best-known, regularly draws upon academic experts for articles dealing with everything from philosophy to sociology. In intellectual level, *Bungei Shunju*'s contents are a considerable cut above what normally appears in, say, *Harper's* or *The Atlantic*. Yet as long ago as 1976 it achieved a circulation of a million copies a month—which in per capita terms is as though *The Atlantic* were almost as widely sold in the United States as *Newsweek*.

Because magazines typically enjoy more pass-along readership than daily papers, it may well be that *Bungei Shunju*'s total audience actually approaches that of *Mainichi* in size. In any case, it is clearly in the millions—which means that a remarkably large percentage of the Japanese population is regularly exposed to highly sophisticated analyses of complex issues. Since so many of its contributors are professors or ex-professors, *Bungei Shunju* inevitably runs many articles written from a leftist viewpoint. But it is also capable of running—as it has done—hard-hitting articles on the ambivalences of the Japanese Communist Party and a wide range of opinion on whether and to what degree Japan should strengthen its military forces.

For all its deficiencies, in short, the Japanese press taken as a whole constitutes an important national resource. Simply by reading his daily newspaper, the Japanese man in the street can keep closer track of the inner workings of his government than readers of most European or American papers can. At the same time, by selective resort to weekly and monthly magazines, he can sample the gamut of intellectual opinion and inform himself at least about the more egregious skeletons in establishment closets. And while all this might seem to require an unrealistically heavy reading load, that is a burden a surprising number of Japanese freely assume: according to a 1979 survey, 52 percent of all Japanese read at least one weekly magazine in addition to their daily paper, and exactly the same percentage read at least one monthly.

Considering the long hours that Japanese tend to work, it is a bit difficult to see how they can read so much and still put in approximately the same amount of time watching television as Americans do. Nonetheless, that is the case. The most recent survey available—one taken in 1975—shows that at that time the average Japanese spent 3 hours and 19 minutes in front of a TV set each workday and 4 hours and 11 minutes on Sundays. Almost certainly, those figures are even higher today—and markedly higher for certain segments of the population. Even in 1975, the typical Japanese woman spent an hour a day more than her husband watching TV, and some schoolchildren were glued to their sets for more than 5 hours a day.

To serve these dedicated viewers, Japan has created what is probably the world's most diverse and highly developed television broadcasting system. As in Britain, there are both privately owned and quasi-governmental channels in Japan. The bulk of the country's television broadcasting stations—there are nearly 1,500 VHF stations and more than 10,000 UHF—are operated by NHK (for Nippon Hoso Kyokai, or Japan Broadcasting Corporation). In structure, NHK is roughly comparable to the British Broadcasting Corporation and, like the BBC, it is largely financed by user fees paid by all owners of TV sets. Half of NHK's stations confine themselves entirely to educational and cultural programming, and even its "general-interest" stations devote less than 30 percent of their time to entertainment. By contrast, the 470-odd VHF stations and 2,900 UHF stations that are privately owned are primarily entertainment-oriented—though even they are supposed to give 30 percent of their air time to educational and cultural programs.

As in the United States, the commercial TV stations in Japan have become the country's biggest advertising medium, and in fact, some of the most sociologically intriguing material on Japanese television appears in commercials. In addition to Japanese models with unusually Western features, Japan's consumer-goods salesmen are addicted to the use of real Westerners in their advertising; scores of anonymous foreign models earn a reasonably handsome living making Japanese TV commercials, and there is also widespread use of Western celebrities, ranging from Sammy Davis, Jr., for Suntory whiskey to Woody Allen for Tokyo's Seibu department store.

By the same token, Japanese commercials make considerable use of English words and phrases, a phenomenon that extends throughout Japanese business. Even Japanese cars produced for the domestic market, for example, almost invariably bear English rather than Japanese model names. (Though it is a fact whose exact significance eludes me, it is also true that there is a pronounced difference between the names U.S. and Japanese automakers tend to give their cars. Where the Americans have a taste for the macho—Mustang, Thunderbird, Cougar, Toronado—the Japanese lean towards the pastoral and/or feminine: Bluebird, Sunny, Violet, Gloria, Carina.)

The heavy use of Western props in TV commercials is in part a simple matter of snob appeal; it is most effective in promoting sales of luxury goods, since Japanese generally still tend to equate the West with elegance and style. But it also reflects a difference in the way Japanese and Westerners respond to advertising. In general, Japanese advertising men are leery of commercials that make utilitarian claims for products or demonstrate their practical advantages. Automobile commercials that emphasize economy and reliability of operation, for example, have been demonstrably less successful in selling cars in Japan than those showing Paul Newman at the wheel of a Nissan Skyline or a handsome Latin-looking type in expensive tweeds barreling across a bucolic countryside in a Toyota. Image creation and skillful appeals to consumer emotions and fantasies, in other words, work even better in Japan than they do in the United States—a fact that may be explained by the psychic pressures imposed upon the average Japanese by high productivity standards, crowded living quarters and the demands of a conformist social order.

Whatever the reason, the world portrayed in Japanese TV commercials is a highly escapist one, full of chic, uncommonly handsome people leading improbably glamorous lives. And escapism is also the keynote of a good deal of Japan's television programming. Much of the entertainment offered on Japanese television is, in fact, almost indistinguishable from U.S. network fare: game shows, lavish variety programs studded with show-biz personalities and the like. But Japanese entertainment programming also contains some piquant and purely native elements: interminable broadcasts of sumo matches, historical epics full of swaggering samurai which are the moral equivalent of U.S. Westerns and, a few years back, a skin show in which the stripteasers were all housewives who had volunteered for the purpose.

Much of this does not travel well, but Japan has nonetheless made its own modest contributions to global TV entertainment. Godzilla the friendly monster is, of course, a Japanese creation, and so is the animated space-war series that appears in the United States under the title *Starblazers*. This last is a spin-off from an immensely successful Japanese movie in which, some two hundred years hence, the World War II battleship *Yamato* is raised from the ocean floor off Okinawa, where it was sunk in 1945, and converted into a space cruiser. At least one Japanese pundit has expressed concern that the fictional resurrection of one of the adornments of the Imperial Japanese Navy could inspire a revival of the *kamikaze* spirit in Japanese children—but like so many of the concerns of pundits, this one seems overblown: my own young son, who has never heard of the Japanese Empire, much less the *kamikaze* spirit, is an ardent *Starblazers* fan.

Taken all in all, however, the frivolities and even occasional vulgarities of Japanese television are no more than minor blemishes. Beyond dispute, the range and quality of programming available to Japanese viewers is much greater than that available to U.S. viewers even since the advent of cable, and as a result, TV plays a far more constructive role in Japanese society than in our own.

As one case in point, television news in Japan manages to be considerably more than a headline service with showbusiness overtones. Instead of being packaged and presented by "personalities" with blow-dry hairstyling, Japan's regular news programs are for the most part presented by essentially anonymous anchormen who determinedly mute their own personalities. Japanese news broadcasts, moreover, are in general superior in depth and thoughtfulness to those offered by the major U.S. networks, and unlike their colleagues in the daily press, Japanese television news staffs strive hard for objectivity. At the same time, there is more and better backgrounding on the news than U.S. television offers. NHK's regular evening news show is commonly followed by a half-hour documentary on some particularly important current topic, and round-table discussions of everything from robotics to the latest Middle Eastern crisis abound on all channels. For the truly masochistic news freak, NHK even offers regular broadcasts of Diet sessions.

The crowning glory of Japanese television, though, lies not in its handling of the news but in its cultural and educational programming. NHK's dramatic productions are on a par with those of the BBC, and like the BBC, it has its own symphony orchestra. In the general education field, it churns out remarkably sophisticated programs on everything from philosophy to computers, often producing accompanying textbooks which sell hundreds of thousands of copies. On a less scholarly level, there are programs on health, nutrition and farming as well as regular instruction in five languages—English, French, German, Russian and Chinese. And quite apart from its offerings to general audiences, NHK furnishes Japan's schools—where nearly every classroom contains a TV set—with a great array of programs carefully designed to supplement the regular academic curriculum.

Japan's biggest experiment with educational TV, however, still lies ahead. Some time ago, the Japanese Diet passed a bill providing for the establishment of a Broadcast University at which any citizen over eighteen will be able to get a B.A. or B.S. through home study. Slated to go into operation in 1984 with an initial class of 10,000, the Broadcast University will offer televised instruction in life sciences, business studies and arts and humanities. For someone who is simultaneously trying to earn a living, the university's requirements will not be easy to fulfill: students will be expected to listen to four or five broadcast lectures a week, make periodic visits to an instructional center, submit regular papers and take examinations. But Japan being Japan, the planners of Broadcast University are already worrying about how to hold its enrollment to manageable proportions: the bill establishing the institution calls for an open admissions policy, and a survey taken during the early stages of the project indicated that 45 percent of the entire Japanese population planned to "attend" Broadcast University lectures.

It is not, of course, mere intellectual curiosity that has led Japan to develop media of such uncommon scope and diversity. For the Japanese, the statement that knowledge is power is not just a pious truism: it is a basic operating principle. Even when it serves no immediate purpose, the Japanese collect information with the compulsiveness of a magpie hoarding brightly colored objects. Dozens of Japanese institutions ranging from the Prime Minister's Office to the All Japan Sugar Refiners Association conduct innumerable polls, surveys and questionnaires covering almost every conceivable aspect of Japanese life. The result is that there are few statistics about Japan so esoteric that someone has not ferreted them out, and sooner or later almost all of these data are put to use: no Japanese Government agency or major corporation would dream of undertaking a new venture until it has acquired mountains of information on every facet of the matter involved and subjected all this material to painstaking analysis and reanalysis.

Partly because of this intense dedication to data, the advent of the computer and the proliferation of radically new communication technologies have played right into Japan's hand. When they talk about it in English, the Japanese somewhat awkwardly describe what is now occurring in the world's advanced economies as the "informatization" of society—the development of a widely dispersed capability to use information far more rapidly, skillfully and purposefully than ever before.

Along with many Westerners, thoughtful Japanese believe that the informatization process will eventually prove as much of a turning point in human history as the Industrial Revolution was.

In mid-1982, Kimio Tsuzuki, who then headed the industrial-electronics division of the Toshiba Corporation, told me that the "information industry"—his overall rubric for computers, electronics and communications technology—already had sales of $100 billion a year on a worldwide basis and predicted that by 1990 that figure would soar to $800 billion a year. Ultimately, Tsuzuki insisted, the information industry will become the biggest business in the world—bigger than autos, steel, oil or chemicals.

In purely commercial terms these are glittering prospects, and as I shall discuss later on, Japanese economic strategy for the next decade and more is heavily focused upon them. But the most sanguine Japanese also believe that properly managed, the "second industrial revolution" can bring social as well as economic benefits—such things as improved public services, more efficient use of natural resources and less pollution of the environment. Most important of all, some say, it will give ordinary citizens increased access to recreation, education and high culture.

In this last respect, in fact, the informatization process has already visibly begun to impinge on daily life in Japan. One of the first harbingers of this was the development of the videocassette recorder—a field in which the Japanese pioneered and in which Japanese manufacturers still account for 90 percent of world production. Still another is Chitoshi's "bilingual TV" set—which is only one of some 3 million such sets already in use in Japan. More properly known as multiplex TV sound receivers, such sets not only make possible simultaneous broadcasting in two languages but can handle stereophonic sound as well.

Like a conquering army, informatization in Japan is advancing on many fronts at once. Sales of home computers and word processors, though still relatively modest, seem certain to burgeon as prices fall—and in the summer of 1982, Noburo Mii, Managing Director for Technical Operations of IBM Japan, told me: "I predict that we will see the day when a computer will sell for five hundred dollars, including printer and everything, and every home will have one."

Meantime, on an experimental basis, thousands of Japanese homes have already been equipped with two-way video systems that permit their owners to bring in at will such things as news bulletins, weather and traffic reports and TV program guides. So far such systems are still rudimentary, but their potential applications are almost limitless: before too many years, for example, they could well lead to the disappearance of the printed telephone directory and its replacement by a single, constantly updated electronic "book" which phone subscribers would consult by means of their video terminals. And since it is possible for the possessor of a two-way video system to make a hard-copy printout of any information that he wishes to retain permanently, the present boundaries between print and electronic media will in time inevitably be blurred. Already, in fact, the Japan Newspaper Publishers Association has rather nervously announced that multiplex broadcasting, as it is called, cannot properly be entrusted to traditional broadcasting organizations alone and that the newspaper industry must be cut in on the action.

None of these innovations, of course, is unique to Japan. Nearly all the basic technology involved was originally developed in the United States, and the American information-processing industry, which is still far bigger than Japan's and in certain respects more highly developed, is pushing rapidly ahead in all the same fields. Indeed, IBM's Noburo Mii, a man intimately familiar with the situation in both countries, suspects that the United States may become a full-fledged "information society" a little faster than Japan does. But the difference is that in Japan the achievement of the information society is a conscious national goal, which is being pursued with a greater degree of governmental coordination than exists in the United States. As a result, it seems likely that Japan's information society will be constructed in a more orderly fashion than our own and with more effective attention to its social and economic consequences.

It also seems possible that by easing some of the constraints under which Japan now labors, informatization will have even more dramatic impact on the life-style and psyche of the Japanese people than upon those of the American people. "Once the information society has arrived," an executive of a big trade association told me, "we Japanese won't have to live all huddled together in cramped little city apartments and houses. And we won't be so dependent on imported fuel either, because we won't have to waste so much of it commuting."

Somewhat skeptically, I asked this enthusiast to explain his sweeping assertions. "It's very simple," he said. "If I want to move far enough out of town so that I can have a comfortable house with a big garden, I'll be able to do that in the future because I'll never have to go to the office—or almost never. Instead, I'll have my office at home: a complete information center with computer, two-way video, printer, word processor and probably a copier, too.

Whatever statistics or information I need I'll be able to call in from my association's central data bank, and if I need a Japanese translation of President Mitterand's latest economic pronouncement, the system will produce that for me too. And the same will be true for entertainment. If I want to see a first-run movie, I won't have to go to a theater in the city; I'll watch it at home."

Though he didn't raise the possibility himself, there are other Japanese who think my friend may well need a multistation information and communications center in his dream house. These people anticipate the day when control of home appliances will be systemized through the use of computers and many household chores will be effectively automated. At that point, even more Japanese women than at present will presumably seek employment or expanded recreational facilities—and for that, they too will have to be plugged in to an information network.

Is all this just pie in the sky? Some of the most intelligent and hardheaded people in Japan are profoundly convinced that it is not. As they see it, there is absolutely no doubt that the information society is coming; the only question is how soon it will arrive.

On that point, no one can offer a certain answer. Parts of the brave new world will probably be in place quite soon. IBM's Mii, for one, thinks it likely that by 1990 most Japanese homes will have a video display terminal. And in mid-1982 a sober young official of the Ministry of International Trade and Industry assured me that "in less than ten years it will be possible at least for technicians to work at home." But the prevailing opinion among the experts appears to be that expressed in the spring of 1982 by Masaru Yoshitomi, chief economist for the Japanese Government's Economic Planning Agency. "To suggest that the information society will be here in ten years is overoptimistic," he said. "We won't be able to stay home that soon. But in twenty to thirty years we will."

11

Machines and Mandarins

Every now and then, some contrary-minded Japanese decides that it is demeaning for his country to be thought of as "exotic" and takes up the cudgels against Westerners who talk of uniquely Japanese attitudes and behavior patterns. Perhaps the best way to deal with this sort of person is to engage him in a discussion of Japanese politics. For what is most deceptive about the way Japan is governed is the fact that on the surface of things it seems totally explicable in Western terms—and in reality is not so at all.

Like Great Britain, Japan has a purely ceremonial monarch, a bicameral parliament known as the Diet in which the "upper house" is largely ceremonial and the "lower house" possesses the lion's share of the power and a Prime Minister who is nominally chosen by parliament rather than by the electorate at large. In addition, like the man who wears both belt and suspenders, Japan reinforces these traditional appurtenances of parliamentary government with a couple of safeguards borrowed from U.S.-style democracy: a written Constitution, whose wording here and there betrays the fact that it was originally drafted in English by members of General Mac-Arthur's staff, and a Supreme Court which is empowered to rule on the constitutionality of executive actions and the laws adopted by the Diet.

Confusingly, however, most of these institutions do not function in Japan in the same way that they do in Britain or the United States. More confusing yet, some of the most important elements in the Japanese political process are matters of practice which do not have constitutional sanction or even, in some cases, any legal foundation at all.

What this means, among other things, is that a Western journalist writing about Japanese politics finds himself in a difficult position. A newspaper or magazine article that seeks to put political events in Japan in their true perspective demands more space and more patience on the part of readers than most editors think warranted. The result, as I can testify from frustrating personal experience, is that more often than not, even reputable American publications settle for reporting the superficialities of Japanese government rather than the realities.

Whatever the deficiencies of Western journalism—and even of some more scholarly Western commentary—it might seem that a reasonably accurate notion of the nature of politics in Japan could be obtained by turning to Japanese writers on the subject. But that is frequently unrewarding too—largely because the people who comment most openly and most often about the exercise of power in Japan are intellectuals. This, of course, is true in most other societies as well, but the difference is that in Japan intellectuals rarely have any firsthand knowledge of government or of the political establishment. The politically involved intellectual of the kind typified in the United States by Henry Kissinger, Zbigniew Brzezinski or Senator Pat Moynihan is a rare article indeed in Japan. Predominantly "progressive"—which is to say leftist—in ideological orientation, most Japanese intellectuals cherish some Platonic ideal of a political order with a purpose far more lofty than ensuring what they contemptuously term the "mere affluence" of its members. And because they see no realistic prospect for the construction of such an order in present-day Japan, the vast majority of intellectuals have chosen to remain aloof from the political fray, retaining their purity and contenting themselves with criticism of things as they are.

This detachment, as *Nihon Keizai Shimbun* editorial writer Kazuo Ijiri pointed out a few years ago, has meant that Japan's intellectuals have consistently failed to articulate principles of leadership acceptable to an overwhelmingly middle-class nation. Almost as bad, it has also rendered most of their analysis of Japanese politics singularly irrelevant. Convinced that the people who govern their country are to a man crass reactionaries, Japan's progressive intellectuals live in vocal fear of "the threat from the right"; even so innocuous an act as a ceremonial New Year's visit to the national Shinto shrine at Ise by a devoutly Christian Prime Minister can be seized upon as evidence of an ominous rightward drift. In fact, sounding a theme frequently echoed by Western observers, many Japanese intellectuals complain that Japan isn't a "real democracy" at all. In so doing, they are basically reiterating a charge made as far back as 1918 by Yukio Ozaki, a wispy little tiger who eventually became the dean of Japanese parliamentarians. Whenever a democratic seed was planted in the minds of his countrymen, Ozaki claimed, "it germinates and grows according to feudal notions."

The reasons for all this paranoia are not particularly hard to find. Given the brutal way in which the "thought police" of prewar Japan suppressed democratic and leftist elements, it is scarcely surprising that Japanese intellectuals still cherish a profound horror of right-wing rule. It is also true that in one conspicuous respect, postwar Japan has not yet acquired what is widely regarded in the West as an indispensable aspect of genuine democracy: the habit of periodically throwing one set of rascals out of office and replacing them with their opponents. Since its formation in 1955, in fact, the conservative Liberal Democratic Party has ruled Japan without interruption or even resort to a coalition Cabinet; for more than a quarter of a century now, election to the presidency of the LDP has been tantamount to election as Prime Minister of Japan.

But while even a paranoiac can have real enemies, the foes with whom Japanese intellectuals endlessly wrestle are largely illusory. There are, to be sure, numerous right-wing groups in Japan; loudspeaker trucks blaring anti-Soviet sentiments or denunciations of the Japanese Government's dealings with Peking are a standard feature of the Tokyo scene, and once in a while a particularly deranged nationalist resorts to violence. (Back in the 1970s, in one of the most clamorous of such episodes, a disillusioned ex-admirer enterprisingly tried to crash a light airplane into the residence of Yoshio Kodama, an unsavory superpatriot who had been fingered in a massive bribery scandal.) Right-wing nationalism has also claimed the allegiance of a certain number of artists and intellectuals, the best-known of these outside Japan having been novelist Yukio Mishima, whose eventual resort to *seppuku* baffled many of his Western admirers. And even among Japanese parliamentarians, there are some who privately hold considerably more nationalistic views than they find it prudent to admit publicly; one Diet member of my acquaintance, an elegant man of cosmopolitan tastes, spent the better part of an evening at a chic Tokyo bar not long ago trying to convince me that the United States should admit that it "forced" Japan to bomb Pearl Harbor, in order that his countrymen might be "cleansed" of what he regards as their crippling and unwarranted sense of guilt about World War II.

All of this, however, is fringe opinion, well outside the mainstream of contemporary Japanese political thought. Poignantly but reassuringly, the speech Yukio Mishima delivered immediately before his suicide—an impassioned appeal for the revival of Japan's ancient "heroic spirit"—evoked only laughter from the Japanese soldiers he was haranguing.

It would, of course, be foolish to rule out entirely the possibility that Japan could turn totalitarian again if it found itself under extreme external pressures. But even then, what form a new Japanese totalitarianism might take is hard to say. Certainly at the moment there would appear to be more potential totalitarians of the left than of the right in Japan—and neither group in any sense constitutes a clear and present danger.

To magnify unduly the rightist threat in Japan, then, is not only misleading but, in my opinion, dangerously so—primarily because it serves to obscure the true strength and nature of Japanese democracy. In an article in the monthly magazine *Chuo Koron* several years ago, a trio of Tokyo University professors charged that Japanese intellectuals typically either ignored or condemned "the Japanese-style collectivism that runs deep in the basic character of the Japanese people." If by Japanese-style collectivism one means the ability to decide upon generally acceptable goals and to pursue them effectively without excessive infringement on anyone's liberties, this seems a highly valid point. Perhaps a better way to put it, however, is the way in which it was stated to me by Taiji Ubukata, the president of Ishikawajima-Harima Heavy Industries. "Both the United States and Japan are democracies, and both are deeply concerned about individual rights," Mr. Ubukata said. "But you must always remember that the words 'democracy' and 'individualism' don't mean the same thing in Japan as they do in the United States."

One of the fundamental differences between democracy as it is practiced in Japan and American-style democracy is that the Japanese version is far more structured and hierarchical. In politics as in everything else, individual Japanese tend to seek self-fulfillment through identification with a group. The kind of politics that has come to prevail in the U.S. House of Representatives—a devil-take-the-hindmost competition for individual power in which "leaders" cannot confidently promise to deliver the votes of their ostensible followers—would strike Japanese as impossibly anarchic. Japanese politicians are, above all, organization men. Once, while traveling through provincial Japan, I asked the mayor of a bustling little manufacturing and market town named Tsubame City where he stood politically. His response was instantaneous and proud: "I'm a member of the [former Prime Minister Kakuei] Tanaka Corps." Even in the heyday of the late Mayor Richard Daley, it is doubtful that a Chicago Congressman would have publicly identified himself as a wheelhorse in the Daley machine—which would be a reasonable parallel.

In the United States, of course, machine politics is traditionally corrupt politics—and so it frequently is in Japan. But the extraordinary political stability that Japan has experienced since World War II does not at bottom rest on gerrymandering, vote-buying or any other form of political hanky-panky. In one very basic respect, democracy *does* mean the same thing in Japan that it does in the United States: it is a system that rests on the consent of the governed. And contrary to the implication of some of its intellectual critics, the Liberal Democratic Party has not somehow hoodwinked or coerced the Japanese public into keeping it in power for so long. It is still in office after all these years because it enjoys the freely given support of more Japanese than any of its rivals.

This is—or at least, should be—a source of considerable embarrassment to most "expert" observers of Japanese politics. Back in the early 1970s it was the consensus of the pundits, Japanese and Western alike, that the LDP's days as Japan's sole ruling party were numbered and that within a few years there would have to be either a major realignment of political forces in Japan or a resort to coalition government—or both.

At the time, it was hard to find fault with the reasoning that underlay these conclusions: Japan's rural population, the LDP's equivalent of what the "solid South" was for our own Democratic Party in Franklin Roosevelt's day, was continuing to shrink, and the party's support among young people and urban residents was steadily eroding. To make matters worse, the world energy crisis that began in 1973 cast doubt upon the policy of rapid economic growth that had been the LDP's crowning glory, and as the decade wore on the party was repeatedly racked by scandals.

All this took its electoral toll, and in the late 1970s the Liberal Democrats did in fact come perilously close to losing control of the Diet. But then, in defiance of all obituary notices, they made a remarkable comeback at the polls: as of 1982, the LDP once again commanded a comfortable majority in the Diet, holding 287 of the 511 seats in the House of Representatives.

Conceivably, this may prove only a temporary reprieve. Because the number of Japanese voters unaffiliated with any party has greatly increased—it now stands at nearly 50 percent of the electorate—the day may yet come when coalition government or a reshuffling of party lines will be necessary. But barring a worldwide economic collapse, that day appears less imminent and inevitable now than it did a few years ago.

To anyone not blinkered by ideological preconceptions, this shouldn't be particularly surprising. For all its manifold imperfections, Japanese society today offers its members a degree of economic and social well-being unprecedented in Japan's history, and the majority of Japanese are understandably reluctant to put all that at risk. They subscribe to the maxim "If it ain't broke, don't fix it"—and this is precisely the kind of pragmatic approach they know they can expect from Liberal Democratic governments. In a 1978 survey of voters' emotional perceptions of Japan's political parties, the LDP ranked close to the bottom on charisma; only the Communist Party was perceived as "grimmer." But where it really mattered, the LDP came out on top: it was seen as the "safest" of all parties and, together with a small splinter group called the New Liberal Club, as the "most dependable."

As this suggests, the LDP owes its long preeminence at least in part to the ineptitude of its opponents. Japanese are fond of saying that they live under a one-and-a-half-party system, by which they mean that all their country's opposition parties lumped together don't carry as much weight as the LDP alone.

One reason this is so is that most of the opposition parties suffer from what the Marxists call internal contradictions. The Komeito, or Clean Government Party, for example, has no real excuse for existence beyond the fact that it was spawned by an evangelical—and highly controversial—Buddhist sect called the Soka Gakkai. In theory, the Clean Government Party no longer has any links to the Soka Gakkai, but it hasn't any clear political purpose either, and were it not for their religious preoccupation, most of its members would probably gravitate to the LDP.

Though it is a considerably more serious organization than the Komeito, the Japanese Communist Party is in some respects even more bedeviled by internal contradictions. Like the Eurocommunist parties of the West, it now soft-pedals traditional Marxist ideology and, at the expense of considerable internecine bloodletting, has endorsed parliamentary democracy and the maintenance of a multiparty system in Japan. It is also in a sense the most nationalistic of all Japanese parties; it favors strong "self-defense" forces for Japan, and while by no means subservient to Peking, it regularly denounces "hegemonism," which is the current Aesopian language for Soviet imperialism in Asia. Yet despite all these efforts to reassure the bourgeoisie, the JCP was rated the "most dangerous" of Japan's political parties in the 1978 survey of voter attitudes and does not exercise in Japanese political life anything approaching the substantive role that the Communist parties of France and Italy do in their countries. In fact, another 1978 poll indicated that the JCP has particular appeal for people who reject conventional Japanese values: paradoxically, many more Communist voters than LDP voters held that individual rights should take precedence over the public interest. In short, it seems quite clear that many Japanese who support the Communist ticket—and 10 percent of the electorate did so in 1980—are simply protest voters and would promptly defect if they saw any real likelihood of the JCP's coming to power.

Grievous as they are, however, the shortcomings of all other Japanese opposition parties pale alongside those of the biggest one, the Japan Socialist Party. If ever a political organization was born with a silver spoon in its mouth it was the JSP. In the national elections of 1947, the first held under the Occupation-imposed Constitution, the JSP won more seats in the Diet than any other party and managed to form a coalition government headed by its then leader, Tetsu Katayama. Its power bases then were impressive ones: it had the backing of Sohyo, the biggest of Japan's four labor confederations, and enjoyed widespread support among intellectuals and public employees, notably including Japan's teachers. All in all, there seemed every reason to think the JSP would alternate in office with its conservative opponents, much as the Labor Party has done in Britain.

In fact, however, the short-lived government which the JSP formed in 1947 marked the last time it has tasted power. For more than three decades now, it has soldiered on as Japan's second party—big enough to be an obstructive force but nothing more.

The chief reason for the JSP's stagnation is that it has been largely dominated by ideologues who have stubbornly insisted on clinging to positions on economic and defense issues that are patently unacceptable to the majority of Japanese. Unlike the West German Socialist Party, the JSP has declined to court middle-of-the-road voters or put together a strong parliamentary coalition by throwing overboard its Marxist baggage.

The result is that like the Japanese intelligentsia as a whole, the

JSP has been relegated to a purely critical role. "Purely," however, may not be quite the appropriate word here. For to some extent, the JSP has become just another political machine. Its parliamentary wheelhorses regularly make back-room deals with their LDP counterparts and figure in corruption scandals with almost the same frequency.

Far more damaging than such peccadilloes, however, is the fact that the JSP has so often made itself look simply foolish. For years, it violently opposed Japan's mutual-security treaty with the United States and the creation of any Japanese military establishment at all. At the same time, it loudly sang the praises of Maoist China. Then, stunningly, these two positions became incompatible. First, Chou En-lai let drop to a Japanese delegation his view that it was only a matter of common sense for Japan to have at least some defensive capability. And subsequently Teng Hsiao-ping compounded the embarrassment: he and his colleagues not only pointed out excesses on the part of the Great Helmsman that had somehow escaped the JSP's attention, but allowed as how, under the existing circumstances, Japan's security treaty with the United States served a useful function. All this left the JSP in the intensely awkward position of having been either wrong in its position on defense or misguided in its enthusiasm for the Chinese—a dilemma which the party characteristically sought to escape by ignoring it.

Thanks in part to this sort of thing, the JSP's luster has been even further dimmed of late. "Those people at the JSP simply aren't serious," a civil servant who deals with them regularly once remarked to me. "If they were told they could take power tomorrow, they wouldn't know what to do. In fact, they'd be horrified." That may be hyperbole, but it is surely true that the majority of Japanese today do not see the JSP—or even any coalition between the JSP and other opposition parties—as a credible alternative government.

In a Japanese context, one of the greatest strengths of the Liberal Democratic Party is that it is the diametric opposite of the Japan Socialist Party when it comes to concern with ideological purity. Though it is universally described as conservative and certainly is so in general predisposition, the LDP cannot properly be accused of having anything so concrete and clear-cut as an ideology. At best it possesses only a kind of amorphous broad philosophy, and that fact enables it to perform a feat indispensable to successful management in Japan: the accommodation of all sorts of seemingly incompatible bedfellows under one blanket.

At bottom, indeed, the LDP is not a unitary political party in the same sense that its European or even American counterparts are. Instead, it is a confederation of *habatsu*—a word customarily translated as "factions" but which might be rendered almost as well by the homelier word "machines." These parliamentary groupings, of which there are currently five, have no legal role in the Government of Japan. Technically, in fact, they sometimes don't exist at all, since they are periodically "dissolved" amid great public fanfare and general professions of righteousness. In reality, however, they are a continuing and central element of the Japanese political system—and another manifestation of its intensely personal character.

To suggest that the LDP's factions are not issue-oriented at all would be an exaggeration. One of the smaller of the current ones is distinctly populist and puts heavy emphasis on such matters as environmental protection. Another is particularly concerned with fiscal soundness, and yet a third with the streamlining of government operations. To a large extent, however, these differences in emphasis reflect the personal preoccupations of the various faction leaders and the dictates of political expediency rather than basic philosophic differences. For above all, the factions are mutual-security groups which exist to advance the political fortunes of their members.

The primary responsibility of a faction member, in other words, is not to serve any particular set of principles but to further the prime-ministerial ambitions of the head of his faction. In return, the faction leader seeks to place as many of his supporters as possible in positions of power and influence. This means that the construction of a Japanese Cabinet is primarily a matter of horse-trading among faction leaders, and since each faction leader wishes to give as many of his supporters as possible at least a brief dip into the cookie jar, it also means that Japanese Prime Ministers are obliged to reshuffle their Cabinets on an almost annual basis. The all-time exemplar of this art, the late Prime Minister Eisaku Sato, actually managed during eight years in office to give Cabinet jobs to more than a hundred LDP parliamentarians—a notable feat in view of the fact that he had only twenty Cabinet-rank jobs at his disposal.

Though they are widely regarded as discreditable—which is why from time to time the leaders of the LDP go through the motions of abolishing them—the factions perform some highly useful functions. Besides offering a more or less orderly way in which to dispense patronage, they also serve as a mechanism through which the root-binding or broad consultative process indispensable to the smooth functioning of any Japanese organization can be conducted. Without them, or something like them, the LDP's leaders would find it far harder and more time-consuming to achieve consensus on major questions of policy.

Nonetheless, the factions undeniably have their dark side. The Prime Minister, who is himself customarily a faction leader, can count on little loyalty from the heads of the other factions; since they all live in hopes of unhorsing him, they pounce mercilessly whenever he commits a gaffe or shows signs of weakness. More destructive yet, the factions contribute significantly to the corruption and influence-buying that defaces Japanese politics.

In Japan as in the United States, running for national office is an expensive undertaking; a first-time candidate for the equivalent of a U.S. Congressional seat can spend a million dollars on his campaign, and the LDP as a whole reportedly spent $100 million on contested seats in the upper house in one election year in the mid-'70s. Unlike the United States, however, Japan does so little to control campaign financing and spending that the relevant legislation is commonly known as "the bamboo-basket law." According to an official government report, political donations in Japan in 1980 totaled nearly half a billion dollars—mostly anted up by business organizations.

There is nothing inherently illegal about this: Japanese corporations are free to contribute to political campaigns, and contributions of less than about $4,500 don't even have to be reported. In the early 1970s, some Japanese corporations actually went so far as to openly "adopt" individual LDP candidates for parliament. That proved a bit too much for even the Japanese to swallow, but corporate funds still continue to flow freely into political coffers—mainly, though by no means exclusively, into those of LDP candidates.

Many of these publicly acknowledged corporate contributions go directly to individual candidates, but large sums are also turned over to the faction leaders, who then proceed to dole them out to their adherents as they see fit. This, of course, gives faction leaders an inordinate and questionable kind of influence over rank-and-file parliamentarians. But what is even less defensible is the so-called "back money" to which some faction leaders have access—money acquired through large undeclared contributions, thinly disguised bribes and, in some cases, outright payoffs. (These last are generally not made directly by a corporation to a politician but pass through the hands of fixers, sometimes with underworld connections, who are known as *kuromaku,* or "black-curtain men.")

Somewhat remarkably, vote-buying is not necessarily illegal in Japan; it is, for example, not punishable in the case of internal party elections. Out-and-out bribery of a public official is, however, most definitely illegal, and whenever it is disclosed there is invariably an indignant brouhaha. But in practice many Japanese accept it as part of the system and see it as no reason to blackball a politician who in other respects has shown himself to be judgmatical and effective. "After all," I was told by a businessman who I am reasonably sure is himself incorruptible, "what matters is the welfare of the nation, not the personal or political finances of Mr. X or Mr. Y."

Given this attitude, it becomes less surprising that there are so many men who are widely rumored to take "back money" or who have actually been formally accused of accepting bribes yet continue to exert great influence in the upper circles of Japanese politics. Here the classic example is former Prime Minister Kakuei Tanaka, who while still in office allegedly accepted a massive bribe from a Japanese sales agent for pressuring a domestic airline called All Japan Airways into buying Lockheed Tri-Star jets. Tanaka's trial on this charge, which began in 1977, still drags on, and knowledgeable Japanese friends assure me that even if he is found guilty in the first instance, the matter will probably be in the courts for at least another ten years. But it is, I think, quite clear that a large number of Japanese believe there's at least some fire underneath all that smoke.

Undeniably, this has done Tanaka great damage. Once charges were formally brought against him, he felt obliged to resign his membership in the Liberal Democratic Party, and it is the consensus among Japanese political experts that unless he is eventually cleared by the courts, public opinion will not tolerate his holding ministerial office again. Nonetheless, he still sits in parliament and is still in all but name the unchallenged leader of the largest faction in the LDP—a faction which has actually grown in size since he was put on trial and which now includes more than a quarter of all LDP members of the Diet. Every day scores of people, including senior government officials, visit his lavish estate in the Mejiro district of Tokyo to court favors or seek policy advice. So pervasive, in fact, is Tanaka's influence that the Japanese press sometimes refers to him as the *Yami Shogun,* or shadow ruler, and it is universally acknowledged that he played a kingmaker's role in the selection of Japan's last three Prime Ministers. Former Prime Minister Zenko

Suzuki was widely regarded as little more than a Tanaka surrogate, and Yasuhiro Nakasone, who succeeded Suzuki in November 1982, surprised even the most hardened observers of the Japanese political scene by giving nearly a third of all the jobs in his Cabinet, including the particularly sensitive post of Chief Cabinet Secretary, to Tanaka lieutenants.

Inevitably, journalistic cliché addicts regularly describe the Lockheed bribery scandal as "Japan's Watergate." There are, however, flaws in that analogy—flaws that say a great deal about some of the essential differences between politics in Japan and in America. Unlike the Liberal Democratic Party, the Republican Party in the United States was thrown out of office by a disillusioned electorate in the wake of Watergate—and unlike Kakuei Tanaka, Richard Nixon no longer has a significant voice in the government of his country.

Though many Japanese politicians are accused of corruption, serious efforts to convict them of it are few and far between. Some cynics, in fact, allege that if Kakuei Tanaka had been part of an "Old Boy net"—specifically, if he had been a graduate of Tokyo University, which produces so many of Japan's top judges and lawyers—he would have been privately informed in advance of the prosecution's strategy in the Lockheed case and how to beat it. That is speculation and impossible to prove or disprove. What is certain, however, is that Tanaka's managerial style had alienated many members of Japan's political establishment. As Prime Minister, he never hesitated to call civil servants directly to inform them of his wishes or displeasure. An activist by nature, he sought quite openly to put his personal mark on the policies and operations of the Japanese Government.

To Americans, that will sound natural enough. But in Japan it is not. Since the retirement of the late Shigeru Yoshida, the brilliant, strong-minded man who presided over his country's emergence from the American Occupation, Japan's Prime Ministers have generally functioned more as chairmen of the board than as chief executive officers. As a rule, in fact, most recent Prime Ministers have taken personal decisions about major matters of state only when their subordinates were unable to present them with a consensus—and not always even then. Some years ago, when Takeo Fukuda was Prime Minister, I had dinner one evening with a man who a few days earlier had attended a Cabinet meeting. At that meeting, he recounted, the head of the Economic Planning Agency had revealed that he and the Minister for International Trade and Industry were unable to agree on a target figure for overall industrial growth in the year ahead. Perhaps, the planning boss had suggested, the Prime Minister would like to adjudicate the matter. At that, my friend related, Fukuda rose from his chair, declared that he had just recalled more pressing business elsewhere and, as a parting shot, announced that he would be glad to consider the question of an industrial-growth target once the two ministers involved could present him with a figure acceptable to both of them.

This, I admit, was a somewhat extreme case, and I do not wish to suggest that the Prime Minister of Japan is merely a figurehead. To some degree, his personal preoccupations often do become those of the Japanese Government, and this seems likely to prove true of the current incumbent, Yasuhiro Nakasone, even though he has altered his views so often that political rivals have nicknamed him "The Weathervane." A World War II naval officer who for some years after Japan's surrender invariably wore a black tie on the ground that "every Japanese should be in mourning," Nakasone is a flamboyant and uncommonly forceful figure by the standards of Japanese politics. (He also possesses a somewhat impish sense of humor; in an interview I had with him back in the mid-1970s, he spoke exclusively in Japanese until I rose to leave, at which point he inquired in quite adequate English: "Well, did I pass my examination?") In his first few weeks in office, Nakasone appeared to have three major preoccupations: improving Japanese–American relations, cutting government spending and strengthening Japan's military establishment. Given the inherent contradictions between some of these objectives, it is doubtful that Nakasone can successfully pursue all of them at once, but it seems reasonable to suppose that he will be able to lend major impetus to whichever one he ultimately decides merits top priority.

This is a safe bet partly because it is not really necessary for a Japanese Prime Minister to display outstanding qualities of leadership in order to have impact on governmental affairs. In sharp contrast to Nakasone, his immediate predecessor, Zenko Suzuki, was a lackluster figure who started his career as an employee of the Japan Fishery Association and was once unkindly described to me by a Japanese foundation executive as "qualified to offer sensible opinions on nothing except commercial fishing—and not even that if it's more than two hundred miles offshore." Yet even Suzuki managed to put his concern for administrative reform firmly on the government agenda. Acting in concert with his Cabinet ministers and the other LDP faction leaders, the Prime Minister of Japan is, in effect, the presiding officer of a kind of executive committee which in broad terms establishes current government policy directions. But what is important to remember is that the terms involved tend to be very broad indeed and are always subject to modifications by countervailing powers within the governmental structure.

In sum, the Prime Minister of Japan does not "run" the Japanese Government in the same sense that even so detached a President as Ronald Reagan or Dwight Eisenhower runs the American Government. And neither, most emphatically, does Emperor Hirohito, who took the only executive decision of his life in August 1945 when in the face of a tied Cabinet vote, he personally decided that Japan should surrender to the United States. Today, although he retains the affection of many of his people, particularly those who are middle-aged or older, the Emperor is exactly what the Japanese Constitution says he is and what his predecessors have in reality been for most of Japanese history: "the symbol of state."

According to the Constitution, in fact "the highest organ of state power" in Japan is neither the Emperor nor the Prime Minister but the Diet. But as a practical matter, the Diet's power too is somewhat circumscribed. Neither its individual members nor its committees are given the enormous staffs the United States lavishes upon its Congressmen. Partly for that reason, very little legislation—and almost none of a policy-setting nature—originates in the Diet itself. And its committees are at best a pale shadow of U.S. Congressional committees. Committee hearings in Tokyo have essentially degenerated to the equivalent of "question time" in Britain's Parliament: they are fencing matches in which the opposition seeks to trap government spokesmen into embarrassing admissions, the government seeks to put the best possible face on its actions and both sides are more concerned with the impact of all this on the next elections than with whatever slight effect it might have on the legislation under consideration.

The Diet does, to be sure, have very real obstructive powers. To amend the Constitution requires a two-thirds vote of both Houses, something which so far has always been impossible to attain. And the Japanese concept of consensual democracy severely inhibits the kind of tyranny of the majority that is regularly practiced in the British Parliament. For a Japanese Government to use its Diet majority to ramrod through a widely unpopular measure or even one that is simply deeply repugnant to the parliamentary opposition is dangerous business. In 1960 when Prime Minister Nobosuke

Kishi shoved through a revision of the U.S.–Japan Security Treaty in an arbitrary, though perfectly legal, manner, he touched off nationwide riots that forced him first to cancel a scheduled visit by President Eisenhower and then to resign from office himself. And on numerous other occasions, government attempts to ride rough-shod over the opposition on less important issues have sparked wild parliamentary brawls and/or a boycott of the Diet by opposition members.

Because of these unhappy experiences, Japanese Governments of late have tended to handle the Diet with circumspection. The views of the opposition are heard at stupefying length, and more often than not concessions, real or token, are made to those views. This has markedly reduced the incidence of flying inkwells and black eyes among Honorable Members; but it also helps ensure that much of the legislation passed by them is so vaguely and artfully worded that it constitutes something closer to exhortation than a blueprint for action.

The comparative ineffectiveness of the Diet in no way displeases the body that in many respects constitutes the most important branch of Japanese Government—which is to say the country's remarkable and unique bureaucracy. It is, in fact, the bureaucrats who write most of the legislation that is submitted to the Diet and virtually all the legislation that is eventually adopted. And it is also the bureaucrats who basically decide how this legislation will be admini-stered, the actual decision-making power in this respect often being delegated to people two or even three levels down in the civil service hierarchy.

This state of affairs is possible essentially because the major minis-tries and government agencies in Japan customarily are run not by elected officials—not, that is to say, by the Cabinet officers nomin-ally in charge of them—but by administrative vice-ministers chosen from the ranks of the civil service. On matters involving patronage and politically sensitive subsidies or welfare payments, a Cabinet minister and his parliamentary vice-minister, who is also a political appointee, are generally given their way. But apart from that, the primary functions of a Cabinet minister are to serve as an upward channel for proposals developed by the bureaucrats and to defend in the Diet the operations of his department. And even in Diet hearings, much of the burden is carried by civil servants, many of whom openly begrudge the time they must "waste" in coping with the questions of parliamentarians.

These arrangements may seem to suggest an extraordinary degree of self-abnegation on the part of Japanese politicians, but that is not the real reason for the latitude they extend to the civil service. Because Occupation-era purges drove so many of Japan's prewar politicians out of public life, the majority of the country's postwar Prime Ministers have come out of the bureaucracy themselves. As a result, they have tended to be respectful of its capabilities and protective of its role and privileges.

In addition, on the infrequent occasions when it becomes necessary, Japan's bureaucrats have effective ways of dealing with politicians who seek to bypass them. Like American Congressmen, Japanese parliamentarians derive much of their electoral appeal from their ability to channel government funds and projects into their districts. But when a politician seriously offends them, the bureaucrats are quite capable of discovering that there is no room in the budget for his pet projects—or, almost as bad, of seeing to it that he is publicly embarrassed during question time in the Diet.

As a result, Japanese politicians commonly treat civil servants with a good deal more respect and even deference than American politicians do. It is by no means unusual for a Diet candidate to boast openly about the good relations he enjoys with the bureaucracy and how much that will enable him to do for his district. Many bureaucrats, in turn, privately harbor something close to contempt for politicians, and occasionally that shows through. In New York some time ago, a senior member of the Diet appeared before an American audience to outline a scheme for Japanese loans to U.S. industry—a project which he obviously had not cleared through bureaucratic channels. In the midst of his presentation, a representative of the Japanese Ministry of Finance preempted the floor and, without a word of protest from his victim, proceeded to "explain" that what the hapless politician had meant to say was almost the exact opposite of what he had in fact said.

To most Americans, the exercise of such great authority by career civil servants would seem intolerable—both a negation of democracy and a sure prescription for rampant red tape and national stagnation. But fortunately for Japan, its bureaucrats—or at least, those who set the prevailing tone—do not fit the American stereotype of the pettifogging, layabout civil servant.

For one thing, the Japanese bureaucracy is an extremely lean one. Japan has fewer public employees in relation to its working population than any other developed nation—fewer than half as many as the United States, West Germany or Britain. And unlike its American counterpart, the Japanese civil service attracts the cream of the nation's youth as far as intellect and ambition are concerned.

Not all public employees in Japan are paragons, of course. The great majority of them are quite ordinary people, and in certain public corporations, most notably the Japanese National Railways, featherbedding and low productivity are serious problems. But within each ministry and major government agency there are a few hundred elite career officers who constitute something akin to the Mandarin corps of Imperial China. And each year, to refresh this corps, organizations such as the Foreign Office or the Ministry of International Trade and Industry recruit a score of so of the top graduates of Japan's best universities. (At one time, the most prestigious ministries focused their recruiting almost entirely on Tokyo University, but now the process has been "democratized" to include graduates of other good national universities and even some private ones.)

From the very start, these handpicked career officers are earmarked for rapid ascent and handled differently from the general run of ministry personnel. Typically, they arrive at the office later than their nonelite colleagues, generally about 10 A.M. But there is good reason for that: an American diplomat who once had to hold urgent talks with a Japanese colleague at 2 A.M. was astonished to discover that even at that hour there were still long ranks of taxis waiting to ferry home career officers of the Foreign Ministry and the nearby Ministry of International Trade and Industry. Such people, in fact, literally live their jobs: Saturday for them is generally just another workday, and much of their "social life" is actually devoted to business.

To ensure that by the time they reach senior positions they will have had wide-ranging experience, the members of the bureaucratic elite are normally rotated through a dizzying variety of jobs, rarely serving in any one position for more than two or three years. Early in their careers they are promoted more or less in tandem, but after ten years or so some have clearly become more equal than others. And by the time they reach their early fifties, the game is over for most of them. One becomes top dog in the ministry—whereupon the remaining members of his "class" customarily leave the bureaucracy for jobs in private industry, a process revealingly known as "the descent from heaven."

It is clearly not material rewards or perks that impel able and intelligent men to pursue so demanding and merciless a career.

Except at the very top level, the members of the bureaucratic elite generally do not even enjoy private offices, but work right alongside their subordinates in cluttered, dingy bull pens. And their salaries do not match those paid people of comparable stature by Japanese private industry—or even by the U.S. civil service. Nonetheless, instances of corruption among elite bureaucrats are extremely rare. They find their satisfaction not in amassing wealth but in the belief that they are the prime guardians of the national interest—which in great degree they are.

Japan's bureaucrats are much more than just watchdogs of the national interest, however; they also play a major role in helping to define it. By unspoken agreement, it is the bureaucracy that is primarily responsible for anticipating the challenges and opportunities that Japan will face in years to come and for articulating the country's objectives.

To fulfill this function, each Japanese Government ministry or agency regularly issues documents surveying the area of society for which it is responsible and proposing guidelines for future action in that field. The best-known of these is the long-range study published each year by the Ministry of International Trade and Industry. Rather than an academic exercise in futurism, this document is a hard-headed analysis of where the Japanese and world economies appear to be headed and what Japanese industry must do in order to cope successfully with these trends.

MITI, however, is not content simply to analyze and recommend; it also takes it upon itself to ensure that its recommendations are implemented. In the early 1970s, for example, when it became apparent that the world would soon be awash in excess shipbuilding capacity, MITI pushed through the Diet a bill exempting the shipbuilding industry from the provisions of Japan's Antimonopoly Law and then encouraged formation of a cartel which proceeded to cut Japan's ship-construction capacity by more than a third. (Instead of being fined or sent to jail, as he would have been in the United States, the industrialist who headed the cartel was decorated by the Japanese Government.) More recently, in a more positive vein, MITI has been working to win a leading role for Japan in computer technology by sponsoring and partially financing a consortium of companies dedicated to development of the so-called Fifth Generation Computer. Scheduled for realization in the 1990s, this project aims at developing computers that can "see" visual images, respond to the spoken word and even do a certain amount of syllogistic reasoning.

Like so much else in Japanese government, MITI's authority to act as a kind of central planning board for Japanese business rests upon somewhat nebulous foundations. To impose its will, the ministry regularly issues to individual industries specific and often very detailed sets of regulations known as "administrative guidance." But these do not in themselves have binding force; to ensure that they are observed, MITI's bureaucrats must rely upon a carefully calculated combination of carrot and stick.

One way in which this process works was outlined for me by my MITI friend Chitoshi a few months after he had been given the task of "rationalizing" a large industry in which Japan is no longer as competitive as it was a decade or so ago. His first step, he explained, had been to assemble an advisory panel from the industry itself and get the members of the panel to agree in theory to the need for reduction in the number of firms in the field and a cutback in overall production. To sweeten the pot, he had then negotiated with the Finance Ministry a significant measure of tax relief for the industry. Now, as the quid pro quo, he was engaged in exacting painful reductions in their scale of operation from individual firms. "It means I have to spend most of my nights drinking in geisha houses," he said ruefully. "That's a tiresome business, and the serious conversation is often very brief—sometimes not much more than 'Okay, I can accept that.' But it's the only way to get the job done."

Flexible and effective as its members are, Japan's bureaucracy is nonetheless composed of fallible and ambitious human beings and, as a result, is far from being a monolith. Like those in Washington, Tokyo's great bureaucratic baronies—its Cabinet ministries, regulatory agencies and public corporations—often engage in internecine warfare, sometimes over matters of principle but sometimes simply to defend or extend their turf. "I occasionally suspect that the people at MITI and the Finance Ministry are at least as interested in shooting down our ideas as in coming up with any of their own," a senior official of the Economic Planning Agency once confessed to me.

To say that Japan's bureaucrats wield enormous power, moreover, is far from saying that there are no constraints upon their power. As World War II recedes into history, a new class of politicians without bureaucratic backgrounds is emerging in Japan, and as a result, the relationship between politicians and bureaucrats is subtly changing. In recent years, according to Tokyo gossip, certain Cabinet members have "interfered" with normal bureaucratic process by attempting to decree themselves who should be appointed administrative vice-minister. So far, the bureaucrats have successfully resisted such attempts to invade their domain, but whether they will be able to do so indefinitely is by no means certain.

More immediately threatening is the fact that MITI, one of the flagships of the bureaucracy, has had the legal bases of its authority rendered even more nebulous than ever. As of the end of 1980, it had lost one of its most potent clubs over uncooperative businessmen: the power to grant or withhold foreign-currency licenses, without which no Japanese company could import raw materials or export finished goods. And that same year the Japanese Supreme Court ruled that even though it was acting in compliance with MITI's decrees, a company might nonetheless be held guilty of violating Japan's Antimonopoly Law.

All this has led some Japanese and a considerable number of foreigners to conclude—often with delight—that the days when MITI could call the tune for Japanese industry are over. But when I suggested as much to Chitoshi, he shrugged. "Of course it's true we don't have as much power as we used to, and we certainly have to take the Supreme Court decision into consideration when we draw up a piece of administrative guidance," he said. "But it's all a matter of interpretation." And then, without missing a beat, he resumed his explanation of how MITI goes about restructuring an entire industry.

As things currently stand, in fact, the most effective restraints upon the power of Japan's bureaucracy are not those formally provided for in the country's political and legal system but totally extraconstitutional ones. Although they are not required to do so, most Japanese Government agencies make heavy use of advisory "deliberative councils" composed of prominent private citizens. In part this constitutes a genuine effort to be responsive to outside opinion, but it is also a device for coping with special-interest groups and lobbies, which are just as active and influential in Japan as they are in the United States.

Overall, the spectrum of special interests represented in Tokyo's corridors of power may be somewhat narrower than it is in Washington: there is, for example, no lobby in Japan for unrestricted use of firearms or the inalienable right of used-car dealers to deceive the public. But the range is still broad enough. Each of Japan's forty-seven prefectures maintains a Tokyo office to advance local interests. So do myriad trade and professional groups, as well as various regional chambers of commerce. And Japan's Central Union of Agricultural Cooperatives, as U.S. citrus and cattle growers can attest to their sorrow, is listened to with respect by bureaucrats and politicians alike.

Undeniably the most potent of Japan's lobbies, however, is the Keidanren, or Federation of Economic Organizations. Composed of more than seven hundred of the largest corporations in Japan, Keidanren is headquartered in an ultra-modern fourteen-story Tokyo office building. In contrast to most Japanese offices, the atmosphere of the Keidanren is hushed and rather churchlike, and a foreigner examining a roster of the organization's leaders might be pardoned for dismissing them as a bunch of superannuated fogies. "The other day," a Keidanren employee once said to me with a giggle, "our president, who is in his eighties, slapped one of the directors, who is seventy-five, on the back and told him, 'You young fellows have more energy than we oldsters.' And do you know, the seventy-five-year-old actually blushed!"

But for all its stuffiness, the Keidanren possesses influence far outstripping that of the National Association of Manufacturers or the Business Roundtable in the United States. Its chairman is commonly referred to in the press as "the Prime Minister of Japanese industry," and the endless documents churned out by its large and highly competent professional staff command close attention in government circles. In early 1982, for example, when the Keidanren publicly declared that it was time to begin a systematic dismantling of the devices used to protect Japanese agriculture from foreign competition, its pronouncement was taken as a major new departure in establishment thinking in Japan and even the mighty farmers' lobby was thrown on the defensive.

Along with the lobbies and special-interest groups, Japanese bureaucrats must also pay close heed to another extragovernmental institution: the press. All governments in free societies must do that, of course, but because it covers the intimate details of day-to-day policy formulation within the government so closely, the press in Japan serves as even more of a sounding board than the press in Britain or the United States. From public reaction to "inside" stories and from the frequent polls conducted by the national dailies, Japan's bureaucrats and politicians can gauge with considerable accuracy the degree of acceptance that any particular course of action is likely to command in the country at large. And in a consensus society, this is more than just a matter of determining what may be popular or politically shrewd; it is a matter of determining what is politically and administratively possible.

To some non-Japanese, the degree to which Japan's leaders defer to minority opinion seems absurd and the diffusion of political power and responsibility in Japan among so many different institutions a dangerous weakness. It has, in fact, been argued that there is no such thing as "the government" in Japan but rather an array of parallel mini-governments whose views and interests must all be reconciled before action can be taken on any particular issue. This, critics argue, makes for slow response to challenges and, in cases where differences of opinion are extreme, can rule out anything except a least-common-denominator approach.

That there is a modicum of truth to such charges is amply demonstrated by the vexed question of Japanese rearmament. In per capita terms, Japan spends upon its armed forces only about 13 percent of what the United States does, and as a result there is increasing clamor among Americans that militarily the Japanese are getting a "free ride" at the expense of the U.S. taxpayer. The implication here—and more and more often the explicitly stated premise— is that the Japanese have slyly conned the United States into squandering billions upon their defense so that they themselves can concentrate all of their resources upon economic growth and the exploitation of American markets.

This, to put it plainly, is ignorant nonsense. Whatever its practical consequences economically, Japan's tippy-toe approach to rearmament has been a product not of clever calculation but of political stalemate. The disastrous upshot of World War II induced in most ordinary Japanese a profound distrust of militarism in any form. With the passage of time, that feeling has faded considerably, but as of 1981, polls showed that 30 percent of the Japanese people still believed their country should pursue a policy of unarmed neutrality. And to buttress its case, this very substantial minority had only to point to the Constitution so thoughtfully drawn up for Japan by Douglas MacArthur and his aides. For Article Nine of that Constitution specifically states: "The Japanese people forever renounce war as a sovereign right of the nation. . . . Land, sea and air forces, as well as other war potential, will never be maintained."

To most of Japan's current leaders, this seems sophomoric foolishness. Partly to appease the Americans and partly for their own purposes, some of the most powerful figures in the Liberal Democratic Party would like to see Japan acquire substantial military capacity and are slowly pushing the country in that direction. The rate at which they can do this, however, is psychologically restricted by the patent unconstitutionality of any rearmament at all—and the cold fact is that the LDP cannot hope to muster the two-thirds majority in parliament necessary to amend the Constitution. Even if it could, moreover, any attempt to do so would set off a political fire storm: though more than 60 percent of all Japanese now approve of some sort of defense establishment, more than 60 percent paradoxically also oppose any tampering with Article Nine.

To reconcile all these seemingly irreconcilable considerations, successive Japanese Governments have resorted to a series of transparent fictions and dubious compromises. Since it would plainly be unconstitutional to do so, Japan to this day technically does not possess an army, navy or air force; instead, it maintains what are religiously referred to as Ground, Air and Maritime Self-Defense Forces. And while per capita military spending is low, the total sums involved are not negligible: Japan's overall military budget is the world's eighth largest—seventh, in fact, if one excludes the obviously aberrant case of Saudi Arabia. What Japan gets for its money, however, is a military establishment clearly too small and too inadequately armed even to defend the Japanese islands, much less protect Japanese interests anywhere else.

Whether it would really be in the U.S. interest for Japan to possess significant military power is, in my view, open to argument. What is not open to argument, however, is that the inability to confront this issue squarely and coherently reflects a potentially worrisome weakness in the Japanese political system.

Nonetheless, it would be a grave error to form a general judgment of the effectiveness of Japanese government on the basis of the great defense muddle. While by no means the only example of governmental inadequacy in contemporary Japan, it does involve a uniquely sensitive issue and is decidedly exceptional. Far more characteristic of the overall performance of Japan's political leadership is the way in which it has responded to the environmental problems that have come to plague all heavily industrialized nations.

Because of its small area and the breakneck pace of its postwar industrial growth, Japan by the late 1960s confronted some of the most grievous pollution problems in the world. Air quality in Tokyo, to cite just one example, was so poor that the city had become actively unsafe for people with chronic respiratory problems and it was not unusual for families that could afford it to send their children off to the country periodically for what were, quite literally, "breathers."

Then, in response to mounting public concern, the government stepped in. By 1975, Japan was spending more of its wealth on antipollution measures than any other country—roughly 3 percent of its Gross National Product. And on the principle that "the polluter must pay," much of this burden was laid squarely on the shoulders of private industry; by the late '70s, Japanese industry was successfully meeting the world's most rigid standards for auto emissions and smoke emissions from new industrial plants. The results have been remarkable: the air in Tokyo is now much cleaner and pleasanter to breathe than that of New York.

Nor is this an isolated example. In an era when transportation systems in the United States have been both shrinking and deteriorating, Japanese transportation facilities have been improved and greatly expanded. Meantime, in terms of ultimate payoff—life expectancy—Japan's healthcare system has clearly been improving faster than America's. Less than twenty years ago, life expectancy in Japan was lower than that of the United States, which in turn was surpassed by several other countries. Today, Japanese life expectancy (seventy-three for men, seventy-eight for women) is the highest in the world. Although improved diet and sanitation are partially responsible for this dramatic change, it also obviously reflects the fact that virtually all Japanese are now covered by health insurance—roughly 60 percent of them through plans provided by their employers, and the remaining 40 percent through a national health plan. As a general rule, health insurance in Japan pays only about two-thirds of a patient's bills, but doctors' fees and hospital costs, which are set by the government, are kept relatively low, so the Japanese tend to visit doctors more often than Americans do. And preventive medicine is more widely practiced in Japan: schoolchildren get mandatory medical and dental checkups, and as a result of vaccinations and inoculations administered at school or through neighborhood organizations, Japanese of every age are better protected against disease than the citizens of most other countries.

Similar success stories abound in other aspects of Japanese economic and social life—and nearly all of them in one way or another reflect the foresight and ingenuity of the men who have ruled Japan since the end of the U.S. Occupation. On balance, in other words, the jerry-built governmental structure that has been erected on the foundation supplied by General MacArthur's somewhat eccentric notions of political science has served the Japanese people remarkably well. There is, I think, no exaggeration in the verdict passed by Richard Rabinowitz, an American lawyer who has practiced in Tokyo for more than twenty years and who regards the Japanese scene with a perceptive but decidedly unsentimental eye. "Of course Japanese politicians and bureaucrats find it hard to adjust to changing circumstances," he says. "All politicians and bureaucrats do. But it seems to me undeniable that Japan's politicial leaders have been far more flexible and far more successful in adjusting to change over the last thirty-five years than any other national leaders I can think of. And I see no reason to think that's going to alter."

12

The Fruits of Industry

It was ten thirty at night, and on the stool next to mine in the Orchid Bar of Tokyo's Hotel Okura a British businessman was sipping moodily at a snifter of brandy. He was, he explained, about to head home to London empty-handed, having failed to land a big contract because the product his company made did not meet the standards of reliability insisted upon by a potential Japanese client. In due course, the Englishman ordered a second brandy and savored it in silence, all the while staring intently at a pair of Japanese bartenders who were deftly mixing and dispensing a bewildering variety of drinks to forty or fifty customers. Finally, his snifter empty, the Englishman abruptly jumped up off his bar stool and, just before disappearing into the night, said loudly to no one in particular: "They are so damned efficient, these people, that it's bloody frightening."

In so saying, the frustrated Briton was of course voicing a sentiment now shared by most of the world's non-Japanese population. Only fifteen years ago, eminent Europeans like France's Jean-Jacques Servan-Schreiber were pointing with alarm to "the American challenge" and glumly predicting the imminent economic takeover of the world by U.S.-controlled multinational corporations. Today all that is forgotten and it is the Japanese challenge that obsesses businessmen, labor leaders and politicians all the way from Detroit to Düsseldorf. How do they do it? Westerners ask in anguished wonderment. How have the inhabitants of a relatively small country with virtually no natural resources managed to build in so short a time the world's second-largest industrial economy? What are the secrets that have enabled Japan to surpass the once-impregnable United States in automobile production, rival it in steel production and unleash upon the world at large a torrent of consumer goods so high in quality and reasonable in price that in one field after another, the developed nations of the West have fallen back upon protectionism, overt or disguised, as the only way to prevent destruction of their domestic industries?

Back in the '60s and early '70s, when they had not yet perceived the full dimensions of the Japanese challenge, most Western businessmen and politicians were inclined to attribute the superior competitiveness of so many Japanese products to some kind of Oriental trickery. Cheap labor was the explanation, they said. Or more darkly yet, they accused the Japanese of widespread dumping—selling goods abroad at prices below their cost of production.

But as the years went by and Japan's great modern corporations steadily expanded their foreign beachheads in one industry after another, the charge of unfair competition became harder and harder to sustain as the primary explanation for Japan's export successes. Clearly, no manufacturer, not even an inscrutable Oriental one, can go on, decade in and decade out, continually selling his products at a loss. And the cheap-labor argument, though still frequently heard, does not stand up to close examination either. For one thing, Japan's most successful manufacturers have for some time been steadily reducing their dependence on human labor: Japan's newer steel mills, auto plants and TV assembly lines are considerably more automated and "robotized" than most comparable Western facilities. In any case, overall labor costs in Japan now equal or surpass those prevailing in most of Western Europe and in some instances actually surpass those in the United States itself. Yet Japanese automakers now sell more cars in the United States than all their European competitors combined.

Faced with these awkward facts, realists in the West began to search for more sophisticated explanations for the superior competitiveness of the Japanese. One reason for it, some people suggested, was that Japanese industry had been fortunate enough to have most of its plants bombed off the face of the earth during World War II and thus, unlike American industry, had been left with no choice but to replace obsolescent factories and mills with more modern and efficient ones. An even more intriguing suggestion was the concept of "Japan, Inc." developed by American business consultant James Abegglen. This was a vision of the Japanese economy as a kind of seamless web in which politicians, bureaucrats and businessmen all worked industriously toward mutually agreed-upon ends. As oversimplified by some of its popularizers, however, it was often reduced to the proposition that unlike the U.S. Government, the Government of Japan invariably seeks, by fair means or foul, to strengthen private industry and advance its interests.

There was some truth to both these suggestions, but again, as time wore on, it became clear that neither of them by itself could fully account for the Japanese miracle. World War II bomb damage, extensive as it was, has very little relevance to the current efficiency of the Japanese auto industry, which existed only in rudimentary form in the 1940s, and it has none whatsoever to Japanese dominance of consumer electronics, an industry which did not exist at all then. And while the Japanese Government has indeed played a vital role in the nurturing of Japanese industry, that role does not, as many Americans appear to believe, involve extraordinarily heavy financial aid to industry. In one important respect, in fact, Tokyo is actually less openhanded than Washington: where the U.S. Government underwrites close to 50 percent of all the research and development efforts of American corporations—including more than 35 percent of all nonmilitary research—only about 25 percent of the R&D money spent in Japan comes from government agencies.

In short, if one is intellectually honest, it is very difficult to find an ego-salving set of excuses for the fact that American industry in recent years has so frequently been outperformed by Japanese industry. In recognition of this, an increasing number of Americans—perhaps the most influential being Harvard professor Ezra Vogel, the author of *Japan as Number One: Lessons for America*—have come up with a revisionist interpretation of the Japanese challenge. The real explanation of the Japanese success story, the revisionists say, is that in a number of respects—social, economic and administrative—Japan operates more intelligently and efficiently than Western societies do. The basic message preached by the revisionists, at least as it gets through to most American businessmen, bureaucrats and politicians, is a simple one: observe what the Japanese do and then try your damnedest to do likewise.

If only because it reflects a sensible degree of modesty—a virtue that has never loomed large in the American national character—the revisionists' approach surely represents a step in the right direction. But as a prescription for concrete action it also carries some inherent risks. To determine what if any economic devices the United States can reasonably hope to borrow from Japan, it is first necessary to arrive at a clear understanding of how big Japanese corporations actually operate—and why they can and do operate that way.

A half century ago, my great-uncle Will Lee lived in a small Connecticut town owned by the Talcotts, an old Yankee family whose ancestors had reputedly acquired the place from a sachem called Uncas the Mohegan.

When I say that the Talcotts owned Talcottville, I mean exactly that. They were more than just the owners of the woolen mill that was the heart of the community and gave employment to most of Talcottville's men. They also owned every house in town, had built the local school and in the manner of eighteenth-century English squires, had appointed the rector of the local church. Talcottville, in short, was at once a business enterprise and a community.

Today, like most of the scores of other such communities that once dotted the United States, Talcottville is no longer a company town—and most Americans would not regret the change. On the contrary, nearly all of us in this country regard the increasing rarity of communities owned or dominated by a single company as a sign of progress. To be dependent on your employer not only for your income but also for your housing, your recreation and even, in a sense, your social life is, by contemporary American standards, an unacceptable infringement on personal freedom. It is therefore somewhat disconcerting to discover that in up-and-coming Japan the state of affairs is almost exactly the reverse. Since World War II, in fact, Japan's major business enterprises have increasingly developed into something approaching self-contained communities. This is not to say that Japan has become simply one vast collection of company towns. What has been happening there is something considerably more complex—something first drawn to my attention by Isamu Yamashita, the chairman of Mitsui Zosen (or, as it is known in English, the Mitsui Engineering and Shipbuilding Company).

Yamashita, a stocky, unassuming engineer who has worked for Mitsui Zosen for nearly fifty years, is one of Japan's most capable and hardheaded executives. Most of our conversation dealt with very pragmatic matters, such as the techniques by which he had achieved a dramatically successful diversification of his company's activities.

But when I asked him a cliché Harvard Business School question—what basic line of business did Mitsui Zosen consider itself to be in—Yamashita suddenly waxed philosophical. Mitsui Zosen, he allowed, was essentially in the business of surviving.

"You have to remember," he went on, "that only fifty years ago we Japanese were still living in an essentially feudal system. As a general thing, people in those days stuck to the communities where they were born. But after World War II, when Japan began reindustrializing, people started to flock to the big industrial complexes, and the old sense of geographic community largely broke down. In a very real way, we in industry spoiled the old community life of Japan, and something had to replace it. So in today's Japan, companies like ours are the new communities, and their managers have a responsibility to create conditions in which people can enjoy a community life. Above all, of course, we managers have the overriding responsibility of keeping the community alive."

At first blush this seemed an interesting but slightly artificial construct—the sort of thing thrown out by a young sociologist desperately seeking a topic for a Ph.D. thesis. But just how true it really is was driven home to me a couple of weeks later when I spent an afternoon with Toru Iijima, a foreman in the Nissan Motor Company's Oppama assembly plant, which sits on the western shore of Tokyo Bay near the great naval base of Yokosuka.

At thirty-seven, Toru Iijima is a lean, handsome man of uncommon dignity and self-possession. I have, in fact, rarely met anyone who struck me as being more in command of his own soul than Iijima. Yet for him the sun rises and sets on Nissan.

A car nut since childhood, Iijima passed up public high school to attend the Nissan Vocational School. From there he went directly to the stamping shop of the Oppama plant. Today, twenty years later, he is still in the stamping shop, but now he has fifteen people working under him.

When he first went to work at Oppama, Iijima lived in a bachelor dormitory that Nissan maintains at Oppama. In due course he married a girl who also worked at Nissan, and for a while they lived in a company-owned apartment. Then a baby came along—today the Iijimas have two sons, thirteen and ten—and Iijima decided to buy his own home. With the help of Nissan's real estate subsidiary, he was able to do so at considerably less than the exorbitant price that housing in the Tokyo megalopolis normally commands. And his payments are relatively easy to handle because of the installment savings program Nissan makes available to its employees—a kind of credit union that pays higher interest than ordinary banks and lends money more cheaply.

A devoted father, Iijima spends much of his free time on barbecues and hikes with his family. But he is also a keen athlete who makes frequent use of the plant gymnasium at Oppama, competing with other Nissan workers in a variety of sports. On vacations he usually drives his wife and children to the mountains in his Nissan Sunny (Datsun 210)—which he bought at an employee discount.

If all this makes Toru Iijima sound like a mindless creation of Nissan, it does him a great injustice. When I asked him if he wanted his sons to go to university so they could become Nissan engineers, he threw me a cool, level look. "I hope they will do whatever they want," he said. "They have to have their own way of life."

Nonetheless, Nissan provides Iijima with the same sense of belonging that Talcottville gave to my great-uncle Will. The thought of looking for a better job elsewhere or, more to the point, of being cast adrift by Nissan literally never crosses Iijima's mind. He knows that unless he commits some heinous offense, he will never be fired. And he knows, too, that if the Oppama plant were ever obliged to reduce production drastically, Nissan would make every effort to find useful employment for any redundant personnel. (Not too far from Oppama, in fact, there is dramatic evidence of the lengths to which a Japanese company will go to take care of its employees: when Nippon Steel was forced to close down one of its furnaces at Kimitsu, on the other side of Tokyo Bay, it promptly set up an agricultural subsidiary in the area and put the displaced furnacemen to work raising cattle.)

For Toru Iijima, Nissan is more than the source of his income. It is a living organism with which he identifies to a degree surpassed only by his identification with his family and his country. "Nissan," he told me, sounding remarkably like Isamu Yamashita, "must survive for long, long years, and the quality of its work must be maintained through all those years." For that reason, he feels great responsibility for the training of younger workers and for ensuring that the members of his shift remain "very active" in suggesting improvements in working methods. He also expects the more experienced members of his shift to spot anything wrong with a car that passes through their hands even if the error was made in another part of the plant. "The whole responsibility for every car we touch is on our shoulders," he says. "If I hear that a car produced by Nissan has any problems, I feel personally guilty."

From casual conversations with people like Toru Iijima, it is tempting to conclude—as many Americans have—that Japanese workers have somehow been brainwashed into utter docility by their bosses. But there is one great flaw in that theory: Japanese executives manifest precisely the same attitudes as their assembly-line workers. Of the scores of Japanese senior executives I have interviewed over the years, I can recall only two who did not sooner or later make a point of informing me that they had spent their entire working lives with one company. And nearly all Japan's current crop of top executives are quick to tell you that they started out on the assembly line or in some equally humble job. (This is a fact that sometimes has rather anomalous results: it is doubtful, for example, that the chief executive of any American corporation can boast, as Mitsui Zosen's Yamashita does, that he was once the leader of his company's labor union.)

The reason for the extraordinary corporate fidelity of Japanese executives is not simply, as foreigners often assume, that they fear change or regard job-hopping as a manifestation of frivolity. Rather, like their workers, they conceive of corporations as communities that, in a certain sense, are collectively managed and hence cannot be successfully led by anyone not intimately familiar with the collective psyche. "In this country you just don't get a company like Chrysler calling in a top Ford executive to run its affairs," one of Japan's most respected businessmen told me. "That would be almost as unthinkable as it would be for New Yorkers to elect a mayor who had lived all his life in Chicago."

Moreover, this sense of the corporation as a unique, continuing entity provides Japanese executives, like their workers, with a high degree of financial and emotional security. Indeed, in a Japanese company, as in the political life of a small American city, dedication and hard work are often more prized than brilliance.

Just how true this is was spelled out for me by Yoshiya Ariyoshi, for many years the elder statesman of the giant shipping line named Nippon Yusen Kaisha (NYK). Heavily influenced by his youthful experiences in Europe—as an NYK representative in Hitler's Germany, he took the risky step of issuing steamship tickets on credit to Jewish families frantic to escape the Thousand Year Reich—Mr. Ariyoshi was unusual among Japanese of his generation in that when he was dealing with Westerners he made his points directly and forcefully. "I know it is hard for Americans to understand," Ariyoshi told me, "but in Japan it's quite customary for a twenty-year-old to receive only a third of the salary of a forty-year-old who is doing exactly the same work. In most companies here all employees except for the top executives are paid according to seniority. To you Americans that would seem to destroy incentive. But in Japan if the other members of your group work hard and you don't, you will eventually be ostracized. And being excluded from the group is the most appalling thing any Japanese can imagine."

As Ariyoshi himself confessed, this reliance on peer pressure can on occasion backfire. "At Japan National Railways, it is the people who work hard that are ostracized," he said ruefully. And an increasing number of Japanese executives feel that as a spur to efficiency and creativity the wage system should be modified so as to put more weight on individual performance. Already some big corporations have begun to edge cautiously away from seniority as the sole criterion of salary, and Taiji Ubukata, president of Ishikawajima-Harima Heavy Industries, foresees the day when "perhaps sixty to seventy percent of wages will be based on seniority and the rest on such things as merit and productivity." But even so limited a resort to the merit system is not a universally popular idea. "It seems to me," one promising young *sarariman* told me, "that our traditional system suits the Japanese character better."

Important as they may be, in other words, financial rewards do not loom as large in corporate life in Japan as they do in the United States—and that is even truer for executives than for workers. It is doubtful that in all of Japan's booming auto industry there is a single person who makes as much as a quarter of the income enjoyed by the top half dozen men in Detroit. The typical big Japanese corporation, in fact, pays its president less than $150,000 a year—partly because he would have to pay out 80 percent of anything over that amount in income tax. And unless he founded his company himself, a Japanese executive cannot hope for stock options, deferred-compensation plans or any of the other gimmicks through which top American managers contrive to become personally wealthy.

In Japanese eyes, this relative deprivation is more than compensated for by the psychic and social security that comes with success. If a Japanese executive reaches the top rungs of his company, the mandatory retirement age—usually somewhere in the sixties for management personnel—will be raised for him or even, as it was in Mr. Ariyoshi's case, effectively suspended entirely. It is by no means uncommon in Japanese business for a man to serve successively as his company's president, then chairman and finally, in extreme old age, honorary chairman.

But even if an executive is only moderately successful and never rises above the bottom rungs of senior management, he does not have to resign himself, as most American executives must, to being put out to pasture in his late fifties or early sixties. Though he will be required to observe his company's mandatory retirement age, more likely than not his colleagues will find him a "postretirement job" in the management of one of the company's subsidiaries or subcontractors. And thus a centrally important element in his life—his membership in the corporate community—remains intact.

To the hardheaded European or American businessman, it may seem a long leap from the institution of "lifetime employment" to the concept of the Japanese corporation as at least a partial surrogate for the traditional geographic community. But only if you make that leap does it become possible to explain, rather than merely describe, some of the aspects of Japanese economic life that foreigners find most mystifying.

Consider, for example, the fact that the typical Japanese labor union represents the workers of only one company and, as a routine matter, adjusts its wage, bonus and overtime demands to the prosperity of that particular company at contract time. Most Westerners who are aware of this phenomenon tend to attribute it either to the passivity of Japanese labor or to the Machiavellian practices of Japanese management. But while both these factors may apply in some slight degree, the fundamental explanation for the close cooperation between unions and management lies in a strongly perceived identity of interest between the two. In many Japanese companies, the union's leadership is treated almost as an arm of management. At Mitsui Shipbuilding, for example, the chief executive officer meets every quarter with the leaders of the company's union (the union president at the time of my visit was a young university graduate who presumably would eventually move into executive ranks himself) and fills them in on all major corporate developments. "So when it comes time for a new wage settlement," Mr. Yamashita told me, "the union already knows the situation of the company and doesn't make exorbitant demands."

Essentially, the reason a big Japanese corporation can operate in this fashion is that its employees accept that their prosperity as individuals is directly dependent upon the prosperity of the economic community to which they belong. Far more than American or European workers, Japanese workers take it for granted that just as an individual must sometimes sacrifice to ensure national survival, so he must sometimes sacrifice to ensure corporate survival.

As Yutaka Takeda, a senior executive of Shin Nippon Steel, once pointed out to me, however, there is an important corollary to this assumption: in the majority of Japanese corporations, the class struggle does not enter strongly into labor-management relations. To be sure, Japanese companies are extremely hierarchical organizations in which everyone is keenly aware of his or her place. But everyone is also made to feel an indispensable part of the community—a fact that many Japanese argue constitutes a crucial difference between American and Japanese industry.

"American executives are too aristocratic," charges a Japanese businessman who knows the United States very well. "Very few of them have ever worked on a production line themselves, and they have little or no contact with their workers, whom they treat as interchangeable parts. Here in Japan it's routine for the president of a big department store, if he has no other engagement, to have lunch in the company cafeteria, mingling with the salesclerks and other employees. And that's not just a gimmick. All of us—every one of us in Japan—believe that the rise or fall of our organization rests on the individual shoulders of each one of us."

It is at least in part this sense of being a valued member of a social unit that explains the extraordinary degree of loyalty Japanese workers feel toward their companies—an attitude closely akin to the civic boosterism of many Americans. For a Westerner it is a sobering experience to hear, as I have, a twenty-three-year-old clerk discourse on the history, products and procedures of her corporation with all the uncritical earnestness of an American high school teacher expounding on the ineffable wisdom of the Founding Fathers.

Still another desirable consequence of the concept of the corporation as a community is the relative immunity of Japanese industry to the plague of mergers and takeovers that has afflicted American industry in recent years. Big Japanese corporations do occasionally merge or absorb one another, but such occurrences are rare—and traumatic. "For one major company here to take over another," a Japanese Government official explained, "is nearly as unsettling as it would be if Connecticut took over Rhode Island. It causes all kinds of psychological and social upheaval."

This is not to say that Japanese industry does not have its own version of the American conglomerate. But Japanese-style conglomerates—the potent collections of twenty to thirty companies such as the "Mitsui group" and the "Mitsubishi group"—are more like loosely linked political confederations than artificial, balance-sheet empires such as Litton Industries.

Typically, at least 50 percent of the stock of, say, a Mitsui company is owned by other Mitsui companies. The performance of the managers of one Mitsui company is, therefore, judged by their peers in other Mitsui companies—and the crucial element in that evaluation is how effectively this particular set of managers has acted to ensure the survival of its company and of the Mitsui group as a whole.

It is precisely here, in my view, that the more-than-commercial role of the major Japanese companies has made its biggest contribution to Japan's economic success. "American managers," Yoshiya Ariyoshi once told me disapprovingly, "are judged by their stockholders on the basis of how big a profit they turned in last quarter and what they can be expected to turn in next quarter. That forces them to focus on the short term, like a baseball player worrying about his batting average. Our system, with its heavy emphasis on the survival of the institution, forces managers to think constantly about the long term."

From time to time, representatives of U.S. cities or states that are trying to attract Japanese investment seek out Richard Rabinowitz to get the benefit of the expertise on Japan he has acquired in the course of twenty years of highly successful law practice there. "I always give them pretty much the same advice," says Rabinowitz. "I tell them to give the Japanese they are wooing reassurances about the existence of a literate work force in their particular region, the degree of physical security the area offers and what it has in the way of cultural facilities and amenities—in short, the kind of reassurances the citizens of any advanced nation want when they are considering a business venture in a less developed society."

Courtesy, of course, does not permit most Japanese to refer openly to the United States as a less advanced nation than Japan. On the contrary, almost every Japanese businessman with whom I have discussed the relative performances of the Japanese and American economies has been quick to tell me of the enormous debt his particular industry owes to "our elder brothers in America." Given the role of the elder brother in the traditional Japanese family, this is an expression of extreme deference; and in thus emphasizing their sense of indebtedness to their American counterparts Japanese businessmen are in no way insincere. An extremely high proportion of the technology currently employed by the most advanced sectors of Japanese industry was originally developed in the United States, and it is no accident that the coveted quality-control award for which Japanese firms bitterly compete each year is named after an American statistician, W. Edwards Deming. "Productivity and quality control are both games we learned from the Americans," admits Ichiro Shioji, the president of the Confederation of Japanese Automobile Workers' Unions.

Such deference is always flattering—until you stop to reflect that very often the Japanese apply what they have borrowed from the United States in the way of technology, managerial devices and manufacturing techniques more effectively than Americans now do. It is this embarrassing fact above all that in recent years has led a certain number of Americans to suggest that it would be wise for U.S. industry to determine what it is that the Japanese do differently and then emulate them.

To support this argument, its most simplistic proponents sometimes point to Japanese companies that have purchased or launched U.S. subsidiaries, have operated them Japanese style (in some cases right down to mass morning calisthenics for employees) and, in the process, have prospered mightily. But while some of these case histories are accurate enough, they tend, in my view, to be deceptive. When you press hard enough, a surprising number of Japanese industrialists privately express reservations about the performance of their American subsidiaries. One deeply pro-American Tokyo executive proudly described to me how his company had acquired a money-losing U.S. concern and rendered it profitable in the space of a single year. In the next breath, however, he confessed that because of sloppy work practices among the employees in his U.S. plant, the number of defective units it produced ran nearly 50 percent higher than in his Japanese plants. Another top Japanese manager confessed with an embarrassed laugh that when his company acquired a well-established U.S. manufacturing company, "we found that the way they were doing things over there was twenty years behind us." Glumly, he added that in his opinion, it would be a very long time before the U.S. operation achieved Japanese levels of productivity—if indeed it ever did.

In the view of many of the Japanese industrialists I have talked with, nearly all Japanese firms that have successfully employed their own style of management in the United States fall into a special category. "They're in fields where they don't have to deal with tough, industry-wide unions," the chief executive of a major Japanese manufacturing company bluntly declared. Somewhat more cautiously, Jiro Tokuyama of the Nomura School of Advanced Management told me: "It's significant, I think, that the Japanese companies that have done best in the United States mostly have American subsidiaries with only a thousand employees or less. In such cases, it's relatively easy to apply what I call Japan's 'lubricant system'—which is to say greater humanism in industrial relations and a greater sense of participation on the part of ordinary workers. But whether this would work in a U.S. company with five or six thousand employees I'm not so sure."

Obviously, it would be foolish to suggest that there is no possibility whatever of successfully transferring Japanese managerial and manufacturing techniques to the United States. Some transfer of this kind is already occurring. A number of U.S. firms have taken a careful look at Japanese business strategies and, as a result, are themselves experimenting with such things as heavier reliance upon subcontractors and "guaranteed" employment. Perhaps the most widespread reimportation from Japan has been the "quality-control circle"—a group of eight to a dozen workers from the same division of a company who are encouraged to engage in regular brainstorming sessions in order to find ways of increasing their own productivity and the reliability of the goods they produce.

But while these and other specific Japanese practices can no doubt be usefully adapted to the American environment, there would seem to be clear limits to the degree to which U.S. industry can hope to remodel itself in the Japanese image. On the strength of his intimate knowledge of both countries, Jiro Tokuyama, for one, has concluded that most of the differences between Japanese and American managerial techniques are merely symptoms of a far deeper and probably ineradicable difference. "The contradiction between the two countries is not basically economic but rather is one of social systems," he asserts. Sounding the same theme, Yoshiya Ariyoshi rhetorically demanded of me: "How can anyone reasonably expect Americans—individualistic and independent-minded Americans—to behave like group-oriented Japanese?"

Because "individualistic" and "independent-minded" are positive words in our lexicon, most Americans instinctively preen themselves when they hear a question like Mr. Ariyoshi's. That, unfortunately, tends to obscure an important fact: it is group orientation that in large part explains the heavy emphasis on long-term planning which many Japanese businessmen regard as the key factor in Japanese managerial strategy.

Nearly all Americans who possess any familiarity with Japanese business freely concede—or angrily charge—that Japanese corporations are far readier than American ones to mortgage the present in order to secure the future. To win a foothold in a promising new industry or market, Japan's major companies routinely make heavy investments that cannot be expected to produce profits for a long time to come. But the fact that Japanese managers take such action far more freely and more frequently than their American counterparts does not stem from greater cunning or superior intelligence. Rather, it is a function of the climate in which they operate.

Unlike his American counterparts, in fact, a Japanese executive would endanger his own career prospects if he sought to maximize short-term profits at the risk of his company's long-term health. There are at least two reasons for this. Where U.S. stockholders for the most part are primarily interested in a company's current earnings and their impact on the price of its shares, the interlocking directorates that exercise effective control of so many Japanese corporations tend, as Mr. Ariyoshi pointed out, to focus on a company's prospects for long-term survival. And this emphasis upon the company as an enduring institution is reinforced by the fact that although they now do far more equity financing than they used to, Japanese corporations still typically rely upon bank loans to meet a much higher percentage of their capital requirements than American corporations do. Inevitably, companies with massive bank loans are inclined to pay close attention to the views of their bankers. But unlike stockholders, bankers do not stand to gain directly from a quick boost in corporate earnings or share prices; their main concern is that a company which has borrowed from them stay in business and go on paying off the interest on its debts.

Besides all these institutional forces, there is another consideration which, I believe, helps significantly to deter Japanese executives from settling for quick and impermanent fixes. Because they identify so completely with one company and rarely indulge in job-hopping, they have a greater stake in the long-range implications of their decisions than America's far more mobile managers necessarily do. Instead of consoling himself with the thought that he can always skip off to greener pastures, a Japanese executive knows that unless in the meantime he has died or retired, he will still be around to face any untoward consequences that his current decisions may ultimately have upon his company's fortunes.

Precisely because it does serve to foster longer perspectives on the part of individual Japanese managers and corporations, group consciousness also contributes mightily to a key element in Japan's overall economic success: long-range planning on a national scale. To some Americans, national planning has come to seem the central achievement of "Japan, Inc.," and occasionally the suggestion is made that the U.S. Government should "follow the Japanese example" by assuming overall responsibility for the management of industrial and technological change in this country.

Such proposals, however, rest upon a basic misunderstanding of the manner in which national planning is conducted in Japan. For as Andrew Osterman, a Harvard specialist in Japanese economic policy, has rightly emphasized: "The Japanese Government is not the primary force in Japan's commercial and technological success."

This is not to say that the Japanese Government is an unimportant or negligible force. Japanese Government agencies, most notably the Ministry of International Trade and Industry, play an invaluable role in analyzing the probable directions of economic and technological change, identifying the dangers and opportunities inherent in such change and coordinating the manner in which private enterprise responds to those challenges. But "central planning" Japanese style is very different from central planning of the Soviet variety or even the kind now practiced in France. It is not, in other words, a rigid process in which ideologically inspired bureaucrats impose upon the productive sectors of the economy arbitrary targets drawn up with scant regard for the realities of the marketplace. Rather, it is a flexible and broadly consensual process in which private enterprise is a willing and highly creative partner.

One reason economic planning can function this way in Japan is, I believe, that the country's private business institutions and their managers are characterized by a strong concern for the national interest—or, if you will, by a strong tribal consciousness. It would be naive in the extreme to believe that Japanese businessmen are all high-minded fellows who invariably put the common welfare ahead of their personal ambitions and corporate profit margins. Indeed, my bureaucrat friend Chitoshi laments that in recent years Japanese corporations have been increasingly prone to pursue what he disapprovingly describes as "selfish interest"; as prime evidence of this, he cites the bitter fight Japanese automakers put up against government acceptance of "voluntary" quotas on Japan's auto exports to the United States. But even Chitoshi has to concede that the auto companies eventually lost that fight and that it is rare for his country's industrialists to resort to a Japanese version of the late "Engine Charlie" Wilson's claim that "What is good for General Motors is good for the United States."

Often enough, to be sure, the greater readiness of Japanese industrialists to subordinate their parochial concerns to the larger concerns of the overall society reflects the fact that they have no other rational choice. This is particularly true in the case of mature industries that have fallen upon hard times—a situation in which standard practice in Japan and the United States differs significantly. The current plight of the U.S. steel industry, for example, is in considerable degree a consequence of the failure of most American steel companies to invest sufficiently heavily in plant modernization over the past quarter century. The U.S. steel industry was the last of any consequence in the world to adopt the highly efficient oxygen furnace, and even its most up-to-date plants are by no means as thoroughly automated as those in Japan. Yet when, as a result of these disparities, Japanese steel began to undersell American steel in the U.S. market, American steelmakers did not respond with massive investment in improved steel technology but instead began to put their capital into unrelated high-profit enterprises ranging from shopping centers to chemical plants. At the same time, however, they demanded—and got—government protection against Japanese and European steel, thereby saddling the U.S. economy with an unnecessarily inflated steel bill.

By contrast, mature industries in Japan mostly can't expect this kind of treatment because the Japanese Government is under such heavy and continuing foreign pressure to eschew protectionism. Accordingly, to stay competitive, mature industries in Japan typically invest heavily in new facilities embodying advanced technology; a senior executive of Nissan Motors, for example, once told me that his company follows a "scrap-and-build" policy under which the equipment in any given plant is continually being improved and all of it is effectively replaced every four or five years. But even employment of the most advanced technology will not always keep an industry healthy in the face of massive foreign competition or sharply increased raw-material costs. In that situation, to the Japanese way of thinking, the proper solution is to follow the course that was taken by Japan's shipbuilding industry in the '70s and that is currently being pursued by its petrochemical industry: with as much government pressure and cooperation as may be required, all the companies in the afflicted industry get together and sharply reduce their productive capacity, spreading out the cutbacks among themselves as equitably as possible.

If old industries fade away more gracefully in Japan than in the United States, new ones also emerge there in a considerably more coherent way. It is, in fact, in the cultivation of promising areas for industrial growth that the contribution of private enterprise to Japan's overall economic development is most dynamic and unforced.

As American economist Eleanor Hadley has pointed out, it is a sobering truth that whenever the U.S. Government has imposed artificial restraints upon Japanese competition in one field of industry, the Japanese have responded by successfully challenging the United States in a higher form of technology. This, of course, is no mere happenstance, and the manner in which these increasingly sophisticated challenges were mounted affords a classic illustration of how private enterprise and the government in Japan interact in the long-term planning process.

Though it has now been half-forgotten by most Americans, the first major industry in which postwar Japan succeeded in posing a serious threat to U.S. producers in their own market was a relatively primitive one: the textile business. But as far back as the late 1950s, the Ministry of Trade and Industry had already identified the far more sophisticated consumer-electronics industry as offering the possibility of major growth—a perception that served both to encourage and to smooth the way for imaginative expansion efforts on the part of Japanese companies in that field. So while Washington haggled with Tokyo over the textile "invasion," Japanese manufacturers of cameras, tape recorders, radios, television sets and hi-fi equipment were investing heavily in product development and making exhaustive studies of the nature of the U.S. market and the tastes of U.S. consumers. The result was that by the early 1970s when Richard Nixon finally cracked down harshly on Japanese textile exports to the United States, Japanese consumer-electronics companies had already established a solid beachhead in the United States and in certain product lines were well on their way to dominance of the American market.

The same story was repeated—but with important variations—a few years later when American television makers successfully prodded the Federal Government into various actions to inhibit U.S. imports of TV sets. This time the Japanese anticipated the protectionist drive and were at least partially braced for it. When the crackdown came, Japan's TV manufacturers had already moved a significant share of their production for the U.S. market into American factories. Perhaps even more important in its long-run implications, however, was the fact that companies such as Sony and Matsushita had consciously begun to focus on the development of products like videocassette recorders that did not yet exist in the United States and whose importation as a result could not—at least initially—be legitimately protested by American electronics firms.

Thanks to these measures, Japan's consumer-electronics industry proved considerably less vulnerable to American exclusionism than its textile industry had. And meantime, to make things even worse from the American point of view, the Japanese had opened up two more fronts in their economic invasion of the United States. In the 1960s, MITI had adopted as its central theme the dictum "Steel is the nation"—and once again private industry enthusiastically rose to the challenge, investing huge sums in advanced production technology and in the acquisition of assured supplies of coal and iron ore in Australia and elsewhere. This, in due course, made it possible for Japanese plants to produce steel far more cheaply than American mills could. And that, in turn, facilitated penetration of the United States by Japanese automakers—although the success of that effort was above all due to the unpredictable energy crisis of the 1970s and the concentration of the Japanese upon supplying high-quality vehicles to a segment of the U.S. market that Detroit's Big Three had traditionally regarded as too small and unprofitable to be worthy of their attention.

Each of these successive Japanese assaults came as a bewildering surprise to an America that had grown comfortably accustomed to enjoying universally acknowledged primacy in technology and manufacturing techniques. The notion that the Japanese might one day set the pace in the television industry, for example, was all but unthinkable as late as the mid-1960s, when a single American company—Corning Glass Works—still produced so large a percentage of all the color TV tubes used in the United States that its executives were loath to discuss the matter publicly for fear of stirring up the trustbusters. So great was U.S. complacency, in fact, that the lessons of the '60s and '70s did not fully sink in until the Japanese-auto invasion peaked at the beginning of the '80s. At that point, substantial numbers of Americans came to realize that up until then they had been largely engaged in locking barn doors after stolen horses and began to pay serious attention to what the Japanese might be planning next. Suddenly, as if on cue, the American media were awash in dramatic forecasts of a looming shoot-out between Japan and the United States in the technologies that were clearly going to reshape the economic life of advanced nations in the waning years of the twentieth century—such things as robotics, computer science, new systems of communication and bioengineering.

Even in this case, however, the American response was somewhat belated. Though MITI did not formally arrive at its famous judgment that "Information is the future" until the late 1970s, it had been putting seed money into many of the new technologies long before that. And far greater sums had been poured into them by Japan's private companies—not so much at MITI's behest as because of their own perceptions of the long-term future. In characteristic Japanese fashion, moreover, much of the development effort by private industry involved what has been described as "patient money." In 1981, Koji Kobayashi of the Nippon Electric Company admitted to me that although his firm had started making semiconductors in the late 1950s, it was only in the early 1970s, after thirteen long years of heavy investment in plant and equipment, that NEC's semiconductor division finally began to show a profit. "In business," Dr. Kobayashi added laconically, "you have to look ahead."

By the time MITI got around to proclaiming the new technologies to be the centerpiece of Japanese economic development, in fact, it had long been apparent to anyone who really was looking ahead that the "information revolution" was likely to rival the original Industrial Revolution in its consequences. What was far less apparent was just how the various arcane technologies involved in that revolution would interact with each other and with traditional economic forces. Partly for that reason it was hard to be sure which of the non-Communist world's two economic superpowers—the United States or Japan—would be more successful in capitalizing upon the opportunities presented by the rapidly changing nature of industrial society.

As of the early 1980s, the United States clearly held the lead in most of the newer areas of high technology—but by no means in all. In robotics, in fact, the palm went to Japan, not so much for its technology, a great deal of which had originally been developed in the United States, as for the speed and decisiveness with which the Japanese had put that technology to use. By 1982, according to Paul Aron, the president of the U.S. branch of Japan's Daiwa Securities Company, there were nearly three times as many advanced reprogrammable robots at work in Japan as in the United States—and Aron fully expected that gap to widen in the years immediately ahead. One reason for his prediction was that while there were only twenty companies manufacturing robots in the United States, there were more than six times that number in Japan—including one that had successfully programmed robots to make other robots. And working against rapid growth of the robot industry in the United States was the attitude of American labor unions: in the best Luddite tradition, they tended to see robots primarily as unwelcome competitors for jobs previously performed by humans.

Robotics, however, is not a technology that stands alone: advanced robots are computer-operated. And in the computer field in general Japan still had a long way to go before catching up with the United States. Though Japanese manufacturers were capable of producing computer frames as good as any made in the United States and were increasing their exports at the rate of 20 to 25 percent a year, the Japanese in 1982 held only 10 percent of the world market in computers; by contrast, IBM alone accounted for an estimated 50 percent of worldwide computer sales that year.

In great part, this enormous disparity reflects the fact that the Americans have been in the computer business in a major way much longer than the Japanese. But it is also widely attributed to the less advanced state of Japanese software, the electronic instructions that tell computers what to do. This deficiency, some U.S. experts argue, basically reflects the cultural differences between Japanese and Westerners; in a sense, Japanese computers "think" differently from American ones and hence are less well adapted to the demands of Western users. But since the Japanese have successfully designed so many other products for Western markets, it seems highly unlikely that they cannot eventually do the same thing with computer software. Moreover, there is at least a possibility that the MITI-organized consortium that is seeking to develop a new generation of computers with something more closely approaching human intelligence may largely eliminate the software problem. "Our ideal," declares Kazuhiro Fuchi of MITI's Electro-Technical Laboratories, "is to create a computer that programs itself."

That the Japanese will ultimately solve the software problem one way or another seems all the more likely in view of their stunning success with semiconductors, the tiny silicon "memory chips" that are the basic building blocks for computers. American companies did the pioneering work in semiconductor development and in the late 1970s still seemed to hold an unshakable lead in the field. But by investing far more heavily in automated production facilities than the Americans were willing to do, Japanese semiconductor manufacturers finally achieved a level of reliability in their chips that their U.S. rivals could not match. As a result, by 1982 the Japanese had captured so large a share of the U.S. market for semiconductors that the Reagan Administration had begun to consider throwing up barriers against the Japanese imports. By then, however, the Japanese were on the verge of pulling off a feat that seemed likely to prolong their dominance of the semiconductor field regardless of what the U.S. Government did: they had moved close to commercial production of a chip vastly more potent than any previously in use—one that could store more than a million bits of information on a piece of silicon the size of a human fingernail.

Weighing all these pluses and minuses, one American engineer familiar with the Japanese computer industry told me in 1980 that he saw no inherent reason why it should not achieve the target MITI had set for it: control of 30 percent of the world computer market by 1990. And to achieve this goal, the Japanese have developed what seems an eminently realistic strategy: to focus initially on the less advanced nations close to home and then spread out. "We have just started to supply systems to Southeast Asian markets," said the managing director of Hitachi, Japan's biggest computer maker, in 1982. "After we acquire the knowledge in nearby markets, we will move elsewhere—step by step."

Far from being an isolated case, moreover, the Japanese drive to overtake the United States in the computer field is symptomatic of what is occurring all across the spectrum of high technology. In advanced communications systems involving the use of fiber optics and lasers, Japanese firms are forging rapidly ahead, and in satellite communications they are already firmly established: nearly half of all the earth stations in use around the world in 1982 were built or partially equipped by the Nippon Electric Company. In genetic engineering, according to knowledgeable Japanese and Americans alike, the U.S. lead was cut from ten years to less than three years between 1980 and 1982 alone. And in one area of technology in which Ronald Reagan's America shows diminished interest, the Japanese continue to push vigorously ahead: all told, Japan is investing some $2.5 billion a year in research into energy conservation and the development of alternative energy sources, most particularly nuclear power. And because of the Japanese vulnerability complex, the widespread opposition to nuclear power that exists in the United States has no parallel in Japan. "All of us—or at least the great majority of us—know that we cannot afford to remain totally dependent on imported oil," a young Japanese woman remarked to me as we threaded our way through the huge crowd that had assembled for a ban-the-bomb rally in Tokyo in the spring of 1982.

Undeniably, then, the progress that Japan has made in high technology in the last three decades has been little short of awesome, and it has been growing more so with each passing year. But even yet, a great many Americans appear confident that the United States will retain its economic and technological superiority over Japan indefinitely. Insofar as it reflects anything more than cultural lag, this belief most often seems to rest on the proposition put to me one night by an Englishman long resident in Japan. "The Japanese," he said flatly, "can't innovate. They're marvellous at adapting, manufacturing and marketing, but they just can't innovate."

The first answer to that, of course, is that up until now the Japanese have seen no reason to go to the trouble of innovating; they've been able to acquire all the innovation they could use by the simple expedient of buying it. In the past thirty years, in fact, Japanese industry has spent more than $10 billion on purchases of foreign technology and in the process saved itself a great deal of time and waste motion.

Now, however, many observers, both foreign and Japanese, argue that this game has been largely played out. "Today the Japanese want to move faster than just borrowing technology allows," says Yale professor Hugh Patrick, a specialist in Japanese economic history and policy.

Whether innovation is quite as indispensable as Westerners would like to think, however, is open to argument. "The Japanese may prove incapable of inventing the next wave of new products, but it is not clear that they need to," Pieter Vander Werf of Cambridge, Massachusetts, wrote *The New York Times* some time ago. "It may be wrong to think that a country can prosper merely by being creative." In other words, as long as Japan retains the ability to make more effective practical use of Western scientific innovation than the West itself does, borrowing technology may remain a perfectly valid strategy for the Japanese.

In any case, the widely held belief that Japanese are inherently incapable of innovation is debatable. That assertion smacks of the kind of baseless ethnic arrogance that led Europeans in the 1950s to proclaim confidently that Egyptian technicians were so inept that they could never keep the Suez Canal functioning. And it also overlooks the fact that there are other kinds of innovation besides scientific innovation and that in some of these other areas the Japanese have shown themselves very innovative indeed.

"If technology is looked on as the ability to get good working products out of the factory door," U.S. computer entrepreneur Gene Amdahl once told a *Business Week* reporter, "I think the Japanese are taking over." When it comes to the art of making products more efficiently, in short, the Japanese have shown themselves masters of innovation. And when it comes to distributing what they make, they have undeniably been innovative in the central role they have given to *sogo sosha*, the giant trading companies that serve as universal go-betweens, dealing in thousands of different products and combining an extraordinary range of business functions: buying, selling, barter, transportation, market research, planning, financing, contracting and the creation of new ventures. An institution that has no real U.S. counterpart—for legal reasons among others—Japan's pervasive network of trading companies serves such a useful function that it has actually become a significant factor in America's own export trade.

Still, inventive as its businessmen have been in these respects, it is undeniably true that Japan has yet to originate "epochal" technologies—the kind that spawn whole new industries. And if the United States and Europe should falter in their development of epochal new technologies—as some Japanese executives believe they have already begun to do—the Japanese would have no choice but to rely on their own scientific resources. Keenly aware of that, both government and industry in Japan have in the last few years begun to earmark increasingly large amounts of money for research and development and to put new stress on inventiveness. "Creativity," writes Masanori Moritani, a senior researcher at the Nomura Research Institute, "is finally in demand."

To many foreigners, all this seems a foredoomed effort, barring radical changes in Japanese life. Such skeptics echo a question American scientist William Shockley tauntingly fired at a Japanese interviewer in 1965: "Do you really think you can establish a Western kind of science and technology on a base of Japanese culture and language?"

Not everybody would accept Shockley's assumption that to be valid, science and technology must be distinctively "Western." But even some Japanese believe that in order to produce any significant number of people capable of scientific innovation, Japan must restructure its educational system and some of its social institutions in such a way as to put more emphasis on individualism and less on deference to superiors and group opinion.

Whether anything so radical as a major revamping of Japanese educational and social institutions is either practical or necessary, however, seems to me highly doubtful. Instead, there would appear to be more promise in the essentially evolutionary approach advocated by Moritani in his book *Japanese Technology*. The centerpiece of the Japanese national research effort, he writes, should be "creativity based on the special characteristics of the Japanese people . . . Japan has long had a custom of incorporating the opinions of group members, particularly of younger members, and of permitting self-assertion so long as it does not disrupt group harmony. High technology development in Japan requires only that this additional self-assertion be given greater scope and that Japanese companies work actively to encourage it."

To Americans steeped in the lore of Thomas Edison and the supreme virtue of untrammeled individualism, Moritani's call for a delicately balanced marriage of self-assertion and group consciousness is apt to sound like a contradiction in terms—a feat impossible of achievement and unlikely, in any event, to produce true creativity. Such doubts cannot be dismissed out of hand; but it is worth bearing in mind that the complexity of contemporary technologies tends to make a collaborative approach to their problems especially fruitful—which may help to explain the fact that although it is in many respects a highly bureaucratic institution, New Jersey's Bell Laboratories is also perhaps the preeminent center of technological innovation in the United States today.

It is also worth bearing in mind that in every area except basic research, Japan's great corporations have already matched or outstripped most of their Western competitors without for a moment abandoning their addiction to group harmony and the consensual style. So while the day when Japan succeeds in developing an effective and uniquely Japanese approach to scientific innovation may not be immediately at hand, it would be foolhardy indeed to assume that it is too far off. For the claim that Moritani somewhat chauvinistically makes for Japan as a nation—that "it will take on any task and create anything necessity demands"—would seem, on the strength of its performance so far, to apply equally well to Japanese industry.

13

Mom, Pop and the Robots

In the heart of the bustling provincial town of Tsubame City, some 150 miles north of Tokyo, sits a handsome house of traditional Japanese architecture. Framed in timber and surmounted by a gracefully curved tiled roof, it is in sharp contrast to the dreary little commercial buildings that surround it, and though the fact is not apparent to the casual passerby, it is also uncommonly large, with a number of interior courtyards and outbuildings in the manner of an old-time compound in Peking.

This is the home of the Tamayama family—and also the site of the "factory" the Tamayamas have been operating for seven generations now. In a single large room housed in a separate structure toward the rear of the property, a score of craftsmen hunched on low benches painstakingly hammer intricate designs into copper pots and vessels. Because of the great amount of skill and handwork required to produce it, Tamayama copperware fetches high prices, but all the same, a city official estimates, it is doubtful that the factory's total sales exceed $500,000 a year.

To suggest that the Tamayama factory is a typical Japanese business would be absurd—but no more so than it would be to make the same statement about Toyota, Sony or Nippon Steel. In some important respects, in fact, the small workshop in Tsubame City is more characteristic of Japan's economic life than the huge and relentlessly efficient corporations that most Americans automatically think of when they hear the phrase "Japanese industry."

A few years ago in a meeting at New York's Lehrman Institute, a particularly outspoken MITI official named Masahisa Naitoh flatly declared that "taken as a whole, the Japanese economy is actually less efficient than that of the United States." Startling though it may sound, that statement is not hard to justify statistically. In certain key fields such as auto- and steelmaking, Japanese labor productivity is unsurpassed anywhere in the world. As of 1982, however, the productivity of American workers as a whole was still more than one and a half times that of Japanese workers.

The chief reason for this is that Japan is cursed or blessed, depending on one's point of view, with what the social scientists have christened a "dual economy." The great corporations most Westerners associate with Japan are only the tip of the Japanese economic iceberg; more than 70 percent of all Japanese industrial workers are employed by companies with fewer than 300 people on staff, and more than half of all Japanese manufacturing enterprises actually employ fewer than 5 people. All told, such small and medium-sized enterprises account for better than 50 percent of Japan's total industrial production.

In two other important areas of the Japanese economy, moreover, mini-sized enterprises are even more prevalent. Almost to a man, the more than 5 million farmers who still survive in Japan cultivate farms so small that they would barely be considered a decent-sized hayfield even in New England. And the outsized Japanese distribution system—with more than 2 million wholesalers and retailers, it is almost twice as large as that of the United States on a per capita basis—is characterized by myriad Mom-and-Pop stores.

It may be true that small is beautiful, but at least as far as the Japanese economy is concerned, it has historically tended to be painfully costly as well. Japanese farmers, for example, produce less than a quarter as much per man as American farm workers do, and in the retailing and service trades generally inefficient operation keeps Japanese prices unnecessarily high.

Even when smaller Japanese enterprises do achieve a high level of competitiveness—and in the manufacturing field many of them emphatically do—it is at a significant social cost. The employees of such firms, an abnormally high percentage of whom are women and older men, often have no formal job guarantees. (The much-vaunted institution of "lifetime employment," which is almost entirely restricted to major corporations, is probably enjoyed by no more than 30 percent of all Japanese workers.) Partly because they generally are not represented by a union, employees of smaller companies on average earn only about 70 percent of what their counterparts in big corporations are paid—and for the nearly 14 million Japanese who work for companies with fewer than 30 employees the figure drops to less than 60 percent. But despite the fact that they pay relatively low wages, and offer few if any fringe benefits such as pension plans, Japan's small companies expect and get long hours of work out of their employees; while the five-day week is now commonplace for workers—though not so much for executives—of Japan's major corporations, it is still a rarity among small firms. As of 1978, in fact, more than 97 percent of Japanese firms with fewer than 100 employees were still extracting five and a half days a week or more out of their staffs, and more than half were still on a six-day week.

Exploitative as all this sounds—and in many cases actually is—what might be called the traditional sector of the Japanese economy nonetheless cannot be written off as an unmitigated evil or an indefensible drag upon Japanese society. For one thing, it reflects in a number of ways, some of which are highly admirable, the attitudes and values which in less conspicuous forms also influence the great corporations that constitute the modern sector of the Japanese economy.

Except perhaps in their country's earliest history, the Japanese have until recently always lived in an economy of scarcity. This had a number of profound effects upon the Japanese psyche and Japanese behavior—one of them, I believe, being the fact that the goods produced in pre-modern Japan, even the most utilitarian of them, were characterized by high standards of workmanship and an elegant simplicity of design. Clearly, this was in part a matter of aesthetics—a manifestation of the same sensibility that gave birth to Zen Buddhism. But at least to some extent it was also a reflection of the fact that material goods and resources were very limited in supply and hence treated with respect.

Today, sadly, simplicity of design is far less prevalent than it used to be in Japan—though some of the most successful Japanese products still possess it. But the high standards of workmanship characteristic of pre-modern Japan are once again the norm. The "junk goods" that Japan produced in its pre-World War II factories—a historical aberration inspired by a developing nation's need to find a niche in foreign markets—have largely disappeared. Ironically, the once-despised label "Made in Japan" has become so synonymous with quality that Japanese industry nowadays must contend with its illicit use by shady operators in Taiwan and other Asian nations.

The long centuries of austerity that Japan experienced surely played a role too in the development of the famous Japanese addiction to work—an addiction dramatically illustrated by the fact that so many Japanese regularly fail to take all the vacation to which they are entitled. When Westerners call them "workaholics," Japanese recognize the word as a pejorative one and sometimes go to extreme lengths to rebut the charge. Thus, economist Masaru Yoshitomi of the Economic Planning Agency somewhat whimsically argues that a major reason Japanese work so hard is that they don't have anything better to do. "Anywhere you go to relax and enjoy yourself in this small country is bound to be congested," he said. "And if you don't have anything exciting to do on the weekend, why not work?"

While there may be a grain of truth in Yoshitomi's argument, it is clearly not a complete explanation—and neither is the suggestion that Japanese work hard primarily to acquire material possessions and a more lavish life-style. Those are things which many contemporary Japanese do in fact crave; yet as Thomas Pepper of the Hudson Institute has pointed out, Japanese also worked extremely hard in feudal times, when the material rewards for doing so were slight. In the end, one is driven back to the conventional explanation that Japan's rampant workaholism is a product of the deep desire of individual Japanese for group acceptance and approval. But it also seems probable that the group orientation of Japanese originated at least in part as an indispensable tool for survival in an environment that offered very limited economic opportunities.

The problem of survival in traditional Japan, however, was not only a matter of scarcity of resources; it was intensified by the frequency with which the Japanese islands are visited by natural disasters—earthquakes, tidal waves and typhoons. (Revealingly, our word "typhoon" comes from Japan; it is simply an English transliteration of *taifun*, the Japanese for "big wind.") Living as they did in an environment that was not only inherently poor but often physically hostile, it is scarcely surprising that the Japanese early on developed what Takeo Doi, Japan's leading psychiatrist, has described as a consciousness of helplessness. This state of mind, which approaches a national obsession, can also be described as a sense of vulnerability—a phrase that is probably more enlightening to non-Japanese. "Helplessness," after all, suggests passivity, but the built-in fear of the Japanese that disaster may be just around the corner actually leads them in many situations to behave more aggressively than they might otherwise.

In economic life, of course, one manifestation of this sense of vulnerability is the tendency of Japanese corporations, both small and large, to compete with great savagery. Far more than their U.S. counterparts, concedes MITI's Naitoh, "Japanese corporations feel a compulsion to maximize their share of expanding market opportunities through cutthroat competition. As a result, it is not uncommon to find selling prices for a particular product dropping below the average cost of production in the industry, with obvious severe consequences for the less efficient producers."

This intense competitiveness born of fear has also had obvious and severe consequences for Japan's relations with the rest of the world. The foundation stones of Japan's international economic success have been hard work, intelligent organization and the creation of excellent products, but just enough of that success has also rested on aggressive—and sometimes even predatory—practices to make it easy for foreigners to tell themselves that they have been victimized. In any case, when a citizen of the world's second-greatest economic power pleads that the need to import most of its raw materials renders his country dangerously vulnerable, Westerners are apt to point out that all nations are economically vulnerable nowadays—or more harshly yet, simply to snort in derision. The trouble is that the Japanese devoutly believes what he is saying.

The impact of the pervasive Japanese sense of vulnerability is all the greater because of a peculiar fact of Japanese history: unlike the United States and the nations of Western Europe, Japan moved almost directly from feudalism into the industrial age. As a consequence, attitudes and behavior patterns characteristic of the feudal society are still more prevalent in Japan than in the West. To any good Western liberal, this is apt to seem ipso facto deplorable, but in reality it has positive consequences as well as negative ones.

A case in point is provided by Japan's welfare system. In old Japan, as in other pre-industrial societies, the aged and incapacitated had to rely for support upon their families or, at best, upon a feudal patron. Today, that is no longer the case. The concept that the general society has a responsibility to care for the old and the unfortunate has been widely accepted in principle in Japan—and to a considerable degree in practice. Nonetheless, welfare responsibilities in Japan still have not been transferred to the government to the same degree as they have been in most Western societies, including even the most staunchly anti-Socialist ones.

Instead, a considerable portion of Japan's welfare burden is assumed by private industry. Through health-care or health-insurance programs, subsidized housing and unemployment insurance in the disguised form of lifetime employment, the big corporations that make up the modern sector of Japan's economy commonly assume functions more often discharged by the government in other industrialized countries. But important as it is, this private welfare system has severe limitations. The smaller companies that constitute the huge traditional sector of the economy simply cannot afford such paternalism. And even in major corporations, "lifetime" employment is not truly a lifetime affair for workers below the executive level; in general practice, they must retire at fifty-five or thereabouts.

This creates a serious problem for older Japanese—and one of growing national urgency, since the average age of the Japanese population is rapidly increasing. Most Japanese workers do not become eligible for the equivalent of Social Security until they are sixty, and to curb the increasingly heavy drains upon the national treasury imposed by the public pension system, the government now wants to up the minimum age to sixty-five. This means that there is a painful gap between the time the typical Japanese retires and the time he can start drawing a pension. And even when his pension payments do begin, they are generally inadequate: in 1979, a worker who retired from a $15,000-a-year job in Japan got a pension of only $4,800 per year. (In the United States, a worker in the same situation was entitled to almost $6,000 in Social Security benefits.)

One response to this problem is for a "retired" Japanese worker to go out and find another job, and a great many do so: close to half of all Japanese over sixty-five are still working, whereas only 25 percent of Americans sixty-five and older are still on the job. But such "retirement" jobs are often poorly paid, and in any case, many older Japanese are unable to find work. As a result, the vast majority of Japanese prepare for old age by squirreling away as much money as possible in their earlier years. "What it comes down to," says economist Masaru Yoshitomi, "is that in thirty years of working life, you have to provide for fifteen years of retirement."

Heartless as this system may seem, it has been of incalculable benefit to Japan in one respect. Between the need to amass a retirement nest egg, the anticipation of heavy educational expenses for his children and his deep-seated feeling that all good fortune is evanescent, the average Japanese puts about 20 percent of his disposable income each year into savings. This is the highest rate of personal savings in any major nation—roughly four times as large, for example, as the share of his income that the average American saves. As a result, Japan has an extraordinarily large pool of capital upon which it can draw to finance industrial growth and development.

Just as Japan's welfare system has both its good and bad sides, so does another legacy from feudal Japan. Where vested economic interests are concerned, whether of groups or of individuals, Japanese often display the kind of mutual protectiveness that was characteristic of medieval guildsmen. Long-standing personal and organizational relationships are taken far more seriously in Japan's business world than they are in U.S. business, and the notion of depriving anyone of his traditional means of making a living arouses much greater repugnance.

In terms of the overall Japanese economy, this has some serious disadvantages. In a number of fields, it has permitted the survival of inefficient institutions and the employment of considerable numbers of people in only marginally useful activities. This, in turn, often results in unnecessarily high prices to the consumer. The concept of the "just price," in fact, has never been strong in Japan; although they resist the kind of constant price increases imposed by U.S. supermarkets, Japanese for the most part seem resigned to being charged whatever the traffic will bear and accept high prices, once established, relatively uncomplainingly.

The quid pro quo for all this, while hard to quantify, is nonetheless of very great importance. For the reluctance to break anyone else's rice bowl serves to mitigate the otherwise fierce competitiveness of Japanese economic life. "Fortunately," says Masahisa Naitoh, "our competitiveness coexists with a willingness to work together in adjusting to change. To the Japanese way of thinking, it is acceptable and natural for companies to cooperate with each other in order to cope with common difficulties."

Though the psychic underpinnings of both the modern and the traditional sectors of the Japanese economy are in many respects identical, some of them are visible in purer forms in Japan's small enterprises than in its big ones. Beyond that, the individuals and institutions that make up Japan's traditional sector fulfill certain social and economic purposes not generally served by small enterprises in the United States. And in at least one key respect, a part of Japan's traditional sector is rapidly becoming very untraditional indeed; it is, in fact, in the forefront of economic change in Japan. For all these reasons, it is impossible to talk meaningfully about the contemporary Japanese economy without taking a close look at the three major subdivisions of its traditional sector—agriculture, the distributive trades and small-scale manufacturing.

Agriculture

For three generations, Yamahei Sato's family have farmed the same land in Niigata Prefecture, a predominantly rural area on the Sea of Japan. By local standards, that is not a particularly long time: Senzo Kihara, who lives a few miles from the Satos, matter-of-factly says that the land he works has been owned by members of his family for four hundred years "that we know of." Unlike the Kiharas, moreover, the Satos were originally tenant farmers; it was only when Douglas MacArthur imposed his land-reform program on Japan that they were able to buy the land they had tilled for so long.

A chunky, balding man of seventy-one, Yamahei Sato enjoys that greatest of all Japanese luxuries: elbow room. Incredibly in the eyes of any Tokyoite, his home, floored with rice-straw mats and pleasantly but sparsely furnished in the traditional Japanese manner, boasts a total of fourteen rooms. He needs all that space, he explains, because he and his wife have six children, and at holiday time it is not unusual for all of them, together with their husbands, wives and a total of twelve grandchildren, to descend upon the family homestead. Apart from the elder Satos, however, the only members of the clan who live on the farm the year around are their thirty-two-year-old-son, Komei, Komei's wife and two children, and the dog Kaoru, a plump little stray whom the children took in and named after the canine star of a TV show.

The average farm in Niigata runs to only about 4½ acres, and by that yardstick the Sato spread is a biggish one. Divided into three separate chunks, the most distant of which is about three-quarters of a mile from the house, it totals 5½ acres—about an acre and a half of which Sato rents from relatives who have given up farming. But even 5½ acres can't produce enough income to warrant much capital investment, so Sato and his neighbor across the street do their farming jointly. Between them they have eleven acres—which has made it economically feasible for them to take out government-subsidized loans from the local agricultural co-op and buy a wide range of machinery, including a tractor, a rice combine and an automatic transplanter. (This last device saves a lot of back-breaking labor every May when rice seedlings must be moved out to the paddy fields from the vinyl-covered hothouses in which they are started.)

Like most of his neighbors, Sato grows vegetables and soybeans for home consumption and a certain amount of barley as a cash crop. But the crop he cares most about is rice, and like everyone else in the area, he is quick to point out that Niigata rice is particularly tasty. (Most Americans would not find it so; Japanese like their rice glutinous and shun the long-grain varieties favored in the United States.) In a good year, Mr. Sato's fields produce about two tons of rice per acre—which is nothing outstanding for the Niigata area, but runs about 50 percent higher than the yield from the average U.S. rice field.

Compared with prewar Japanese farmers, Yamahei Sato lives very well indeed: he owns a car, and his income almost certainly tops the $20,000 that is about average for Niigata farmers. But he and his family could not live nearly so comfortably, and perhaps could not make it all, if they relied upon farming alone. So the Satos' daughter-in-law works full time in a nearby nursery, and Komei, though he pitches in with the farm work at planting and harvest time, is basically in the welding business; in a small shop behind the house he works as a subcontractor to a subcontractor for a manufacturer of agricultural machinery. And even the elder Satos have what Yamahei calls "our senior citizens' work": more than half their time the year around is spent in a corner of Komei's shop polishing and packaging stainless steel pots for a local manufacturer of housewares.

If he chose, Yamahei Sato could avoid having to work so hard: land in his part of Niigata currently fetches in the neighborhood of $100,000 an acre, which means that on paper he is worth $500,000 or so. But if he were to sell his farm, taxes would eat up a great deal of his profit—and anyway, what would he do with himself then?

Yamahei Sato is an atypical Japanese farmer, not only because he owns more land than most but also because of his readiness to share equipment and the use of his fields with his neighbor. For efficiency's sake, the Japanese Government has tried hard to promote such arrangements, but with the stubborn independence of peasants everywhere, the majority of Japanese farmers still prefer to remain the unquestioned lords of their own little plots of earth.

The fact that even Sato cannot live by farming alone, however, reflects an almost universal situation in rural Japan: only 13 percent of Japanese farm families still make their living entirely from the land. More than 70 percent of them, in fact, now earn more of their income from outside work than from such farming as they do. The great majority of Japanese farmers, in other words, are really only farmers on the side.

Even so, it still takes massive government intervention to keep Japan's agricultural population economically afloat. Left to themselves, Japanese farmers are simply not competitive in international terms. Even though Japan's overall agricultural output is far smaller than that of the United States, there are more than twice as many farm workers in Japan as there are in America. For this and other reasons, including extremely intensive use of fertilizer, agricultural production costs in Japan are inordinately high. To produce a ton of rice in the United States, for example, costs $420; in Japan, the figure is $1,200.

Theoretically, this problem could be at least partially cured if the innumerable mini-farms created by MacArthur's land reform were merged into larger and more efficient units. Politically, however, that is out of the question, so as a poor second best, the Japanese Government subsidizes the bulk of the nation's agriculture. The entire rice crop each year, to take the most egregious case, is purchased by the government at a figure well above the world price and then resold to consumers at a loss. And where there are no direct subsidies, there are sometimes indirect ones: Japan's cattle raisers, who are second only to rice farmers in the dollar value of their production, are protected by import quotas on foreign beef, and tangerine growers are similarly insulated from competition from citrus fruit produced abroad.

The burden that all this imposes on Japanese society is great. Direct subsidies to agriculture have been estimated to run as high as $20 billion—which in 1982 amounted to nearly 30 percent of the Japanese Government's budget deficit. And that is only the beginning of the story: the high prices paid for food by Japanese consumers add incalculably to the cost of keeping Japanese agriculture alive. Even the prices of such staples as rice and bread in Japan regularly run two to three times the world average. As a result, food purchases accounted for 32 percent of all consumer expenditure in Japan in 1980; in the United States the comparable figure was only 17 percent.

In recent years, some headway has been made in combating the worst excesses of Japan's wasteful agricultural establishment. To ease the enormous financial strain of the rice subsidy, the government has been enforcing reductions in the amount of land devoted to rice production. Under heavy pressure from the United States, import quotas on beef and citrus fruits have also been eased and seem certain in due course to be eased still more.

Such efforts, however, have run into strong resistance at almost every turn. Despite the fact that they make up so small a share of the Japanese population, Japan's farmers have great political clout: because Japan's current electoral districts were established more than thirty-five years ago when the farm population was much larger than it is now, rural areas were heavily overrepresented in the Diet. This, of course, gives special weight to the farmers' opposition to liberalization of agricultural imports—which not only is implacable but sometimes borders on the irrational. When I visited him in 1982, Senzo Kihara, the Niigata farmer whose family has been tilling the same land for four centuries, argued that it would be highly dangerous to permit imports of U.S. rice, even though most Japanese won't eat it. Brandishing a bottle of California sake—which he rather unhappily admitted to be of excellent quality—he explained that Japanese sake brewers use a lot of rice and that in a free market they might well find California rice cheaper than the homegrown variety and just as well suited to their needs.

Despite their disproportionate political influence, the farmers by themselves might not have been able to stave off free trade in food for so long. But because of the national vulnerability complex, they have found many allies in the nonfarm population. Although it produced 90 percent of its food requirements in 1960, Japan today is only about 70 percent self-sufficient. That is one of the lowest ratios for any major nation and clearly means that any major interruption in food supplies from abroad would be highly painful for Japan.

A growing number of Japanese, mostly in the bureaucracy and in the modern sector of the economy, accept this as inevitable and regard the dream of agricultural self-sufficiency for Japan as an archaic survival. Isao Nakauchi, Japan's biggest supermarket operator, even goes so far as to call it "ridiculous." And so it is—not just because all developed nations now are vitally dependent upon imports of one kind or another but because anything approaching genuine self-sufficiency in food is unattainable for Japan without radical changes in its society and living standards. Indeed, even the 70-percent self-sufficiency level officially claimed by Japan is illusory, since without imported animal feed and fertilizer made from imported petroleum the country's present levels of beef and grain production would instantly start to plummet.

Such arguments, however, still do not carry much weight with the mass of Japanese. Remarkably, the gradual progress Japan is making toward more rational agricultural policies has essentially come in response to American insistence rather than to any pressure from the long-suffering Japanese consumer. By American standards, Japanese consumer organizations are extremely restrained in their demands even in their most aggressive moments, and when it comes to high food prices they have virtually leaned over backward.

On a conscious level, this is primarily because of a widespread fear that foreign food suppliers might for their own purposes arbitrarily cut off shipments to Japan—a fear powerfully reinforced by Richard Nixon back in the early 1970s when, in response to a temporary shortage in the United States, he abruptly suspended U.S. soybean exports to Japan. Though the ban was short-lived, its memory lingers on. "We cannot deposit our lives with the United States just because her food is cheaper," declared Naokazu Takeuchi of the Japan Federation of Consumers in May 1982. "Even if we have to pay high prices for self-sufficiency, we will have to bear it."

In less conscious fashion, two other factors help explain the acquiescence of so much of Japan's urban population to the coddling of the country's farmers. One of these is that some of the items whose high prices most outrage foreign visitors to Japan—steak and oranges, for example—are not part of the everyday diet of most Japanese and, as occasional luxuries occupying something of the role that lobster might in a middle-class U.S. household, are expected to be costly.

Probably even more important—although impossible to measure statistically—is the sentimental and increasingly unrealistic belief of many Japanese city-dwellers that farmers lead a hard life and so deserve special consideration. "You have to remember that a very large proportion of middle-aged Japanese originally came from the country themselves," says Mark Popiel of Dodwell, an English trading company that has been operating in Japan for more than a century. "Inevitably, such people have retained something of the farmer's mentality." Presumably, too, they retain conceptions of farm life shaped in the days when rice seedlings were transplanted not by machine but by backbreaking human labor and when the possibility that a farmer might become prosperous enough to own a color TV or even an automobile seemed as remote as the prospect of a Martian invasion.

| Distribution |

A slim, handsome man in his early thirties with a perennial expression of faint surprise, Ken Shioya is the heir apparent to a liquor store in the city of Niigata. The Shioya store, which was started by Ken's grandfather and is now owned by his father, has always been in the same part of Niigata's Furumachi district—although, as Ken notes, somewhat amused by his own precision, city authorities lost track of exact property boundaries after a great fire destroyed much of downtown Niigata in 1957, "so we may have moved four or five yards in one direction or another at that time."

While it is very small—not more than 15 feet wide and 20 feet deep—the Shioyas' shop has an uncluttered contemporary air, largely because its stock is beautifully organized. Its display racks include not only sake, beer and a full range of Japanese spirits but a considerable array of imported items as well: Scotch, English gin, French brandy and even some European wines. (Japanese wine, though it does exist, is for the most part indifferent stuff.) Ken confesses, however, that the Shioyas don't sell any great amount of the more expensive foreign brands, except at holiday times when people buy them as gifts for their friends. And when it comes to the less prestigious imports such as run-of-the-mill Scotches, most of the Shioyas' customers prefer to spend their money on Japan's own Suntory Reserve or Suntory Old—the latter of which, somewhat incredibly, is now the single largest-selling brand of whiskey in the world.

To some extent, Ken Shioya blames the lack of enthusiasm for the more modestly priced Scotches on Japan's supermarkets, which by selling such brands at a discount have deprived them of some of their status value and thus made them less attractive as gifts. In general, Ken adds laconically, the advent of supermarkets in the Niigata area "hasn't helped" his business. "We can always tell when they are having sales," he says, "because then our trade falls off some."

But Ken isn't really too worried about losing the loyalty of his customers because of the extra convenience he offers them. Whereas the big stores close at 6 P.M., the Shioyas always stay open till eight and sometimes until nine. And while they call Sundays their day off, the Shioyas stay open the last Sunday of every month, and they remain open seven days a week in July and August, when it's festival season and the gift-shopping is heavy.

That schedule isn't quite as punishing as it first sounds, however.

All told, there are five people who take turns tending counter in the shop—Ken, his wife, his parents and his younger sister. And nobody has to waste time commuting: everybody in the family, including Ken's young children, lives above the store.

Even upon casual acquaintance, it is clear that Ken Shioya is a person with an active mind and considerable intelligence. Because of that, some of his attitudes would come as a surprise to most Americans of similar caliber: he has no apparent desire to be anything more than a small shopkeeper and no visible disposition to experiment with new ways of doing business. Most of the seven wholesalers with whom the Shioyas deal they have been doing business with for years, and Ken takes it for granted that there should be two levels of wholesaler between him and the original importers of the Scotch that he sells. On one point, however, Ken shows no passivity at all: the liquor vending machines permitted in Japanese cities, he explains, are equipped with timers which are supposed to ensure that they operate for only a certain number of hours a day. Sometimes, however, unscrupulous vending-machine operators try to cheat the law by disconnecting the timers. To prevent such unfair competition, says Ken Shioya firmly, he and other liquor-store owners regularly patrol the machines in their areas.

There are hundreds of thousands of Ken Shioyas in Japan—not to speak of hundreds of thousands of other shopkeepers whose stores are even smaller, less well stocked and less up-to-date than his. All told, according to a study made by the business-research division of Dodwell, Japan has 1,673,000 retailers—which is only 10 percent fewer than the United States has to serve a population twice as large. "At a lot of these shops," says Dodwell's Mark Popiel, "the entire staff consists of Mom and Dad, and there aren't any storage facilities at all. What you see on the shelves is their total stock. Quite often, in fact, they just put the stuff out in front of the shop in the daytime and pull it in at night. In many cases, just as is true of farmers, the market value of their little piece of real estate is probably enormous nowadays, but they're not interested in that. All they're interested in is making a living and having something to do. Their shop is their life."

One of the rewards of that life is the psychic comfort Japan's shopkeepers find in the personal relationships they build up with their wholesalers over the years. "Historically," says Saburo Okita, a leading economist and onetime Foreign Minister of Japan, "our distribution system is based on intermediaries—as many intermediaries as possible." By Dodwell's reckoning, there are nearly 369,000 wholesalers operating in today's Japan, nearly as many as there are in the whole of the United States. What this means, among other things, is that each retail sale made in Japan is preceded by more than twice as many wholesale transactions as is customary in America.

The inevitable upshot of Japan's swollen wholesale establishment is swollen prices. It is by no means unusual to find Japanese products on sale in Los Angeles for less than they cost in Tokyo simply because the markups involved in moving an item across the Pacific and through U.S. customs are smaller than those involved in moving it a few miles through Japan's mind-boggling network of domestic wholesalers.

Unfortunately too, the peculiar nature of the Japanese distribution system helps make it uncommonly hard for foreign manufacturers to sell their goods in Japan and thereby embitters Japan's relations with its major trading partners. Part of the problem here is that both in business and in government there are still many Japanese who are simply not prepared to see a foreign product take over a major share of the Japanese market and actively seek to prevent that from happening. Another major source of difficulty is that a great many foreign firms, out of either ignorance or indignation, fail to master the intricacies of the Japanese distribution system and, as a result, approach it in a manner that ensures their failure to penetrate it effectively.

It would be simplistic, however, to place all the blame in this situation upon either foreign manufacturers or Japanese wholesalers. The fact is, as Ken Shioya suggested, that most consumers in Japan instinctively follow a kind of modified "buy Japanese" policy; for all their addiction to Western-style products, Japanese tend to purchase goods that have actually been manufactured abroad only when they are primarily concerned with status value.

Because of this attitude, foreign companies that aspire to sell any large volume of goods in Japan quite frequently find themselves ensnared in a Japanese version of Catch-22. Since consumer buying patterns have taught them to regard most imported products as small-volume items, Japanese wholesalers tend to mark them up extremely heavily—thereby helping to ensure that they will in fact remain small-volume items.

To regard all this as immutable, however, would be a great mistake: Japanese retailing practices in particular are in a state of flux—the most visible symbol of change being supermarket operator Isao Nakauchi, whose Daiei chain now includes some 170 stores scattered all across Japan. A brash and disturbingly outspoken man by Japanese standards, the sixty-year-old Nakauchi bypasses the traditional wholesaling network wherever possible and buys a great deal of what he sells from foreign suppliers. By such means and by the use of U.S. supermarket devices such as private labels and generic brands, he keeps his prices well below those of the Mom-and-Pop shops; his markup on food, he says, averages 12 percent, as opposed to 25 percent in most smaller stores.

All this has made Daiei, which began with a single store in 1857, far and away Japan's single biggest retail business. (It captured that title from the three-hundred-year-old Mitsukoshi department-store chain more than a decade ago.) Even in socially conservative farming communities, most women now confess to doing at least some of their shopping at the local supermarket. And in major cities super-markets have become so much of a fixture that a few years ago a Tokyo primary-school teacher reported he could no longer reliably test his students' general intelligence by asking them where one should go to buy various items such as meat, vegetables and toothpaste. Instead of giving the traditional answers—the butcher's, the greengrocer's and the pharmacy—some kids now answered all such questions with one phrase: "the supermarket."

For the foreseeable future, though, it is highly unlikely that the rise of supermarkets, discount stores and the like will revolutionize Japanese retailing to the same degree or even in exactly the same ways that it has affected retailing in the United States. For one thing, Japanese retailers operate under certain inherent limitations that their American counterparts don't—such as the fact that shop-ping by car is less practicable in Japan's constricted cities than in most U.S. communities. "You can't use a ten-ton truck to deliver goods to a store on a narrow alley," Nakauchi points out. "And we have to build stores in places like that to get to our customers."

Reinforcing these inherent limitations are some artificially imposed ones. Since the mid-1970s, the Japanese Government by a variety of devices has restricted the number of supermarkets that can be built in a given area as well as the size of those that do get built. To some extent, such restrictions simply reflect the massive voting power of Japan's small retailers; local merchants' associations, in fact, are actually given formal veto power over the construction in their areas of stores above a certain size. But just as important is the Japanese bureaucracy's fear that without government interven-tion the pace of change in the distributive and retail trades would become socially disruptive. "We can't just let all these small stores be wiped out at once," argues the Economic Planning Agency's Yoshitomi.

In an attempt to reconcile this interventionist attitude with the general free-market philosophy that his government professes, Yoshitomi also claims, however, that Japan's existing distribution system largely reflects public demand. "Our consumers' tastes remain so finicky," he says, "that retailers have to specialize." There's at least some truth to that; Japanese, for instance, insist upon—and get—fruit and vegetables in their stores of markedly higher quality than is generally available in the United States. It is also true that the average Japanese home has far less storage space for food than an American home and that shopping affords young mothers in Japan one of their rare chances to get out of the house. As a result, most Japanese women still do their food shopping in daily dribs and drabs—which makes it more feasible to patronize local specialty shops.

But beyond all this, Japan's myriad wholesale and retail establishments are widely perceived to serve an important social function. The fact that unemployment consistently remains so low in Japan—as of 1982, it amounted to only a little over 2 percent of the work force—is recognized to be due in large part to the extremely large number of people engaged in marketing the nation's goods. Many of these people are obviously underemployed by rational economic standards, and a number exist in something close to a state of disguised unemployment. But at least they enjoy the self-respect that comes from holding a job, however nominal; and no less important in the Japanese scheme of things, they are not a charge on the state. In short, as Isao Nakauchi likes to point out, his country's traditional wholesaling and retailing industries constitute, along with farming, "part of the Japanese-style welfare system."

Manufacturing

Toshio Iguchi, a compact, square-faced man of thirty-one, is in many ways the kind of "modern" Japanese husband featured in TV commercials for barbecue grills and the like. He and his wife have the ideal Japanese family in terms of size and sex—one girl, one boy—and live in solid middle-class comfort on the outskirts of Tokyo in a pleasant house graced with a handsome rock garden. There are, in fact, only two respects in which the Iguchis' life-style departs a bit from the norm: their yard is an unusually large one, and unlike the majority of Tokyoites, Toshio doesn't commute to work.

Both these circumstances stem from the fact that Toshio is his own boss. Under the corporate name of Iguchi Seisakujo, he is a subcontractor for a company that manufactures toy watches for children. His "factory"—which is actually a large metal shed set in one corner of his yard—consists basically of three injection-molding machines with which he produces plastic parts for the kiddie watches.

At one time, Toshio employed four workers to tend his molding machine. This, he confessed to *New York Times* correspondent Henry Scott Stokes, wasn't a totally satisfactory arrangement, since he could never be sure that his workers would actually show up when they were supposed to. Nevertheless, it was a real blow when the oldest of the four—and the only skilled hand among them—was lured away by another company in the same business. Then, to make matters worse, Toshio's younger employees began drifting off to better jobs in offices and coffee bars, and by the spring of 1980 he was left with no workers at all.

At one time that probably would have been the end of Iguchi Seisakujo. But no longer. To solve his problem, Toshio turned to Japan's newest labor pool: robots. In the rapidly developing technology that the Japanese have christened "mechatronics"—a word coined to describe the marriage of electronics and mechanical engineering—the robots that Toshio acquired to run his molding machines represented a rather primitive stage. Unlike the most advanced robots, which are controlled by computer tapes, Toshio's are operated by a fixed sequence of electrical switches and hence cannot easily be "reprogrammed." Even these relatively simple machines carry a price tag too steep for a company with a total capitalization of less than $40,000. Fortunately, however, Toshio was able to lease the equipment he needed from a company named Japan Robot Lease—and to do so at a cost that represented only a fraction of the wages he used to pay his human workers.

Becoming a one-man band has simplified Toshio Iguchi's life considerably. All he has to do these days is keep the molding machines fed with plastic, collect the parts the robots make and package them for shipment to the assembly plant. He no longer has to worry about absenteeism and keeping track of wages, the robots never make mistakes and, because his costs are lower, his company is more competitive. "This," he says, "is certainly the most effective way to deal with the present labor situation."

But expensive and unreliable as his human workers were, Toshio has to admit that he misses their companionship—and the fact that he can now spend more time than he used to with his family somehow doesn't totally fill that void. So just to have other men to talk to, he has taken to playing golf quite a lot.

Inevitably, the hundreds and thousands of small and medium-sized manufacturing companies scattered around Japan differ vastly in what they make and how they make it. Perhaps 10 percent of them are still engaged, like the Tamayama copperware shop in Tsubame City, in the hand production of traditional goods ranging from rice paper to porcelains. At the other end of the scale are firms such as the Mitsumi Electric Company near Tokyo, which uses high-precision equipment to turn out extremely sophisticated integrated circuits.

Whatever they make, however, Japan's small manufacturing enterprises tend to be family businesses or firms controlled by a single man. And the majority of them—an estimated 60 percent—do not make finished consumer products but, like Toshio Iguchi, are subcontractors, who manufacture parts that are subsequently assembled by larger firms. Like the Japanese distribution system, manufacturing in Japan is often a highly complex affair involving many invisible hands: an item that bears a famous brand name is very apt to be in reality the composite product of layer upon layer of subcontractors.

In many cases, these small subcontractors sell all or virtually all of their output to a single bigger company and, in effect, become a part of its industrial "group." For the subcontractor this has the advantage that it eliminates the expense and uncertainties of marketing. But it also leaves him little alternative but to comply when his sole customer presses him to cut the price and improve the quality of his product. "This isn't a matter of give-and-take," says Dodwell's Mark Popiel. "The big company simply sets the terms. It pays the subcontractor a price just high enough to enable him to survive if he cuts costs to the bone. A big company won't push one of its subcontractors over the edge if it can help it—but it will push him right to it."

For the great Japanese corporations that have flooded the world with their exports this arrangement constitutes an invaluable economic cushion—and one of which they take maximum advantage. Where Ford and General Motors, for example, produce about two-thirds of what goes into their cars themselves and rely on subcontractors only for the remaining third, Toyota and Nissan operate on exactly the reverse ratio.

In a variety of ways, this heavy reliance on subcontractors helps Japan's industrial giants to keep their costs in check. To begin with, it permits them to operate with far smaller parts inventories than most major U.S. corporations. This, in turn, means that they don't have to tie up as much capital in warehouses and real estate or pay the wages of as many stock clerks and transport personnel. Instead, these functions are in large part farmed out to smaller firms that can perform them more cheaply.

In general, in fact, the subcontracting system allows a major Japanese company to operate with minimal staff of its own and to get much of the work that goes into its finished products performed by relatively low-cost outside labor. For unlike the country's big corporations, Japan's small subcontractors do not seek to attract the cream of the work force through guarantees of lifetime employment and other expensive benefits. Rather, they tap the lower levels of the national labor pool, often relying heavily on so-called part-time workers. (Somewhat confusingly, hundreds of thousands of the latter are what is known as "full-time part-timers"—people who actually work an eight-hour day five or six days a week, but who are less well paid than they would be if they were technically classified as full-time employees.)

Still another advantage of the subcontracting system from the point of view of Japan's big corporations is that in times of trouble it provides them with a built-in—and to them, more or less painless—cost-reduction mechanism. "When a recession strikes or the competition gets really tough," says Mark Popiel, "the first thing a big corporation in this country does is put the squeeze on its subcontractors." Simply by decreeing a reduction in the prices it will pay its captive suppliers for parts and services, the big corporation can instantly chop its costs without inflicting morale-destroying wage cuts on its own personnel.

This system makes it possible for Japanese companies to respond quickly to changes in the economic climate and at the same time serves to inhibit the kind of suicidal wage inflation that has sapped the competitiveness of so many U.S. industries. Perhaps equally important, extensive use of subcontractors and the disproportionate number of small manufacturing firms in Japan have helped the Japanese escape some of the rigidities that tend to characterize big business elsewhere in the world. With no hint of complaint, Masato

Tsuru, managing director of Nippon Oil Seal, one of Japan's biggest subcontracting firms, pointed out to me that a big manufacturer can often exact improvements in product quality more easily from an outside supplier than from his own employees. Similarly, when the demands of the market dictate a change in product design, it is often easier to turn around a number of small firms than a single big one with its elaborate managerial hierarchy. And of necessity, small firms are more prepared than huge ones to gamble their entire existence on a product that may or may not prove successful.

Often enough, of course, such gambles fail. In 1981, in fact, more than 17,600 Japanese companies with total liabilities of nearly $12 billion went bankrupt. From an economist's point of view, that was not necessarily cause for unalloyed sorrow: in theory, as MITI's Masahisa Naitoh notes, it is almost as important for "senescent" or uneconomic industries to die as for promising new ones to be born. But however desirable that process may be in overall economic terms, the death of an industrial giant inevitably causes great social disruption. Here again, Japan is well served by its abundance of small enterprises: it is they rather than the country's major enterprises that do virtually all the dying—a fact which considerably mitigates the social costs involved.

In human terms, the environment in which Japan's small manufacturers and their employees exist is a difficult one at best, and not infrequently downright harsh. Without disputing that, many Japanese will nonetheless argue that it has played a key role in their country's emergence as an economic superpower. "It provides a sort of vitality that we must retain in order to keep our country competitive," insists Masaru Yoshitomi. And the most enterprising of Japan's small manufacturers now quite clearly constitute the vanguard of a revolution that seems likely to infuse even greater vitality into the Japanese industrial structure.

Though never so heavily overmanned as the country's farms and distribution system, Japan's small manufacturing enterprises have also in a sense been part of the informal welfare system. Specifically, they have served as a source of employment for the nation's less desirable workers, those who because of age, lack of education or some other handicap—such as simply being married and female—could not find a place in a big company. To some extent, this is still true, but it is becoming less and less true every day. At a very rapid pace, Japan's small factories are radically changing their labor patterns.

Two factors—one economic and the other primarily social—have conspired to produce this change. The relentless pressure big corporations have put upon their subcontractors to reduce costs and simultaneously improve the quality and reliability of their goods has necessarily driven the smaller companies to seek greater worker productivity. And this, quite clearly, is a goal most likely to be achieved through the use of energetic and relatively well-educated workers—which is to say young people with high school diplomas.

But even as the demand for productive young workers has mounted, Japan's birthrate has been falling: where the average Japanese woman in the 1960s had 2.1 children, today she has only 1.7. As a result, the percentage of young people in the overall Japanese population is steadily diminishing. Inevitably, this has increased the competition for their services and made them less willing to accept the inferior wages and working conditions that generally prevail in small companies.

The upshot of all this has been that in recent years more and more of Japan's small manufacturers began to face the same problem that Toshio Iguchi did: an intractable shortage of effective and affordable workers. But at this point, characteristically, the Japanese Government stepped into the picture. With a little courteous arm-twisting here and there, Tokyo's mandarins persuaded nearly three dozen of Japan's burgeoning robot manufacturers to set up a joint company to lease their products. For the robot makers this had the advantage that it significantly expanded their potential market. Even more important for the overall economy, however, it enabled a small manufacturer who could not afford to buy, say, a $45,000 robot outright to lease one for as little as $750 a month. What's more, it gave him the assurance that he could freely trade his robots in for new and improved models as they came along.

With the way thus paved, throngs of small Japanese entrepreneurs like Toshio Iguchi have now switched—at least in part—from human labor to robots. While Americans still tend to think of robots as complex devices suitable only for giant operations like an automobile assembly line, it has now become routine for small Japanese firms to use them for such tasks as welding, spray painting and metal grinding. As of 1980, an estimated 41 percent of all Japanese companies with between 30 and 100 employees were already employing at least some robots, and that figure seems certain to snowball as companies that have not yet "robotized" begin to find themselves unable to compete with those that have. Though he laughed as he said it, Masaru Yoshitomi clearly was not joking when, in the spring of 1982, he suggested to me that in the typical Japanese family enterprise of the future, Mom will keep the books, Pop will tend the robots and Junior will do the programming for them.

Besides manufacturing, there is at least one other sector of Japan's traditional economy where robotization is likely to have dramatic impact. Sooner or later—most probably within the next generation—some of Japan's service trades too seem virtually certain to be revolutionized by robots.

Historically, service jobs in Japan have been what the economists like to call labor-intensive. As anthropologist Lionel Tiger pointed out in a paean to Japanese food a few years ago, to prepare and serve Japan's seemingly simple traditional cuisine properly involves far more human labor than is required for anything short of haute cuisine in the West. Similarly, Japanese businesses of every description have traditionally maintained serried ranks of receptionists, gofers, tea makers and assorted other spear carriers of various types. In all my time in Japan, I cannot recall ever having visited a business establishment that did not immediately dispatch one of a corps of demure maidens to fetch me tea, juice or coffee—and not infrequently, all three in succession. And on a fair number of occasions, I have had a car and chauffeur pressed upon me to ferry me to my next appointment.

But while it lends a welcome graciousness to what in the West are often brusque and impersonal transactions, this profligate use of human resources has become too expensive to maintain in many areas of the contemporary Japanese economy. So, in an effort to preserve the form if not the substance of their traditional behavior patterns, the Japanese have once again turned to robots. As early as the mid-1970s, robot "greeters" clad in kimono or waitress costumes began turning up in stores and restaurants. And instead of straightforward automatic signals, robot flagmen and traffic cops became a familiar sight on Japan's highways.

All signs are that these are only the first modest steps in the dehumanization of services in Japan. In late 1981, in a deadly serious article in the respected publication *Ekonomisuto*, a university professor named Tetsuo Ihara conjured up a vision of Japan in which people will have their hair attended to by robot barbers and beauticians and will get their washing done at "a robot-operated laundromat that returns the dirty clothes fed into it as cleanly and neatly as your local laundry service now does." And when the

Tokyoite of tomorrow decides to dine out, Ihara suggested, he may well go to a "tastefully decorated" restaurant in his own apartment building where robot chefs will "cook whatever dish you command by the insertion of an order card."

To many Westerners, the world Professor Ihara envisages will surely sound depressingly sterile and dehumanized. But this is not a concern most Japanese would share. Japanese in general actively like robots. A few years ago at a seminar in Tokyo, Ichiro Shioji, the head of Japan's watered-down version of the United Auto Workers, noted that the humans who labor on Japan's automobile assembly lines treat the robots they work with like partners. "They talk to their robots, pat them on the arm and even give them affectionate nicknames," Shioji said with an indulgent smile. At that, some of the Europeans and Americans present exchanged quizzical glances, but their skepticism was unwarranted: a subsequent visit to a big auto plant demonstrated to me that Shioji was simply reporting literal fact.

Japanese sociologists and psychologists like to attribute their countrymen's receptivity to robots to the influence of Buddhism—which, unlike Christianity, does not place man at the center of the universe and, in fact, makes no particular distinction between the animate and inanimate. As a result of this outlook, the theory goes, Japanese do not instinctively feel threatened by machines with human attributes as Westerners tend to do.

There is probably a large element of truth in this explanation. But whatever special psychological affinity the Japanese may have for robots has surely been reinforced by the fact that up until now robots have to a great extent been employed in Japan to perform jobs that human workers find unusually arduous or distasteful. More important yet, the introduction of robots has not so far thrown any significant number of Japanese out of work. At the moment, in fact, robotization is not even meeting the overall requirements of the Japanese economy for additional labor. As of 1981, Japanese industry was creating new job openings at the rate of 600,000 a year while robot production amounted to only about 20,000 units a year—and while "intelligent robots" that will perform the work of two or three men are in the offing, the general rule of thumb in Japan is still that it takes one robot to fill the shoes of one human.

If the optimists are right, moreover, there is no reason to expect that robotization will ever create widespread unemployment in Japan in the foreseeable future. From an overall economic point of view, the optimists argue, the results of robotization in Japan will be like those of the Industrial Revolution in nineteenth-century Europe: it will create economic growth matching—or more than matching—the increases it makes possible in labor productivity. This, in turn, will lead to increased demands for goods and services and hence to a general increase in employment opportunities.

By no means all Japanese are totally convinced that things will work out that neatly. For one thing, the Doubting Thomases point out, the world economy in general shows worrisome signs of becoming a zero-sum game in which demand cannot be expected to expand automatically; and although the Japanese economy is still growing, it is now doing so at a far slower rate than it did in the go-go 1960s. And in any case, no matter how rosy Japan's overall employment picture may remain, an overly rapid mass resort to robots by Japan's small manufacturing and service enterprises could well cause a great deal of individual hardship and disruption. For while Japan's big corporations can—and do—retrain workers replaced by robots for other jobs, no such safety net exists for the millions of Japanese employed by little companies.

On balance, though, the prevailing Japanese attitude on this issue appears to be that expressed by economic journalist Keiji Ikehata: "Too much brooding over the impact of the spread of robots . . . will probably lead to groundless fears." Just as it has protected farmers and shopkeepers against the ravages of unrestrained competition, so the Japanese Government would almost certainly intervene if the robotization of small factories and service enterprises clearly threatened to cause excessive economic and social disruption. So far, however, the enthusiasm with which Toshio Iguchi and his counterparts all over Japan have embraced robots has been an almost unalloyed blessing: its key effect has been to enhance the efficiency and flexibility with which Japan's small entrepreneurs serve the great corporations that constitute the cutting edge of the nation's economy. Robotization, in short, is bringing the productivity of the Japanese work force as a whole closer to the U.S. level and may indeed herald the day when the only economic advantage the United States has over Japan will be as a producer of food and raw materials.

SECTION FIVE

Looking Ahead

14

A Talent for Survival

Some years ago an eminent econometrician undertook to explain to me how he and his colleagues went about constructing a computer "model" of a country's economy in order to predict its future performance. When I inquired how he built into such a model the various possible political developments that might radically alter a country's economic course, my instructor patiently pointed out that future political events were too unpredictable to make it practicable to factor them into a computer's calculations.

Clearly, though I did not have the courage to say so at the time, this is one of the major reasons econometric prediction so often proves faulty: it consists essentially of extrapolation from current circumstances, and these all too often are ultimately cancelled out or even reversed by the advent of an Ayatollah Khomeini.

This Achilles' heel of econometrics is, of course, the basic problem with all futurology: the unpredictable, by definition, cannot be incorporated into a mathematical formula. All that a futurologist has to offer in the last analysis is his personal insights—and however brilliant they may be, individual insights necessarily rest more upon intuition than upon scientifically demonstrable propositions.

In Japan, to make matters worse, the inherent difficulty of all prediction is intensified by a special circumstance—which is that, to a degree unusual for a great nation, the choices open to the Japanese are circumscribed by events outside their own country. Because postwar Japan has hitched its wagon so firmly to the U.S. star, both militarily and economically, it seems likely that the way in which Americans conduct their affairs in the years ahead will shape the future course of Japanese history at least as much as anything the Japanese themselves may do.

For this reason, there is very little point in trying to predict what Japan will be like tomorrow simply by making projections based upon the forces at play in the Japan of today. Certainly such an exercise will not enable anyone to assert with assurance that there is high probability that Japan will evolve along one particular set of lines. Instead, I believe, it is necessary to draw up two broad scenarios concerning the future of Japan, each resting on a different set of assumptions about the role the United States will play in the world in coming years.

In April 1980 in a speech that he somewhat pointedly chose to deliver in Hiroshima, the late Prime Minister Masayoshi Ohira declared: "The United States has changed from a superpower to just another power." Then, in seeming paradox, he added: "The time has come for Japan to work more closely with the United States and take the initiative in further strengthening Japan–U.S. ties."

Despite their apparent illogic, Ohira's comments faithfully mirrored the mixture of cold-eyed realism and anxious dependence with which Japanese now regard the United States. The average Japanese is keenly aware—more aware than the average American—that the brief era when the United States had sufficient military power to be able to impose something like a Pax Americana upon much of the world ended with Vietnam. He is also keenly aware that the United States faces serious long-term economic problems and that no matter how successfully it may cope with those problems, its relative weight in the world economy can hardly fail to diminish as that of other nations increases. Indeed, a high-level advisory group set up by the Japanese Government has self-confidently predicted that in Japan itself per capita Gross National Product—the value of the goods and services produced by each citizen—will be 20 percent higher than in the United States by the year 2000.

As Ohira made plain at Hiroshima, however, none of these developments has yet led Japan's leaders to begin edging out from under the U.S. wing. Partly because any conceivable alternative would require painful changes in Japan's internal life and partly out of sheer human addiction to the familiar, the men who rule Japan still insist that it is in their country's best interest to remain a U.S. client. Their reasoning was neatly summed up a few years ago by Hisahiko Okazaki, a handsome, self-assured Cambridge graduate who is the Japanese Foreign Ministry's leading specialist in military matters. "The cardinal task of Japan's diplomatic and defense policies," Okazaki explained, "is to maintain the country's security, provide access to resources and markets and enhance the stability and prosperity of the people's livelihood. It follows as a matter of course that the most advantageous foreign policy is to preserve Japan's security ties with the United States. . . . Possibly for the next thirty years we have no choice but to place our bets with the Anglo-Saxon world."

Implicit in Okazaki's statement, however, are two conditions upon which Japan's continuing loyalty to the U.S. alliance rests. One of these is that if the Japanese are to rely upon the United States as the ultimate guarantor of Japan's security, the United States must maintain enough military strength to cope with Soviet adventurism in areas of vital concern to Japan—and must make credible American willingness to use that strength if necessary. The second precondition for a continuing Japanese–American alliance is an American economy strong enough to enable the United States to go on playing an active international role. "In my view," former Japanese Foreign Minister Saburo Okita told me in the spring of 1982, "a strong U.S. economy is even more important in the long run than U.S. military power. Because without a strong economic foundation your military power may not be very effective." What Okita did not bother to add—perhaps because he thought it too obvious to require mention—was that an economically weak America would also be likely to resort to trade restrictions so extreme as to play havoc with Japan's own economy.

Understandably, the way in which the United States has managed its economy and its foreign policy in recent years has aroused in some Japanese fears that America may have lost both the will and the ability to maintain the kind of international environment which Japan needs in order to survive and prosper as a free society. Since the mid-'70s, articles with titles such as "When Will America Bounce Back?" and "Glorious America, Where Are You?" have become staple fare in Japanese magazines. Nonetheless, Japan as a nation is still following Okazaki's prescription and gambling its fate on the proposition that the United States will in the end show itself "reliable."

Even if that gamble proves justified, however, Japan is by no means automatically assured of a halcyon future. As inveterate worriers, the Japanese detect potential threats to their long-term well-being not only from abroad but also in the internal workings of their own society. Perhaps the greatest of their domestic concerns is that Japan will lose much of the competitive economic advantage that underlies its present prosperity. The rationale behind this fear is a widespread belief that the productivity of the Japanese work force will finally cease to grow, either because of the steadily increasing age of the average Japanese worker or because Japan ultimately succumbs to "the British disease"—that erosion of the work ethic which tends to afflict highly developed societies.

A large number of Japanese, in fact, gloomily assert that their country has already contracted the British disease. As older people everywhere in the world are apt to do, many senior Japanese of my acquaintance lament that "the younger generation" is going to hell in a handbasket. Even so judicious a man as NYK's Yoshiya Ariyoshi once resignedly told me: "Japanese industry is doomed to be Americanized. Our youngsters nowadays are born with silver spoons in their mouths. They are taking things easier and have begun to think, 'Why should we sacrifice for the company?' " And some time later, Kazuo Nukazawa, a career Keidanren official in his mid-forties, echoed Mr. Ariyoshi's plaint. "People my age used to work Saturdays even if we weren't paid," he said. "Today's young people still work hard, but they don't work on Saturday at all and don't do overtime even on weekdays unless they are paid. We suffer from the same syndrome you Americans do. It's just that since we came later to industrialization, our symptoms aren't yet as acute as yours."

Such glum appraisals, moreover, do not rest solely on anecdotal evidence and subjective impressions. As I noted earlier, recent polls attest to the fact that young Japanese attach considerably more importance than their elders to self-gratification and a privately centered value system. By Western lights at least, this is not entirely deplorable: it helps explain, among other things, the fact that young Japanese husbands often devote more time and attention to their families than their fathers did. But the new emphasis on self-gratification has also helped spawn the mindless materialism of the members of Japan's Crystal Generation—the kind of people who made it possible for Louis Vuitton to open six successful boutiques in Tokyo and Osaka within the space of a single month in 1979.

Perhaps even more far-reaching in its implications than the desire for self-gratification is the fact that the willingness to postpone such gratification is clearly eroding. Executives of Japanese finance companies, for example, report that they do a disproportionate amount of their business with people under thirty-five; instead of saving for years to buy a car as their parents did, many young Japanese are quite prepared to go into debt to buy the things they want right now. And in another manifestation of the same phenomenon, some young Japanese, particularly in high-technology fields, have grown increasingly frustrated with the rigidities the seniority system imposes on their career development. Though it may have been a cloud no bigger than a man's hand, it nonetheless startled Japan's industrial establishment when in early 1980 several dozen computer technicians walked away from safe jobs with Ishikawajima-Harima Heavy Industries to become stockholders in their own systems-design company.

No doubt there will be more such incidents in the Japan of tomorrow. No doubt too, the average workweek will grow shorter, and the importance Japanese workers attach to leisure time and recreation will continue to increase. Nonetheless, I believe that Japan has considerably less to fear from the British disease than its own doomsayers suggest and a number of spiteful Westerners hope. For to succumb fully to that ailment, the Japanese would have to adopt individualism as the dominant value system of their society. And for the foreseeable future at least, the upbringing of Japanese children and the nature of Japanese education would seem to render such a mass conversion highly improbable.

Instead, what seems more likely to occur is some intensification of a state of dynamic tension described by a senior MITI official named Naohiro Amaya in a perceptive essay that he published in 1980. The thesis of this essay is that ever since Japan opened itself to Western influences more than a century ago, Japanese society has had a dual structure similar to that of the human brain. Western values and Western-style relationships based on the sanctity of individual rights, Amaya says, exist on the surface of Japanese society, which he compares to the neopallium, or outer portion, of the human brain. But it is the structure and ethics of the traditional Japanese village, he insists, that dominate in the lower stratum of Japanese society and constitute its equivalent of the paleopallium, or inner core, of the brain, where instincts are generated. "Such groups as the so-called progressive intellectuals, the worshipers of America and Europe, the majority of journalists and the progressive opposition parties," Amaya concludes, "seem to think that the surface layer represents the ideal Japan. . . . But whether we like it or not, the paleopallium inside the Japanese brain is still alive and kicking. And in this part of our brain, community values take precedence over individual values."

In short, while the young Japanese workers of tomorrow will not work as hard as those of the 1960s and '70s, there seems every prospect that they will continue to work harder than their American and European counterparts. And in any case, there is one very concrete reason why neither the "decadence" of Japanese youth nor the infirmities of Japan's increasingly numerous older workers are apt to impair Japan's overall economic competitiveness. This lies in the pace at which Japan is embracing robots—a pace, as we have seen, unmatched in any other industrial nation. Like any other investment in machinery, investment in robots increases human productivity—only enormously so. At the most modern robot-equipped plants in Japan, a $30,000-a-year human worker accounts for an annual output of nearly $500,000 worth of goods—which means high profits for the manufacturer. And by the end of this century, according to expert estimates, Japan is likely to have a million robots in service, many of them capable of performing far more sophisticated tasks than the robots of today. Along about that time, to take just one example, Ichiro Shioji of the Japan Auto Workers Union forecasts that nearly 90 percent of the current production jobs at Nissan Motors will have been taken over by robots. And since robots turn out more consistently perfect products than humans, this presumably will make the caliber of Nissan's human work force somewhat less crucial than it now is.

It is, of course, conceivable that Japan's rush to robotics could be slowed down or even stalled if it began to produce widespread unemployment. Recently, in fact, there have been signs that some Japanese labor unions are having uneasy second thoughts about their initial unhesitating acceptance of robots; even Shioji has moderated his original enthusiasm sufficiently to warn that with the slowdown in Japan's auto exports, "the view that robots will not affect employment is open to question."

But as Masaru Yoshitomi of the Economic Planning Agency points out: "Higher productivity doesn't necessarily mean unemployment. If you have an adequate rate of economic growth, that's no problem. And so far, our markets have continued to expand at a rate which has made it possible for us to create enough new jobs to compensate for the increased productivity achieved by the machines." All in all, Yoshitomi says, he is optimistic about the continued growth of the Japanese economy, at least over the next decade.

One man's rosy vision, however, can be another man's nightmare.

And a fair number of thoughtful Japanese are in fact increasingly concerned about a hazard which, ironically, is almost the exact opposite of the British disease. What concerns these people is the risk that the Japanese will succeed in doing what my friend Jiro Tokuyama describes as "turning strength into weakness." The overriding danger, according to this school of thought, is that Japan will maintain such high levels of competitiveness in foreign markets as to render itself an outcast among nations and provoke a worldwide repudiation of the principle of free trade.

To a degree, of course, this concern echoes the primary complaint that so many Westerners make about Japan. In the steadily escalating rhetoric of international trade negotiations, it has now become routine for American and European spokesmen to assert that Japan has "abused" the free-trade system—a system, they add with debatable accuracy, from which Japan has benefited more than any other nation. In my own experience, this "Jap-bashing," as the Europeans cheerily call it, reached some sort of apogee when a senior official of the U.S. Foreign Service impatiently instructed me that it didn't really matter whether the particular trade-liberalization measures the United States was then pressing upon Japan would actually serve to reduce the American trade deficit to any significant degree. What was vital, he said, was for Japan to take these steps as a token of good faith—a demonstration that it recognizes the potentially calamitous economic and political consequences of any global return to the "beggar-thy-neighbor" protectionist policies of the 1930s.

This quasi-theological approach to a practical problem of political and economic management has, of course, about as much chance of proving effective as a rain dance has of changing the weather. Nonetheless, it would be foolish to pooh-pooh the fear that inspires it. It is, in fact, quite conceivable that the adoption of autarkic economic policies by many national governments will finally put an end to the continuing growth of international trade that has characterized the postwar era. And should that happen, the long-term political consequences could well be disastrous for the entire world. But if such a tragedy does occur, it will, I believe, be caused by the shortsightedness of American and European statesmen and not by a heedless drive on the part of the Japanese to maximize their exports at the expense of other nations' economic health.

I rest this prediction primarily upon what would seem to be the likeliest political prospects for Japan—assuming, as we are for the moment, the continuation of the U.S.–Japanese alliance and a reasonably healthy U.S. economy. Given those circumstances, I share Masaru Yoshitomi's belief that the Japanese economy too will remain strong. Specifically, it should remain strong enough to create more than enough jobs to accommodate all the young Japanese who will be coming into the labor market in the years immediately ahead—particularly since young people are diminishing not only in proportion to Japan's total population but also in absolute number. (In 1970, there were more than 2.4 million Japanese who turned twenty; by 1980, the number of new twenty-year-olds had fallen to fewer than 1.6 million.)

All this suggests that Japan should be able to forestall the development of the yeastiest and most dangerous element a society can be afflicted with—a large and indigestible body of "overeducated" youths frustrated by their inability to find suitable employment. This, in turn, would seem to portend a considerable degree of political stability in Japan over the next decade or so. Provided they are reasonably content with their economic lot, the Japanese seem likely to go on electing the same sort of government they have been electing ever since the end of the U.S. Occupation. Even then, it may well prove that future Japanese governments will not always be exclusively composed of Liberal Democrats—although for some time to come that is not inconceivable. But they would seem likely to be broadly conservative regimes characterized by the same kind of caution, pragmatism and adaptability that have characterized the LDP regimes of the past. And such governments can be expected to go on relying heavily upon the elite bureaucracy, with its inbred distaste for adventurism and addiction to compromise.

A Japan thus governed could, I believe, readily find effective ways to mitigate its trade tensions with the rest of the world and, in my view, will almost inevitably do so. Already, in fact, the policies necessary to do this either exist in nascent form in Japan or have been widely discussed there.

Largely because Japan's exports have made themselves so conspicuous by affecting particularly sensitive industries in other advanced nations, foreigners often assume that Japan is more dependent upon its export trade than any other great industrial power. In one limited sense, there is some truth to this: because of excessive competition in the domestic market, a fair number of individual Japanese companies and even some entire industries depend upon foreign sales for their margin of survival. But for Japan as a nation, maintaining an extremely high level of exports is not a make-or-break matter. As of 1980, in fact, exports accounted for only 12.5

percent of Japan's Gross National Product—which was half again as high as the figure for the United States, but substantially lower than that for any other industrialized Western nation. (The comparable figure for West Germany, for example, was 23.4 percent and the figure for Great Britain 22.2 percent.)

What this means is that a significant reduction in the size of Japan's trade surpluses—whether through a reduction of exports, an increase in imports or a combination of the two—need not be as destructive to Japan's overall economic health as many Japanese are in the habit of asserting. Such a development would, to be sure, cause painful dislocations in certain specific parts of the Japanese economy; but with good management, these effects could be offset in a number of ways.

One of these would be for the Japanese Government to give active encouragement to private investment abroad on a scale comparable, at least in relative terms, to the massive foreign investments made by U.S. industry in the '50s and '60s. Such a large-scale resort to manufacturing overseas would admittedly reduce Japan's own exports, but it would also—as it has for the United States—produce foreign earnings that would help prevent excessive deterioration of Japan's overall balance of payments.

Another possible offset would be a gradual increase in Japan's defense spending to something approaching the modest percentages of national income that now prevail among the European members of NATO. While this would not transform Japan into a major military power, it would have a significant impact upon the nation's economy. If Japan chose to manufacture most of its own weapons, this would offer a number of Japanese corporations a profitable alternative to their present reliance upon export sales. And if, on the other hand, Japan chose to buy the bulk of its weapons abroad, its imports of manufactured goods would increase. In either case, the net effect would be to reduce the size of Japanese trade surpluses.

By all odds the most effective way in which Japan could offset a diminished emphasis on exports, however, would be to expand its own internal economy. And here there are needs crying out to be met. In highways, housing, sewers, public recreational facilities and many other social amenities, Japan is still far below the levels considered acceptable in most developed nations. A concentrated national effort to remedy these deficiencies would inevitably produce a surge in domestic economic activity. This in turn would enable ordinary Japanese to satisfy more of their cravings for consumer goods—which would provide Japanese manufacturers with larger domestic markets and perhaps spur larger imports from abroad as well.

Stated as baldly as they are here, the measures just outlined may sound both obvious and easy to put into effect. But the latter, at least, is far from the case. Evidence of that can be found in the fact that while the Japanese have debated all these possibilities and actually dabbled with some, they have so far rejected all-out adoption of any of them. And in every case they have had plausible reasons for inaction: domestic political pressures, fear of fueling inflation, a healthy dread of the cumulative effects of greatly increased government budget deficits and, above all, that perennial bugaboo, the "special vulnerability" of Japan.

Deep-seated as all these concerns are, however, there is good reason to hope that over the next decade the Japanese will overcome them and take the corrective measures I have described—not, surely, as rapidly and completely as the rest of the world would like, but rapidly enough and thoroughly enough to prevent today's trade tensions from turning into a trade war. This will happen, in part, because as realists, Japan's rulers will have to come to terms with the relentless foreign pressures upon them to change their economic habits—pressures which, when not irrationally or intemperately applied, some members of the Japanese establishment privately welcome. "There are times," my bureaucrat friend Chitoshi once told me with a wry smile, "when the only way our politicians can be led to take steps that are painful but in our own long-term interest is if they can argue that you Americans leave them no choice."

Productive as they sometimes may be, however, external pressures can equally well backfire if they are carried to the point of injuring national pride. So it is fortunate that Japan's realistic politicians will also be under internal pressure to expand their domestic economy. While Japan's young people may still be willing to work hard, more and more of them are demanding greater rewards for doing so. "If Japan is such a rich country," a newly married office worker asked rhetorically when I last visited Tokyo, "why is it that my wife and I have to live in a one-room apartment without a private bath?" This kind of question is being posed with increasing frequency and insistence in today's Japan, and that fact should incline Japan's leaders, if only for reasons of electoral survival, to pay more attention to living standards and somewhat less to trade statistics.

Meantime, a different kind of pressure for change will come from within the Japanese establishment itself. More and more Japanese businessmen and politicians now favor a considerable strengthening of Japan's military forces, and in the last few years they have become far less hesitant about pressing their views. "This is a highly emotional issue, and the debate won't be a particularly rational or consistently sustained one," a senior MITI official predicted to me in late 1980. "It will flare up from time to time, die down and then flare up again. But I believe that by the end of this decade it will have been resolved in favor of rearmament."

With intelligent management, the new economic and political directions in which a stable Japan seems likely to proceed could have great positive effects. An easing of trade frictions should ameliorate the image of the Japanese as nothing more than a nation of "transistor salesmen"—the contemptuous phrase with which Charles de Gaulle once dismissed the late Prime Minister Hayato Ikeda. And that, together with greater conventional military capabilities, should permit Japan to play a more assertive and effective role in international politics.

Already, in fact, Japan has helped ease the U.S. taxpayer's burden by making geopolitically motivated loans to Pakistan and Turkey—two countries that loom large in American strategic planning. Presumably, if it continues to enjoy the confidence of the Japanese, the United States can expect even more such assistance in maintaining the world balance of power from a diplomatically active Japan.

By the same token, there is every prospect that the military relationship between the United States and Japan will gradually cease to be as one-sided as it is now. And this change will not necessarily be limited to a simple increase in Japan's armed forces or a greater Japanese role in countering the great buildup of Soviet naval power that has occurred in the Far East. Even more far-reaching, I believe, is the kind of change envisaged by Keidanren's Kazuo Nukazawa. "As I see it," says Nukazawa, "the United States will still be a bigger power than Japan in every sense twenty years from now and we will still be ultimately dependent upon you for our survival. But because we will be so advanced technologically you will also be dependent upon us for some crucial elements of your military power—microcircuitry or whatever the newest thing will be by then. And that's precisely what the relationship between our two countries ought to be: mutual dependence for mutual survival."

★

It would be pleasant indeed to be able to assert with complete assurance that the Japan of twenty years hence will be the one Kazuo Nukazawa envisages: a stable democratic country inextricably linked with the United States and actively contributing through its vast technological and economic resources to the maintenance of world peace. But there is, unfortunately, no inevitability about Nukazawa's scenario. It is, in fact, disturbingly easy to construct an alternative and far more pessimistic scenario concerning Japan's future. For side by side with the many encouraging phenomena visible in today's Japan there exist some potentially ominous ones: trends and attitudes which, under certain circumstances, could intensify and ultimately combine to reshape Japanese society in ways that would be extremely painful not only for the Japanese themselves but for the rest of the world as well.

Perhaps the most conspicuous of the disturbing trends is the change that is occurring in the way Japanese respond to the ceaseless foreign pressures upon their country to reduce its exports and increase its imports. For anyone who does not regularly see the world through the eyes of the Japanese media, it is difficult to imagine the preeminent position that trade frictions now occupy in public consciousness in Japan. It is doubtful that there has been a single day in the last several years when the Japanese press has not carried a story in some way reflecting European or American dissatisfaction with Japan's economic behavior.

For many years after such complaints began to become commonplace, the characteristic response of the Japanese was to ask themselves what errors they had committed to provoke such wrath and how those errors could best be repaired. As late as March 1978, for example, Takeo Fukuda, who was then Japan's Prime Minister, indignantly rebuffed one of his ministers who suggested that perhaps the time had come to point out to the Carter Administration that a lot of America's balance-of-payments problems were of its own making. Even today, that accommodating attitude is by no means completely dead: particularly among older members of the Japanese economic and political establishment the predominant view still is that Japan must do whatever it can to appease its critics. But such humility is now far from universal and is frequently mixed with defensiveness. In large numbers of Japanese, in fact, the continuing drumfire of foreign complaints and demands has induced something akin to a siege mentality—a sense that their country is under assault from every side.

This, of course, is a particularly painful state of mind for people who at the best of times are uncommonly sensitive to the way in which their society is regarded abroad. Before World War II, as Tadashi Yamamoto, the director of the Japan Center for International Exchange, points out, "Europe was always the teaching model for Japan." So it hurts Japanese in a way in which it could never hurt Americans when a prominent European industrialist publicly suggests, as the president of Volvo once did, that Japan's economic successes have been achieved at the cost of unjust social policies. And given the elder-brother role in which so many Japanese have psychically cast the United States since the end of World War II, it hurts even more when a leading American political figure declares, as Tip O'Neill did during a visit to Detroit in 1982, that Japan has been "extremely unfair" to the United States and that if he were President he would "fix the Japanese like they've never been fixed before."

Inevitably, hurt feelings have bred resentment. With considerable justice, more and more Japanese have come to write Western Europeans off as hypocrites who inveigh against allegedly unfair trade practices on the part of Japan simply in order to justify their own protectionism. Even a lifelong diplomat like Nobuhiko Ushiba, Japan's most practiced and prestigious negotiator in matters involving international trade, is no longer prepared to give Western Europeans any credit for good intentions. "The Europeans are doing nothing to maintain free trade," Ushiba complained in late 1981. "France, for instance, is already closed to Japanese products. We have nothing more to fear from them."

Where the United States is concerned Japanese feelings are far more ambivalent—partly because Japan has a great deal more at stake in America than in Europe and partly because the majority of Japanese continue to cling to the belief that sooner or later U.S. industry will solve its productivity problems and thus automatically ease the trade frictions between Washington and Tokyo. In the meantime, however, there is an increasingly widespread conviction that the nub of the U.S. complaint against Japan is not that the Japanese have violated the rules of free trade but that they have prospered too mightily by playing the game according to those rules.

This is a charge that I had never heard a responsible Japanese make until the mid-1970s, and even then it was made only by innuendo. By 1982, however, variations on it were being openly voiced by some of the most pro-American figures in Japan. In May of that year, Jiro Tokuyama of the Nomura School of Advanced

Management expressed to me almost in passing the belief that "from the U.S. viewpoint the Japanese standard of living is already too high, and Americans don't want to see it go any higher." And only a few days later former Foreign Minister Saburo Okita asserted that because of economic difficulties of their own creation and their concern over Japanese competition in high technology, Americans were using Japan as a scapegoat. "Unfortunately," he added drily, "Japan has a high degree of goatability."

These, to repeat, were views held by responsible men dedicated to the preservation of the Japanese–American alliance. Among less responsible Japanese, it is easy these days to find something akin to paranoia concerning U.S. behavior toward Japan. Just how suspicious some Japanese have become, in fact, was clearly demonstrated in the summer of 1982 when, within a period of six weeks, the FBI charged two major Japanese computer makers with conspiracy to steal trade secrets from IBM, the U.S. subsidiary of the Mitsui trading company was indicted for "dumping" steel in the American market and the Justice Department disclosed that it was investigating six Japanese semiconductor manufacturers for possible conspiracy to drive up the price of computer chips in the United States. Pouncing on the rapid-fire order in which these charges were made, the Japanese press—and most ordinary Japanese—promptly concluded that government and industry in the United States were engaged in a concerted drive to "punish" Japan and blunt competition by Japanese companies in American markets. And even government officials in Tokyo, although they dismissed the notion of a centrally orchestrated American campaign, pointedly noted one peculiar fact: only a few months before the Reagan Administration suggested that Japanese semiconductor makers were charging unduly high prices, it had voiced the fear that they might be selling chips at artificially low prices. "We would like," said one Japanese bureaucrat sourly, "to see some consistency from the American Government in this matter."

Pent-up resentment is, of course, always a dangerous emotion, and because their abhorrence of confrontation makes it hard for them to turn anger to constructive ends, it is, I believe, particularly dangerous in Japanese. Even more than other peoples, they are apt to respond to what they see as prolonged unfairness not simply by concluding that their adversaries are wrongheaded but by writing them off as hopelessly malign or contemptible. And in today's Japan it is not hard to find manifestations of contempt for Europeans and Americans—a contempt sometimes epitomized in the saying "Europe is a boutique and America is a farm."

As that comment suggests, it is Western Europe that bears the brunt of Japanese contempt as well as Japanese resentment, and that fact has increasingly affected dealings between the Europeans and the Japanese. At one meeting over trade problems in 1981, a group of Japanese businessmen totally abandoned the customary courtesies and read the Europeans present a no-holds-barred lecture on European laziness and laxity. "You get the feeling that they really think we are decadent," a top European negotiator later reported in outrage and astonishment.

A similar, though less extreme, condescension toward the United States has also begun to surface in a manner unthinkable even half a dozen years ago. "Every moment the U.S. delays in putting its house in order inconveniences the entire world," wrote Tetsuya Ozaki of Jiji Press in June 1982. "Shape up, America!" And for all his commitment to continued Japanese–American partnership, Keidanren's Kazuo Nukazawa bluntly told me over drinks one evening: "Japanese used to regard Americans as teachers, but now we see them as equals. So these days, when the United States complains or makes demands upon us, Japanese want to say: 'Look, in economics we are both students. Your marks are bad; my marks are better. So don't tell me what to do!' "

From the assertion of equality it is a short step to assertions of superiority—and that is a step some Japanese have in fact already taken. There is growing feeling in Japan that political scientist Yatsuhiro Nakagawa and economic commentator Nobumasa Ota are right when they proudly claim that "the Japanese economic system is a valuable model for the free world's advanced industrial societies." And while it is still emphatically a minority view, there is growing sentiment too that Japan's economic might should be backed up by the ultimate in military might. Within the last three years two highly intelligent and eminently respectable Japanese friends—one an elite bureaucrat and one a well-known public figure—have confided to me that they personally believe Japan should go ahead and build nuclear weapons. "After all," said the more outspoken of the two, "you can't expect people to join an army that they know has no chance of winning."

In itself, there is nothing particularly surprising about this. All along, there have been a certain number of unreconstructed—or at least only partially reconstructed—nationalists inside Japan's industrial and political establishments. What is different now is not so much that these people have become more numerous—though that is probably the case—but that they feel somewhat more at liberty to act upon their views.

Undoubtedly, the most dramatic evidence of this to emerge so far occurred in the summer of 1982 when Tokyo's Ministry of Education approved for school use new history textbooks which described Japan's attempted conquest of China in the 1930s as an "advance" rather than an "invasion," soft-pedaled the horrors committed by Japanese troops in the 1937 "Rape of Nanking" and downplayed the excesses of Japanese colonial rule in Korea in the first half of this century. Predictably, this nationalistic rewriting of history outraged Japan's major newspapers and the political opposition in general, but it was not until China, Taiwan and South Korea entered vehement official protests that the Japanese Government finally announced that the offending passages would eventually be corrected. Even then, however, the government acted with visible reluctance, and the fact that it was forced to backtrack under foreign pressure may actually have done as much to fan nationalism as to deter it. "If we have to consult with foreigners on what we want to teach our children," grumbled one avowedly "dovish" Liberal Democratic Diet member, "this is something we cannot easily swallow."

The great textbook controversy touched a particularly raw nerve in Japan since, at least by implication, it raised the vexed question of whether the Japanese are by nature or conditioning particularly prone to cruel or brutal behavior. This, I believe, is a matter which most Westerners find it nearly impossible to discuss without lapsing, however unconsciously, into some degree of racism. During World War II, one officer with whom I served was fond of asserting that Nazi savagery was even more inexcusable than Japanese savagery since "the Germans know better." This struck me then—and does now—as ethnic condescension of the purest ray serene. But so on the other hand does the assumption, often unrecognized or unadmitted by those who make it, that barbarities committed by Orientals are somehow more reflective of national character than barbarities committed by Westerners.

That Japanese have in the past committed acts of unspeakable awfulness is a simple fact: besides such horrors as the Rape of Nanking and the Philippine Death March, there is a long, ugly roll call of less well-known atrocities, including the infamous medical experiments carried out upon prisoners of war by Japanese Army doctors in China. At the same time, it is difficult to think of many nations, large or small, whose citizens have not been guilty of indefensible cruelties within reasonably recent history. Frenchmen in Algeria, Americans in Vietnam, Russians in half a dozen countries including their own, Hindus and Moslems in the Indian subcontinent—all these and too many other "civilized" peoples to list have shown themselves capable of barbarity on a massive scale. And while comparisons are even more odious in this connection than in most others, no excess ever committed by Japanese rivals what Germans did in the Holocaust. Nor is there any real parallel in contemporary Japanese society to the random violence and savagery now so prevalent in the great cities of the United States.

But to say that there is nothing in the nature or social conditioning of Japanese that renders them as individuals any more predisposed to cruelty than other peoples does not totally dispose of the problems raised by Japan's behavior as a nation before and during World War II. All imperialisms are brutal, but Japanese imperialism in its heyday was markedly so. To my mind, the most convincing explanation for this fact is that group orientation, latent xenophobia and the concept of morality as relative rather than absolute all conspired to make it comparatively easy for Japanese to be mobilized for ventures in which violence and brutality were presented as means to a glorious end.

It can, in short, be argued—as some Japanese themselves do argue—that by its very nature Japanese society has what might be described as a higher potential for totalitarianism than societies based on individualistic values. Considering all that has happened in Japan in the last thirty-five years, my own estimate would be that this is far less true now than it was before World War II. But that the totalitarian potential survives in some degree also seems clear. The insensate displays of mass violence that characterized the great student riots of the 1960s certainly suggested that the capacity of Japanese to indulge in consensual irrationality was still alive then. And that it has not yet entirely disappeared is indicated by an incident that occurred one night in the fall of 1980 when I was invited to dinner at the home of a knowledgeable American resident of Tokyo. Over cocktails, my host passed along the latest neighborhood sensation: the previous evening, the members of an obscure leftist organization had trapped five young men in a street only a block or two from where we were sitting and had beaten them to death with steel rods. When I asked what had prompted the massacre, my friend matter-of-factly remarked that it was a dispute over some point of Marxist doctrine so complex that he really did not understand it.

To devote so much attention to Japan's potential for totalitarianism may seem, in the context of present-day Japanese society, rather like conjuring up a bogeyman to scare the children. At the moment, the lingering manifestations of that potential, like Japan's increasing resentment of foreign pressures and the desire of some Japanese for a greater degree of national self-assertion, are no more than ripples on the surface of a generally tranquil pond. And for as long as Japan remains economically and politically stable, it is reasonable to expect that this will continue to be the case.

The thing that could change all this and transform what are now merely ripples into raging waves is the possibility that the majority of Japanese themselves most fear: a radical deterioration in the present relationship between Japan and the United States. And that relationship, as I have emphasized before, requires that the United States provide Japan not only with a defense umbrella but, in a sense, with an economic umbrella as well.

As the experience of the last decade plainly indicates, weakness in our domestic economy tends to drive the United States to adopt protectionist devices—which in turn encourages greater protectionism on the part of other advanced nations. In a perennially troubled and decreasingly competitive U.S. economy, this process would surely be intensified and the present world drift away from free trade speeded up.

This would, among other things, lead to a contraction of Japan's foreign markets, and that, carried far enough, could scarcely fail to have grave repercussions for Japan. Exaggerated as the Japanese vulnerability complex may be, it does have this much substance: while Japan doesn't necessarily need its present high level of exports in order to remain economically healthy, it has even less prospect than other industrial nations of successfully creating anything remotely resembling a self-contained economy. Since the Japanese have so few material resources of their own, they must somehow earn at least enough money abroad to pay for the raw materials required to meet the needs of their domestic economy.

The needs of the Japanese domestic economy are not, of course, immutable; there is no natural law which says that they must be maintained at present levels or better. But I have yet to meet a Japanese who does not believe that the political consequences inside Japan would be severe if a broad exclusion of Japanese goods from foreign markets—above all the U.S. market—were to force a major reduction in Japan's domestic economic activity and a decline in Japanese living standards. Whether the Liberal Democratic Party, which has rested its reputation so heavily upon successful economic management, could survive anything like a true depression is, in my view, highly questionable—and it is almost equally doubtful, I believe, that a viable democratic alternative to the LDP could be constructed under such circumstances. What's more, it is by no means clear that the U.S.-Japanese alliance could long endure in the face of serious economic difficulties that most Japanese perceived as U.S.-induced.

As Saburo Okita points out, however, there are two inextricably linked elements in the Japanese–American alliance. Vital as the economic aspect of the relationship is, the United States cannot retain Japan's loyalty simply by showing itself a strong and reliable economic partner. It must also maintain sufficient military power to guarantee Japan against Soviet nuclear blackmail and, no less important, give credible evidence of its willingness to use that power in extremis. What is crucial in this respect is not so much assertions of U.S. readiness to come to Japan's aid in the event of a Russian attack upon the Japanese islands as a display of strength and determination sufficient to deter Russian leaders from even contemplating such a step. "The days when MacArthur could keep resistance alive by saying 'I shall return' are long gone," an influential Liberal Democratic parliamentarian told me some time ago. "Nobody in this country wants to live three or four years under Soviet occupation while waiting for the United States to sort things out."

Beyond all doubt, the men who rule Japan are somewhat less confident today than they were a decade ago that American power and will are adequate to constitute a totally reliable deterrent. And if the time ever came when they were forced to conclude that the U.S. deterrent clearly was not reliable, it would be irresponsible of them not to consider alternative ways of achieving some degree of strategic security for Japan. Such inaction, in fact, might also prove unwise in purely political terms. Deeply as the great majority of Japanese abhor war, an increasingly large number of them appear to share the sentiments of a Tokyo security analyst who told a seminar in Aspen, Colorado, a few years ago: "If the Russians come, I don't want to have to just skip away."

The most obvious alternative for a Japan that had lost confidence in the American umbrella would be a kind of East Asian version of Gaullism. This would essentially rest upon the creation of an independent Japanese nuclear strike force—one at least strong enough to be able to inflict unacceptable damage upon any potential aggressor. That Japan has the technological capability to develop such a force relatively quickly cannot be doubted, and it is hard to conceive that a Japanese Government that decided to "go nuclear" would not also undertake a major buildup of the country's conventional military forces.

Such behavior would inevitably alarm many of Japan's Asian neighbors, some of whom, with their bitter memories of World War II, have already expressed concern at even modest strengthening of the Japanese Self-Defense Forces. A few years ago, when Prime Minister Takeo Fukuda explained that Japan merely wanted to become a "hedgehog" with just enough power to repel the attacks of its enemies, a Southeast Asian diplomat in a dubious bit of zoology responded that a hedgehog that throws its weight around in a chicken coop, no matter how inadvertently, can still injure the chickens. And all-out Japanese rearmament would set the chickens to squawking even louder. It could, in fact, provoke an East Asian arms race, with countries such as South Korea, Indonesia and even Australia seeking to ensure their security through the acquisition of their own nuclear weapons.

So great is Japan's economic and technological superiority over its neighbors, however, that it would be difficult for them to live in a state of permanent hostility with the Japanese. Some of them at least might ultimately find it the lesser evil to accept Japan as the paramount regional power. And particularly in the event of a global reversion to protectionism, there would be strong impetus for Japan to try to create its own informal East Asian sphere of influence and thereby ensure its access to the raw materials of Australia, Indonesia, the Philippines, Malaysia and Thailand.

There is, of course, yet another alternative to the U.S. alliance theoretically open to Japan—one that as far as I can discover was never publicly alluded to by any responsible figure in postwar Japan until early 1982. At that point, when a foreign newsman asked him what Japan would do if protectionism in Europe and America "went all the way," the Vice-Director of the Ministry of International Trade and Industry replied: "We would be forced to join the Communist bloc."

Though it received minimal attention in the United States, that remark created dismay inside the Japanese Government. When I flew into Tokyo shortly after it was made, longtime friends in the bureaucracy nervously hastened to explain it away as everything from "a purely hypothetical comment" to "an inept joke." And up to a point, they were right to dismiss it so summarily. Year in and year out, the Soviet Union tops the polls as the nation the Japanese man in the street most dislikes and distrusts. To conceive of circumstances in which the Japanese would voluntarily accept Russian domination is difficult indeed. And to conceive of a Soviet Government flexible enough to offer Japan an alliance free of ideological constraints and based on something akin to equality is even more difficult.

What is not inconceivable, however, is the possibility that, as it distanced itself from the United States, a "Gaullist" Japan might seek close ties with Communist China. This is an eventuality generally written off by conventional political thinkers, on the ground that in economic terms the impoverished Chinese multitudes would offer Japan no effective substitute for the highly developed markets of the United States and Western Europe. If Japan were to find itself largely excluded from American and European markets, however, it could no longer hope to maintain its present living standard in any case and might find China the most acceptable economic partner available. Even now, China possesses natural resources of interest to Japan, and with sufficient investment and exploration it could very probably become an even more significant supplier of raw materials. "In my opinion," U.S. Ambassador Mike Mansfield tells visitors to his huge, sunny office in Tokyo, "the world's next big oil field will be off the China coast."

Economically, then, China could in the future prove a more useful partner than it currently appears. And a rapprochement with China would also carry psychological rewards for Japan. "When Japanese are associating with Americans, there are always tensions somewhere," Jiro Tokuyama once confessed to me. "But when Japanese are associating with Chinese, they can relax."

Most important of all, a Gaullist Japan would presumably find a close relationship with Peking almost a geopolitical necessity. In the absence of a solid U.S.–Japanese alliance, the Japanese would find even more dismaying than they do now any possibility of a revived Sino–Soviet alliance. Rather than run that risk, it would clearly be in Japan's interest to marry Japanese technology with China's vast manpower and land mass—and thereby create a new deterrent to Soviet expansionism in Asia.

In light of America's somewhat erratic economic and strategic policies over the last decade, some Western students of foreign affairs suspect that Japan's leaders must already have given at least some consideration to possible alternatives to the American alliance. The few Japanese who will discuss the matter at all, however, stoutly insist that this is not so. "It's far too early to consider such possibilities," a longtime friend in the Japanese Foreign Office flatly assured me when I last visited Tokyo. "That's sci-fi talk."

Most Japanese, in fact, won't even go that far. Shortly after the signing of the Sino–Japanese Treaty of Friendship in August 1978—an event, significantly, which marked the first time in postwar history that Japan moved more quickly than the United States on a major diplomatic issue—I suggested to a group composed mainly of members of Japan's foreign-policy establishment what I have been suggesting here: that in the worst conceivable circumstances, the time might come when events would force Japan to reassess its ties with the United States and move closer to China. When I had finished, two foreign diplomats—one American and one Russian—somewhat irascibly challenged my thesis. Not a single Japanese in the audience, however, directly commented on it in any way.

Four years later, I recalled all this to a Japanese who had been present on that occasion and asked if things had changed enough since then so that senior Japanese policy-makers were now discussing Japan's strategic options among themselves. "Ambiguously perhaps," my friend replied. "But you must remember that whatever they may be thinking inside, Japanese never speak out on subjects like this—particularly to Americans. In fact, even among Japanese we wouldn't talk openly about this kind of thing; we're unconsciously conditioned not even to think specifically about such matters."

For a moment, my friend hesitated and then, with a slightly ironic smile, asked if I intended to quote him by name. When I promised not to do so, he said: "Okay, I'll tell you this, then: if the light of nationalism is ever rekindled in this country, nobody will be able to put it out. I don't want to see that happen, but it's certainly imaginable under the circumstances you've mentioned. And if it should happen, there's a big possibility we could go along with China."

Sadly, in my view, Washington is just as devoid as Tokyo is of any serious discussion of this scenario. Those American officials who will even consider it—like their Japanese counterparts, most of them regard it as "sci-fi talk"—brush off the notion of any such radical Japanese change of course as so destructive of Japan's own national goals as to be unthinkable. That judgment, however, ignores one crucial consideration: Japan's current dedication to democracy, an open society and material affluence is not something that grew inexorably from purely Japanese roots; it is the product of a particular set of international circumstances and under other circumstances might well be superseded by other imperatives.

The course taken by Japan in the aftermath of World War II was an extraordinary one for a proud nation to adopt: as a people, the Japanese quite consciously decided to restructure their society, modeling it as closely as practicable upon that of the United States. At bottom, the collective reasoning of the Japanese was very straightforward: because the United States had so clearly established itself as the world's strongest power, it followed that American practices and institutions must be superior to any others.

Up till now, that reasoning, however simplistic it may appear, has paid off handsomely for Japan. But only if it continues to pay off will there be solid reason to hope that the first and infinitely more desirable of my two broad scenarios concerning Japan's future will become reality. It cannot be overstressed that there is one indispensable precondition to Japan's continued stability—and that is for the United States itself to maintain a healthy economy and enough national power and resolution to defend both its own vital interests and those of its principal allies.

To prescribe what the United States can or should do to achieve these objectives is obviously beyond the scope of this book. But assuming that they are in fact achieved, it still cannot be expected that America's relations with Japan will then take care of themselves. Under the best of circumstances, there are several ways in which the United States would be wise to change its policies in order to put the Japanese–American alliance on a sounder footing.

To begin with, the United States ought to take prompt action to alleviate insofar as possible Japan's sense of vulnerability concerning food and energy supplies. In the matter of food, it should be feasible to develop arrangements that would give Japan guaranteed long-term access to American agricultural products. And as far as energy is concerned, there are several readily available measures Washington could take. Simply by agreeing to permit the sale of Alaskan oil to Japan, the Congress could reduce Japanese dependence on volatile Middle Eastern supplies—and at the same time significantly reduce our trade deficit with Japan. If only for psychological reassurance, the U.S. Government should also work out with the Japanese

Government contingency plans for maintaining the maximum feasible flow of crude oil into Japan in the event of another Arab oil embargo or similar international upheaval. Finally, the United States should never again seek to play the role of nanny with respect to Japan's nuclear development program. A Japan that was determined to acquire nuclear weapons could surely do so no matter what technical roadblocks Washington might throw up, and the fact that the Carter Administration's ban on fast breeder reactors materially delayed the Japanese nuclear-energy effort is still recalled with resentment in Japan as an example of American indifference to the Japanese energy plight.

What applies in the nuclear field, moreover, applies even more strongly and incontrovertibly in some others. Useful as it would be to reassure the Japanese of the strength of the U.S. commitment to their country, it would be more useful yet if American officials would simply abandon their public hectoring of Japan on defense issues. Even if these pressures should succeed in stimulating a major Japanese military buildup, their ultimate consequences could well be quite different from those envisaged by policymakers in Washington. Besides creating new political tensions in Asia, Japanese rearmament could cause new economic tensions between Japan and the United States. Instead of buying more arms from the United States, Japan might very well create its own defense industries and become a major competitor in the international arms trade; already, it is said, U.S.-designed missiles built in Japan with largely Japanese components are superior in quality to American-made versions of the same weapons.

In any case, it is highly questionable whether public demands upon Japan to beef up its armed forces even serve the immediate purpose the American officials who make them have in mind. Such open American pressure clearly complicates the political task of those Japanese who actively favor an increased defense effort by making it appear to the man in the street that they are advocating something the United States wants for its own benefit rather than something that meets any need of Japan's. "Whether you favor Japanese rearmament or oppose it," says one U.S. diplomat with long experience in Asia, "there's nothing to be gained and a lot to be lost by our trying to tell the Japanese what to do about rearmament. The smartest thing the United States could do is relax and let them proceed at their own pace—which is just what they've been doing anyway."

By the same token, it is long past time that U.S. officials ceased to complain so loudly and incessantly over Japan's trade surpluses with the United States. In focusing as heavily as they do upon this single issue, American politicians and diplomats are guilty not only of unnecessary exacerbation of Japanese–American relations but of intellectual dishonesty as well. In international economic terms, what is of prime importance to the United States is not its balance of trade with any particular country but its worldwide balance of payments. Though no one whose knowledge of the economic condition of the United States was based solely upon the statements emanating from Washington could be expected to realize it, the fact is that in both 1980 and 1981 the U.S. global balance-of-payments position was substantially better than that of Japan. And even in the late '70s when the United States did have balance-of-payments difficulties, Dr. Lawrence Klein, at one time Jimmy Carter's principal economic adviser, flatly assured me that our trade deficit with Japan was "not a principal reason" for those troubles.

It is, of course, undeniable that important American industries have lost a painful share of their domestic and, in some cases, foreign markets to Japanese competitors. But even here Washington's obsession with the Japanese trade balance serves both countries ill. In its own interest, the United States should be making sustained and vigorous efforts to exploit its economic strengths more effectively and to remedy its economic weaknesses: it should devise carrot-and-stick programs to induce ailing industries like steel and autos to take the tough, expensive measures necessary to restore their competitiveness; it should seek to devise mechanisms for maintaining a more realistic exchange rate between the yen and the dollar—the absence of such mechanisms being, in the opinion of some economists, a principal cause of Japanese–American trade imbalances; and beyond argument, the United States should seek more aggressively and intelligently to increase its exports. (The export efforts made by U.S. industry in Japan, for example, have been far less effective in recent years than those made by Western European industry.)

Unfortunately, however, by setting up the Japanese trade balance as a kind of straw man, successive U.S. administrations have distracted public attention from our real problems and enabled Americans to take refuge in the notion that their problems are primarily the creation of "unfair" foreigners. In particular, Washington's myopia has made it possible for U.S. businessmen and labor unions to wrap themselves in the cloak of national interest and whip up support for protectionism. This, of course, simply diminishes the incentive for mismanaged industries to come to grips with their own shortcomings. At the same time, the constant U.S. denunciations of Japan and increasingly frequent U.S. resorts to artificial restrictions on Japanese imports serve to encourage and justify the even more nakedly exclusionist attitudes of the Western Europeans. And the arrant protectionism of the Europeans, by impelling Japanese exporters to focus even more heavily on the U.S. market than they otherwise might, further stimulates frictions between Japan and the United States.

In short, a vicious circle has been created by the high-handedness—sometimes conscious but more often unconscious—with which the United States has become accustomed to treat Japan. And the only way to cure this destructive situation is for the United States to begin to treat Japan with at least the same respect that it accords to substantially less dynamic allies such as France and Britain. The United States can only damage itself when its leaders insist upon extracting from Japanese leaders—as the Reagan Administration did from Prime Minister Suzuki in 1981—concessions that are clearly going to cause political turmoil in Japan. And it is sheer folly to humiliate a sovereign nation—as the Carter Administration did Japan—by demanding that it promise to achieve a fixed rate of economic growth dreamed up by a set of obscure foreign functionaries to suit their own purposes.

None of this is to say that the United States should not attempt to influence Japan's behavior. Clearly, it is a legitimate and necessary function of American diplomacy to seek to persuade the Japanese to pursue economic, political and security policies as compatible as possible with U.S. interests. Clearly too, there are sure to be times when, in order to overcome political inertia in Japan, the United States will have no recourse but to reinforce persuasion with pressure. But such pressure should be applied with due regard for Japanese national pride and with a minimum of public ultimata. Whenever possible, Washington should content itself with getting Tokyo's agreement upon the ends to be sought and leave the precise means by which those ends are achieved up to the Japanese. And when the United States does feel obligated to meddle in Japan's internal affairs to the extent of specifying detailed means and objectives, it should do so with more sophistication and subtlety than at present.

One possible recipe for achieving this is that proposed by Kazuo Nukazawa. Arguing that the Japanese press consistently distorts U.S. positions on trade issues, he argues that to offset this the

United States should establish in Tokyo what he calls a "trade council" with the sole function of presenting the American case to influential Japanese. "It should put out lots of handsome, well-reasoned documents written in beautiful Japanese," says Nukazawa. "And together with the U.S. Embassy, it should lobby members of the Diet in terms of their local interests. It could point out to members from Niigata, for example, that if they want their region to maintain its highly profitable tableware exports to the United States, they would be smart to plump for greater imports of American beef and oranges. That's the kind of thing we Japanese do in the United States. Why don't you Americans do it here?"

The answer to that question, in my view, is that the United States should indeed be doing that kind of thing in Japan—and not just in connection with trade issues. At one time or another, the United States has had some outstandingly effective representatives in Tokyo: perceptive "amateur" ambassadors like Edwin Reischauer and Mike Mansfield and topflight career diplomats like Richard Sneider, who played a large role in negotiating the return of Okinawa to Japanese rule. Far too often, however, the work of such people has been largely negated by political and bureaucratic heavy hitters who fly in from Washington determined to "lay down the law" to the Japanese. And even among the general run of U.S. diplomats stationed in Japan something akin to an Occupation mentality is frequently visible. Time and again over the years, I have heard U.S. Embassy personnel lecture Japanese with all the condescension of an impatient teacher explaining a self-evident proposition to a slow student.

This was never a particularly ingratiating technique, and today it is a completely counterproductive one. One of the most striking changes in attitudes in Japan in recent years has been the increasingly open desire of Japanese to be accorded some measure of respect by the United States. In this changed climate, American representatives in Japan should be seeking to influence opinion in a much broader range of Japanese society than they now do and to elicit from Japanese themselves ideas on what contributions their country can best make to the solution of mutual economic, diplomatic and security problems.

To deal with the Japanese in this way—as equals who must be convinced rather than as little brothers who can be summarily ordered about—calls for a degree of realism about the U.S. position in the world that some Americans will find hard to swallow: just as most Japanese still tend to think of their country as weaker than it really is, most Americans still tend to think of theirs as more powerful than it now is. But the potential rewards of such sensible humility on America's part can scarcely be exaggerated. There are a great many highly intelligent and knowledgeable people who agree with Mike Mansfield when he says: "The next century will be that of the Pacific." Whether the shift from an Atlantic-centered world to a Pacific-centered one will be quite as complete as some geopoliticians theorize can be debated. But what cannot be questioned, in my view, is that the peoples of East Asia will play an important role—possibly even the most important role—in shaping the history of the decades ahead. And of all the nations that have been major actors in a Europe-oriented world, only two—the United States and the Soviet Union—are geographically and otherwise equipped to exercise comparable influence in an Asia-oriented one.

At a luncheon in Washington back in the 1960s, McGeorge Bundy, who was then Lyndon Johnson's National Security Adviser, told his fellow guests: "Of all the allies the United States has, West Germany is the last one we would surrender." In those days, when few doubted that Western Europe was far and away the most critical area of contention between the United States and the Soviet Union, Bundy's statement seemed logical enough. But in time to come, as the dynamic peoples of East Asia take their place at center stage, I believe it will be the Japanese alliance that will prove most vital to America's continued well-being.

To justify that judgment, one can cite a variety of economic, political and strategic considerations. But there are also other, less tangible considerations to be borne in mind. Regardless of whether one's dominant emotion toward Japan is fear or admiration, it is impossible to deny that the Japanese are a truly extraordinary people. To an extent unmatched by the inhabitants of any other nation, they have succeeded in marrying the social discipline that is the chief virtue of a strong collective consciousness with the sense of personal responsibility that Westerners customarily regard as inseparable from rugged individualism.

It is this unique blend of attributes, I believe, which largely explains the one Japanese national achievement universally recognized by foreigners: the fact that within the space of half a lifetime Japan, against all odds, has established itself, together with the United States, as one of the two dominant economic powers in the non-Communist world. But the same combination of attributes also serves to explain some other Japanese achievements to which the rest of the world has not, in my view, paid enough attention. Unlike the Communist societies, Japan has managed to achieve formidable strength while maintaining tolerable levels of political and personal freedom. Yet unlike the industrialized nations of the West, it has maintained those freedoms and made steady progress toward the creation of a more equitable society without paying a worrisome price in social fragmentation and lost economic dynamism.

Finally, like so many individual Japanese, Japan as a nation is a quick study. If any single characteristic can be fairly described as the most important asset Japan possesses, it is the ability to adapt to radically changed circumstances without sacrificing a distinctive sense of identity. Were I obliged to lay a bet as to which of the world's major national societies is most likely still to be functioning in 2050 in a form reasonably recognizable to its present inhabitants, Japan would be my choice.

The Japanese, in short, have an uncommon talent for survival—which may in the end be the most compelling of all the many reasons that it is in America's interest to bind them to us as closely as possible.

Index

Abe, Kobo 176
Abegglen, James 217
abortion 57
Acheson, Dean 17
advertising
  Japanese vs. Western 184–5
  in newspapers 179
  see also television commercials
age, status and 134
agriculture 241, 247–51
  cooperative efforts in 247, 248
  food prices and 117, 249, 250, 251
  mechanization of 247–8
  productivity in 249
  protectionism and 117, 249, 250
  self-sufficiency of 251
  subsidy programs in 119, 247, 249
  U.S. imports and 24, 289
  see also farmers
Ainu 40
Allen, Woody 184
All Japan Airways 201
amae (dependency syndrome) 62–3
Amaya, Naohiro 271

Amdahl, Gene 237
Americanization 162, 289
  changing role of women and 98
  consumer fads and pop culture in 29, 50
  of family life 55
  fear of "backwardness" and 50–1
  of managerial techniques 29–30
  see also Westernization
Anderson, Mori and Rabinowitz 150
Antimonopoly Law 208, 210
archery 138
Ariyoshi, Sawako 176
Ariyoshi, Yoshiya 63, 222–3, 226, 228, 229, 270
Aron, Paul 234
Asahi Shimbun 100, 101, 177–8, 180, 181
Association of Home Economists and Consumer Affairs Professionals 100
auto industry, Japanese 218, 223, 241, 258–9
  foreign markets for 217, 230, 233
  robots in 217, 263, 272

auto industry, U.S. 30, 233, 258–9
  Japanese influence on 31
  Japanese market for 20
automobiles, model names of 184

baby-sitters 59
Ball, George 49
bars
  English conversation 89
  karaoke (solo singing) 143
  see also hostess bars
Beautiful People 128
beef prices 117, 251
Bell Laboratories 239
Benedict, Ruth 154
Blumenthal, W. Michael 20
bonsai culture 48
books 175–7
  buying of 176
  fiction, popularity of 176
  publishing of, 175–6
  translated from Japanese 176
  translated into Japanese 176–7
British Broadcasting Corporation
  (BBC) 184, 186
Broadcast University 186–7
Buddhism 41, 44, 64, 136, 242
Bundy, McGeorge 294
Bungei Shunju 167, 181, 183
Burakumin (Eta) 44–5
bureaucracy 205–11
  constraints on power of 209–11
  in defining and implementing of
    national interest 208–9
  elite career officers in 207–8
  internecine warfare in 209
  legislative power of 205
  motivations of 207–8
  politicians' relationship
    with 205–6, 209–10
  quality of 207
  size of 206

status of 131–2
  see also Japanese Government;
    specific ministries
Bureau of Statistics 118
business and industry,
  Japanese 107–8, 216–64
  amae (dependency syndrome)
    in 62–3
  bank loans to 229
  capital availability and 246
  college graduates recruited by 77,
    84, 88, 105
  common welfare as concern
    of 230–1
  competition within 244, 246
  consensus decision-making in 19,
    48–9
  conglomerates in 225
  English used in marketing by 184
  erosion of work ethic and 270–2
  executives' attitudes
    toward 219–20, 221–2, 229, 230
  foreign technology purchased
    by 237
  future well-being of 273–7
  governmental nurturing of 217–8,
    234
  group orientation in 228–9
  guilt principle in 66–7
  as indebted to U.S.
    counterparts 29–30, 226
  "information revolution"
    and 187–8, 233–6
  innovation in 237–9
  "junk goods" produced by 242
  labor costs of 217
  labor productivity in 241
  labor unions and 224–5, 227
  "latent ability" syndrome of 84,
    88
  lawyers in 149, 150

lifetime employment in 220–2, 241

lobbies for 211

long-term planning in 226, 228–30, 234

mature, difficulties faced by 231–2

mergers and takeovers in 225–6

multinationalism suggested for 169–70, 275

mutual protectiveness in 246

national planning and 208–9, 210, 229–30, 231, 232, 233, 234

new, emergence of 232–3

Oriental trickery ascribed to 217

peer pressure and ostracization in 222–3

political campaigns financed by 200–1

"quality-control circles" in 228

research and development for 218, 238

responsiveness to market pressures of 259

retirement practices in 133, 223–4, 245

robots in 217, 234–5, 257–8, 261–4, 272

"scrap-and-build" policy in 231

sense of community provided by 219–22, 224–6

small enterprises in 240–2, 246–62

societal changes and future of 238–9

sogo sosha (trading companies) in 238

standards of workmanship and 242

subcontracting system in 257, 258–61

superior competitiveness of 216–8

U.S. emulation of 218, 227–8

U.S. revisionists' views on 218

U.S. subsidiaries of 227–8

vulnerability complex and 243–4

wage system in 222–3

welfare burden assumed by 244–5

women in 94–5, 95–6, 98, 99–100

workers' attitudes toward 220–1, 224–5

World War II destruction and 217, 218

see also specific industries

business and industry, U.S.

company towns in 219

complacency of 233

criticisms of executives in 225

emulation of Japanese proposed for 218, 227–8

government's relationship with 218

inferior competitiveness of 217–8

Japanese borrowings from 29–30, 226

Japanese takeovers of 227–8

mature, difficulties faced by 230–1

protectionism urged by 231, 232–3, 291–2

short-term planning in 226, 228–9

supremacy of 216, 237

wage system in 223

workers' skills and productivity in 72, 227, 241

see also specific industries

Business Roundtable 211

Business Week 237

calendar 163

Call Us Crystal (Tanaka) 121–2

Canada 71, 161

"capsule hotels" 139

Carter, Jimmy 20, 22, 23, 28, 278, 290, 291, 292

cattle raising 117, 249

Central Union of Agricultural Cooperatives 211

Century Magazine 61

children, Japanese 55, 104, 271
  activities outside home of 121
  changes in physical appearance of 117–8
  character formation of 63–5
  conformity inculcated in 63
  day-care centers for 68–9, 99, 102
  evaluation of upbringing of 65–6
  foods preferred by 116
  foreigners as treated by 164
  male, favored treatment of 60–1
  maternal love for 61–2
  number of, in typical family 57, 261
  permissiveness in upbringing of 61, 63
  preventive medicine for 214
  transferring of personal status to 135
  young mothers as prisoners of 59
  see also educational system, Japanese; teen-agers, Japanese

China, Imperial, Japan's borrowings from 41–2, 163

China, Nationalist 282

China, People's Republic of (Communist China) 22, 282
  Japanese newspapers and 179
  JSP ties to 198
  potential for Japanese alliance with 287–9

Chinese language, infused into Japanese 35–7

Chinese minority in Japan 45

Chinese people, Japanese disliked by 159

Chira, Susan 120

Chisso Corporation 149

Chitoshi (pseudonym) 110, 114, 134–5, 150–1, 156, 188, 209, 210, 276

Chou En-lai 21, 198

Christians, massacres of 42

Chrysanthemum and the Sword, The (Benedict) 154

Chuo Koron 194

Clean Government Party (Komeito) 196

clothing
  of "upscale" men 134
  Westernization of 115

colleges
  junior, attended by women 76
  see also universities

Common Market 161

communication revolution *see* informatization process

commutation
  acceptable distances for, 111
  information process and 189–90

computers 187–8
  Fifth Generation 208–9
  home 188, 189–90
  semiconductors for 234, 235, 280
  software for 235
  U.S.—Japanese competition in 234–6

Confucianism 41–2, 47, 74

Congress, U.S. 24, 32, 122, 149, 195, 204, 206

Constitution, Japanese 95, 191, 197, 204, 213

consumer-electronics industry 218, 232–3

continuing education
  English language studied in 89
  as prevalent among women 89
contraception 57
contracts, Japanese relativism
  and 150–1
convenience foods, prevalence
  of 116
Corning Glass Works 233
Crihfield, Liza 92
crime 145–8
  deterrents to 147
  drug abuse and 146
  juvenile 82, 146–7
  statistics on 146–7
  in U.S. vs. Japan 82, 145–6
  yakuza (gangsters) in 146
Crystal People 121–2, 128, 270

Daiei supermarket chain 254–5
daikon (radish) legs 117
Daley, Richard 195
danchi (apartment blocks) 112, 128
Davis, Sammy, Jr. 184
day-care centers 68–9, 99, 102
Defense Department, U.S. 26
de Gaulle, Charles 277
Deming, W. Edwards 226
Denman, Sir Roy 110
Depression, Great 27
Dewey, John 71, 75
Diet 149, 151, 186, 197, 250, 293
  bureaucracy's relationship
    with 205–6, 208
  committee hearings in 204, 205
  LDP members of 195, 201
  legislative process in 204–5
  power of 204
  structure of 191
  women in 94, 96–7

  see also Japanese Government;
    politics
Dingell, John 157
distribution and retailing
  industries 241, 246–7, 252–6
  consumer habits and 256
  foreign manufacturers and 254,
    255
  governmental limitations
    on 255–6
  markups in 254, 255
  Mom-and-Pop stores in 241,
    252–4, 255
  social function of 256
  supermarkets in 252, 254–6
  in U.S. vs. Japan 253–4
  wholesalers in 253–4, 255
divorce 56–7
Dodwell 251, 253
Doi, Takeo 65, 243
dokushin kizoku ("unmarried
  aristocrats") 94
drug abuse 146

eating habits 116–18
  changes in physical appearance
    and 117–8
  economic constraints on 117, 251
  nutritional evaluation of 117
  Westernization of 116–7
  see also foods; restaurants
econometric prediction 267
Economic Planning Agency 202–3,
  209
educational system, Japanese 64,
  70–90, 238, 271
  academic achievement required
    in 79–80
  automatic promotion in 74
  boys vs. girls in 60, 76
  classroom behavior in 74–5

educational system, Japanese
  continued
  competitiveness in 76–9, 80–2
  continuing education and 88–9
  criticisms of 82–3, 100
  curriculum in 79
  educational TV in 186–7
  effectiveness of 72–3, 83, 175
  ethics taught in 74
  familial sacrifices and 80
  graduate study and 88
  homework in 79
  mothers' role in 60, 79–80
  organization of 73
  politicization of 71–2
  private or parochial schools in 73
  psychic stresses of 82–3
  rote memorization in 81
  socialization process in 74–5
  spending on 71
  students responsible for cleaning
    in 75
  textbook controversy in 282
  thinking abilities and 73
  time spent in school in 79
  tracking avoided in 73–4
  tutoring in 80
  uniformity in 73–4
  see also teachers; universities;
    university graduates; university
    professors
educational system, U.S. 74, 80
  classroom behavior in 74–5
  ineffectiveness of 72–3
  limited role of teachers in 75
  organization of 73
  spending on 71
  time spent in school in 79
Eisenhower, Dwight D. 87, 204,
  205
Ekonomisuto 262–3

elderly people, Japanese:
  homes of 119–20
  support of 57–8, 244–5
energy-related industries 236
English-conversation bars 89
English language, study of 79,
  89–90
  Americans' assumptions on 90
  bad teaching methods and 89
  bilingual TV and 114
  cultural gap and 90
  living abroad and 89–90
English words and phrases, in
  Japanese marketing 184
Eta (Burakumin) 44–5
Eto, Jun 102
Eurasian minority in Japan 45
Europeans, Western:
  Japanese disliked by 158–9
  Japanese resentment
    against 278–9, 280, 281
extramarital sex 56, 61–2

family life 55–69
  Americanization of 55
  current changes in 68–9, 119–23
  fragmentation of 120–1
  living conditions and 112–13,
    119–23
  as matriarchal 58–60, 95
  sacrifices for children's education
    and 80
  trend toward nuclear family
    and 58, 98, 119
  see also children, Japanese;
    fathers, Japanese; homes;
    marriage; mothers, Japanese
farmers 247–51
  earnings of 248, 249
  life-style of 247–8, 251
  political clout of 250–1

small-sized farms of 241, 247, 248
  see also agriculture
fast foods, proliferation of 140
fathers, Japanese
  absence from household of 59–60
  changes in role of 68, 99, 270
"Fatter Japan Is a Safer Japan,
  A" 119
Federal Bureau of Investigation,
  U.S. (FBI) 280
Federation of Economic
  Organizations (Keidanren) 211
feminism, *see* women's movement
festivals 135–6
feudalism 27, 47
  legacies of 244–6
foods
  convenience 116
  fast 140
  prices of 117, 249, 250, 251
  see also eating habits; restaurants
Forbis William 136
Ford, Gerald R. 160
Ford Motor Company 258–9
foreigners 153–71
  assimilation impossible for 45,
    167–8
  attention attracted by 164
  books about Japan written by 177
  changes in attitudes toward 170–1
  cultural borrowings from 41–2,
    162–3, 168; *see also*
    Americanization; Westernization
  difficulties of Japanese language
    and 38
  difficulty in distinguishing
    between 163–4
  disdain for contact with 51, 163,
    164–6, 170–1
  exclusionary attitudes and 45,
    166–8

gaijin complex and 162–71, 180
  Japanese disliked by 157–60
  Japanese in residence
    among 164–6
  Japanese superiority complex
    and 51–2, 167–9
  Japanese tourism and 164–5
  Japan sealed off from 42–3
  multinational industries
    and 169–70
  press coverage made difficult
    for 180
  problems in interactions
    with 153–5, 160–1
  as seldom invited to Japanese
    homes 118
  self-delusion in dealings
    with 168–9
  TV commercials and 162–3,
    184–5
Foreign Ministry 88, 207
Francis Xavier, Saint 35
Freud, Sigmund 65–6
Fuchi, Kazuhiro 235
Fukuda, Takeo 20, 180, 202–3,
  278, 286

gadgets, obsession with 114–5
gaijin (outside person) 164
  see also foreigners
gambling 137, 146
geisha 92–3
  sexual functions of 93
  trained in traditional arts 92–3
geisha parties
  female guests at 140
  political and business affairs
    conducted at 93
General Motors Corporation 250–9
genetic engineering 25, 233
Germany, Nazi, brutality of 282,
  283

gift exchanges 154
Godzilla 185
Goldman, Sherwin 158
golf 138
graduate education
  going abroad for 88
  Japanese institutions inadequate
    for 88
Graham, Katharine 140
Great Britain 71, 169, 184, 211,
  275
  government of, compared with
    Japan 191, 197, 204, 206
Greater East Asia Co-Prosperity
  Sphere 159

Hadley, Eleanor 232
Hagiwara, Emiko 120
haragei (visceral
  communication) 39–40
Harajuku Bamboo Shoot
  Tribe 70–1
hara-kiri 66
Harper's 183
health care 214
health insurance 214
Hemingway, Ernest 177
Hickman, Herman 23
Hiraizumi, Wataru 106, 107
Hirohito, emperor of Japan 129,
  163, 204
Hitachi 236
Hodgson, James D. 156
homes 106–23
  central heating uncommon in 112
  classlessness of neighborhoods
    and 128
  commutable distances and 111
  cost of 110–11
  cramped space of 106, 110–11,
    112, 119–21

danchi (apartment blocks) as 112,
  128
  decorative objects in 113–14
  dream of acquiring of 106
  employers' assistance in acquiring
    of 111, 220
  entertaining in 118, 121, 139
  family life affected by 112,
    119–23
  foreigners seldom invited to 118
  ingathering in Tokaido
    megalopolis and 107–10
  Japanese embarrassed by 118
  kitchens in 20
  "luxurious," described 110
  shortage of usable land and 106–7
  social spending on 119
  typical contents of 113–15
  Westernization of behavior
    in 115–17
homosexuality 56
hostess bars 58–9, 62, 93, 142–5
  drinking at 142–3, 144–5
  laughter in 143
  as private clubs 142–3
  sexual badinage at 93, 143
hotels:
  "capsule" 139
  "love" 120
household appliances, proliferation
  of 98, 114–15
Hoveyda, Fereydoon 24

IBM 235, 280
Ichikawa, Fusae 94
Iguchi, Toshio 256–8, 261
Iguchi Seisakujo 257–8
Ihara, Tetsuo 262–3
Iijima, Toru 220–1
Ijiri, Kazuo 192
Ikeda, Hayato 277

Ikehata, Keiji 264
illiteracy, in U.S. vs. Japan 72
Imperial family 129
industrialization, disorderly, in
    Third World 24–5
Industrial Revolution 187, 234,
    263–4
industry *see* business and industry,
    Japanese; business and industry,
    U.S.; *specific industries*
informatization process 187–90
  as conscious national goal 189
  economic goals of 187–8
  Japanese dedication to data
    and 187
  social consequences of 188–90
  U.S.–Japanese competition for
    markets in 233–6
  in U.S. vs. Japan 189
insurance, health 214
International House of Japan,
    Tokyo 113
International Women's
    Decade 103
I.Q. scores, in U.S. vs. Japan 175
Isamu 134–5
Ise, Shinto shrine at 192
Ishikawajima-Harima Heavy
    Industries 271
Iwata, Ryushu 84, 87

Japan
  atomic attack on 46
  birthrate in 261
  as classless society 127–8, 131
  distribution of wealth in 128, 130
  "dual economy" in 241
  energy needs of 28, 46, 160, 189,
    236, 289–90
  environmental problems in 213–14

expansion of domestic economy
    in 275–6
Gross National Product of 268,
    274–5
image problem of 157–62
life expectancy in 214
natural disasters in 46, 243
political history of 26–7
population density of 166
population distribution in 107–9
pre–World War II imperialism
    of 283
residential land prices in 110
scarcity in 166, 242–4, 284
self-imposed isolation of 42–3
usable land in 106–7
Japan Air Lines 148
*Japan as Number One: Lessons for
    America* (Vogel) 218
Japanese, The (Reischauer) 167
Japanese–American
    relations 18–33, 203
  adapting to Japanese patterns
    in 67, 157
  changes in industrial patterns
    and 24–5
  continuation of Japanese loyalty
    in 268–9
  cultural misunderstandings
    in 159–60
  decline in U.S. world power
    and 268–9, 293–4
  differences in logic and values
    and 19, 34–5
  economic interdependence
    and 23–4, 30–2
  erosion of U.S. goodwill in 157–8
  future trends in 267–9, 277,
    284–9
  guilt feelings in 66–7

Japanese–American relations
  continued
Japanese influence on American
  life and 30–2
Japanese knowledge of U.S.
  and 32–3
language skills and 89–100
military ties and 23, 25–6, 179,
  198, 204–5, 212–3, 269, 277,
  285–6, 290
potential for Japanese turnabout
  in 27–8, 284–9
problems in, blamed on
  Japanese 21, 161
public relations failure in 157–8,
  161–2
respect for Japanese needed
  in 292–4
scholarly expertise ignored in 18
strikes by Japanese students
  and 85
suggestions for improving
  of 289–93
superiority complexes in 21–3,
  51, 281
trade frictions in 161, 278–81,
  284–9, 291–2
U.S. ignorance of Japan
  and 18–21, 23–4
see also Americanization
Japanese Communist Party
  (JCP) 71–2, 77, 183, 196–7
Japanese Government 108, 155–6
agricultural programs of 117,
  119, 249, 250–1
assessment of 212–15
budget deficits run by 119
Cabinet formation in 199, 202
Cabinet ministers' functions
  in 205
ceremonial monarch in 191, 204

collective decision-making in 20,
  199–200
college graduates recruited 77,
  84, 88, 98, 207
industrial planning by 208–9,
  229–30, 231, 232, 233, 234
industry nurtured by 218, 233–4
kisha kurabu (press clubs)
  of 180–1
newspapers overly critical of 179
organization of 191–2
press as sounding board for 211–12
Prime Ministership in 191, 193,
  199, 200, 202–4, 204–5, 206
retail trades limited by 255–6
robotization and 261–2, 264
social spending by 118–19
women in 94, 96–7, 98–9
women's rights promoted by 103
see also bureaucracy; Diet;
  politics; *specific ministries*
Japanese language 35–40, 176
Chinese infused into 35–7
haragei (visceral communication)
  and 39–40
as imprecise 37–9
kanji (pictographs) and phonetic
  alphabets in 36–8
kinship with other languages
  lacked by 35
shift to Latin alphabet in 37–8
spoken, difficulties in 35–6, 38
Western words in 43–4
Japanese National Railways 207,
  223
Japanese people
adaptability of 26–8, 49–50, 295
aesthetic traditions of 112–13,
  136, 242
aggressive feelings poorly
  handled by 68, 280–1

antisocial behavior of 144–7
"buy Japanese" policy of 254
change in physical appearance
  of 117–18
clothing of 115, 134
collective responsibility felt
  by 46–7, 75
conformity of 63, 70–1
confrontation avoided by 39, 47,
  48, 102, 159, 161, 280
consensus emphasized by 20,
  47–9, 102, 105, 211–12
cosmopolitanism as viewed
  by 165–6, 169, 170; *see also*
  foreigners
cruel or brutal behavior ascribed
  to 282–4
as deceptively compliant 155–6
dependency syndrome of 62–3,
  65–6
eating habits of 116–18, 251
economic and social mobility
  of 131
ethnic and cultural homogeneity
  of 40–4, 74, 168
exclusionary attitudes of 44–5,
  166–8
in expatriate communities 165
as foreign tourists 164–5
friendships among 154–5
group acceptance sought by 243
guilt as experienced by 63–4,
  66–7
as highly emotional 28
humor and laughter of 143
individualism among 47–8,
  122–3, 166, 194, 238–9, 271
intelligence of 175
materialism of 98, 135, 243
misbehavior of 142–5
nationalism of 193–4, 281–2

plain speaking avoided by 38–40,
  161–2
political ideologies of 49
principles of universal validity
  lacked by 64
progenitors of 40
psychic health of 65–6
reading habits of 175–83
reciprocity concept of 63
relativism of 150–1, 160
saving habits of 245–6
self-assertion disdained by 67,
  131
self-gratification as goal of 121–2,
  270–1
sleeping habits of 115
social fragmentation of 128
superiority complex of 51–2,
  167–9, 281
tribal identity of 45, 46, 49, 51,
  64–5
as unable to hold liquor 144–5
unfamiliar problems or
  environments difficult for 64–5
uniqueness asserted by 37, 167–9,
  191
vagueness of 156
vulnerability complex of 46, 51,
  243–4, 250
as workaholics 243
Japanese Technology
  (Moritani) 238–9
Japan Housing Corporation 112
Japan Newspaper Publishers
  Association 189
Japan Robot Lease 257
Japan Socialist Party (JSP) 197–8
Johnson, Lyndon, B. 294
journalism
  Western, deficiencies of 192
  women in 100–1

journalism *continued*
  see also magazines; newspapers
juku (tutoring school) 83
Justice Department, U.S. 280

Kahn, Herman 107
kamikaze (divine wind) 42, 185–6
kanji (pictographs) 36–7
karaoke (solo singing in public) 143
Katayama, Tetsu 197
Kawabata, Yasunari 176
Kawaguchi, Yoriko 60, 69, 77,
  99–100, 102
Kawashima, Takeyoshi 38, 151
Kayashima, Atsushi 74, 75, 76
Keidanren (Federation of
  Economic Organizations) 211
Keio Kindergarten 78
Keio University 78
Kihara, Senzo 247, 250
kimonos 115, 117
Kimura, Shosaburo 120
kisha kurabu (press clubs) 180–1
Kishi, Nobosuke 204–5
Kissinger, Henry 21, 192
Kitamura, Haruo 120–1
Klein, Lawrence 291
Kobayashi, Koji 234
Kodama, Yoshio 193
Komeito (Clean Government
  Party) 196
Korea, South 24, 286
  Japanese disliked in 159
Korean minority in Japan 45
Kosawa, Heisaku 65–6
Krishner, Bernard 85
Kublai Khan 42
Kunihiro, Masao 39, 89
Kurita, Yasuyuki 113–14
kuromaku ("black-curtain
  men") 201

Kurosawa, Akira 177
kyoikumama (education
  mama) 79–80, 82
Kyoto, spared from bombing 16
Kyoto Ceramic Company 133
Kyoto University 77, 165

lawyers 149–50
Lee, Will 219, 221
Lee Kuan-yew 138
legal system 147–52
  criminal cases in 147
  judicial interpretation of laws
    in 38, 151–2
  lawyers in 149–50
  litigation infrequent in 148–9
  public apologies or confessions
    in 147, 149
  relativism and 150–1
Le Rat Mort, Tokyo 142
Liberal Democratic Party
  (LDP) 95, 97, 180, 274
  campaign financing and 200
  clear-cut ideology lacked
    by 198–9
  economic and societal well-being
    under 196, 285
  habatsu (factions) in 199–200, 201
  opposition parties' shortcomings
    and 197–8
  rearmament issue and 213
  temporary decline of (early
    1970s) 195–6
  uninterrupted rule of 193, 195–7
Lin Piao 179, 182
Little, Frances 61
living together 55–6
Lloyd George, David 112
Lockheed bribery scandal 201–2
"love hotels" 120
Lynn, Richard 175

MacArthur, Douglas 15, 21, 57, 130, 151, 191, 212, 214–5, 247, 249, 285
magazines 181–3
  general-interest weeklies 182
  investigative reporting by 181–2
  monthly 182–3
  number and range of 182
mah-jong 137
Mainichi Shimbun 178, 180, 181, 182, 183
Mamagon (dragonlike mother) 66
Mansfield, Mike 287, 293, 294
manufacturing, small-scale 240–2, 244, 256–62
  bankruptcies in 260
  robots in 257–8, 261–2, 264
  in subcontracting system 257, 258–9
  vitality of 260
  work force in 259, 260–1
Mao Tse-tung 179
Marcos, Ferdinand 138
marijuana 146
marriage 55–60
  between American men and Japanese women 155
  arranging of 57, 62, 104
  childbearing and 57
  cramped living conditions and 119–20
  expected of all Japanese 56
  living together vs. 55–6
  men's dissatisfaction in 61–2
  sexual roles in 58–60
  as social and practical matter 57
  women's career goals and 96, 98–9, 100
"Married Women: Weak Link in Japan's Family" (Kimura) 120
Marxism 85

Matsuda, Taeko 95–6, 97, 135
Matsushita 232
"mechatronics" 257
Meiji Emperor 27, 129
Meiji Restoration 27, 163
meishi (calling cards) 133–4
men, Japanese
  clothing of 115, 134
  dependency syndrome of 61–3
  as dominant in professional and public life 58–9, 60–1
  favored upbringing of 60–1
  male chauvinsim of 92, 101, 102–3
  matriarchal nature of family life and 58–61
  sexual bolstering of 93
  sexual freedom of 56, 57, 144
  study space desired by 120
  tensions relieved by 142–5
  time spent on job by 59, 68
  as unaware of feminist successes 103–4
  see also fathers, Japanese
Mii, Noburo 188, 189, 190
Miki, Takeo 58
military
  East Asian Gaullism and 285–6
  Japanese–American alliance and 23, 25–6, 179, 198, 204–5, 212, 213, 277, 285
  nuclear weapons proposed for 281, 286
  rearmament issue and 212–13, 290
  trade surpluses and 275
  U.S. demands on 290–1
Miller, Glenn 50
"Minamata disease" 149
Ministry of Education 73, 79, 282
Ministry of Finance 206, 209

Ministry of International Trade and
   Industry (MITI) 88, 99, 108,
   203, 207
   constraints on power of 210
   in defining and implementing of
   national interest 208–9, 230,
   232, 233–4, 235–6
   Electro-Technical Laboratories
   of 235
Ministry of Labor 96, 97, 103
Mishima, Yukio 66, 176, 194
mistresses 62, 93
Mitsubishi group 225
Mitsubishi Motors
   Corporation 158
Mitsui group 225, 280
Mitsui Zosen (Mitsui Engineering
   and Shipbuilding
   Company) 219, 224
Mitsukoshi department-store
   chain 255
Mitsumi Electric Company 258
mizushobai (floating world) 92
Mom-and-Pop stores 241, 252–4,
   255
Mori, Hanae, 128
Morinaga, Ichiro 111
Morita, Akio 128
Moritani, Masanori 238, 239
Moriyama, Mayumi 96–7, 140
mothers, Japanese
   caricatures of 66, 80
   education of children and 60–1,
      80
   -in-law, power lost by 58
   permissiveness of 61, 63
   sons' relationship with 60, 61–2,
      93, 100
   values inculcated in children
      by 63–4, 65

working, day-care centers
   and 68–9
young, as oppressed 59
multiplex broadcasting 188–9

Nagai, Michio 82–3
Nagasaki, Dutch trading post
   at 42–3
Naitoh, Masahisa 240–1, 244, 246,
   260
Nakagawa, Yatsuhiro 281
Nakasone, Yasuhiro 202, 203
Nakauchi, Isao, 250, 254–5, 256
Narita Airport, Tokyo, closure
   of 85, 86, 145
National Association of
   Manufacturers 211
nature-savoring, as national
   pastime 136
Navy, U.S. 27
Nelson, Horatio, Lord 47
nemawashi (consensus
   method) 48–9
New Liberal Club 196
Newman, Paul 185
newspapers 177–82, 183
   areas inadequately reported
      by 179, 181–2
   circulations of 177–8
   decentralized production of 178
   financial resources and staffs
      of 178
   foreign coverage by 178
   homogeneity of 180–1
   kisha kurabu (government press
      clubs) and 180–1
   multiplex broadcasting and 189
   as overly critical of
      government 179
   strengths of 178–9, 180
Newsweek 162, 178, 181–2, 183

New York, N.Y. 214
 crime in 147
 Japanese residents of 165
 mah-jong games in 137
New York *Daily News* 178
New York Times 119, 179, 237
New York Times Magazine 17
Nihon Keizai Shimbun 178
Nikko Research Center 72
Nippon Electric Company
 (NEC) 234, 236
Nippon Hoso Kyokai (Japan
 Broadcasting Corporation;
 NHK) 184, 186
Nippon Oil Seal 260
Nippon Steel 221
Nippon Yusen Kaisha (NYK) 222
Nissan Motor Company 111, 231,
 258–9, 272
 Oppama plant of 220–1
Nixon, Richard M. 22, 28, 156,
 202, 232, 251
nuclear energy 236
nuclear weapons 281, 285–6
Nukazawa, Kazuo 270, 277–8,
 281, 292–3

Occupation, U.S. 50, 73, 151, 202
 hunger and disease in 16–17
 "old" wealth redistributed in 130
 political reforms in 197, 202,
 214–15
 as success 21
 superiority complex and 21–2
 women's equality and 95, 96
"Occupation mentality" 161
Ochiai, Ryo 99–100
Office of International Research
 and Development
 Cooperation 98–9
Ogata, Sadako 57, 103, 104

Ohira, Masayoshi 268
oil crisis of 1973 28, 101
Okazaki, Hisahiko 268–9
Okita, Saburo 253, 269, 280, 285
on (favor or debt) 154
O'Neill, Tip 279
orange prices 117, 251
Osterman, Andrew 230
Ota, Nobumasa 34, 281
Ozaka, Tetsuya 281
Ozaki, Yukio 193

pachinko (pinball machines) 137,
 163
pain principle 158
Pakistan, Japanese loans to 277
Palestine Liberation
 Organization 160
Pao, Sir Yue-kong 138
parliament, *see* Diet
Parrott, Lindesay 17
Patrick, Hugh 237
Pearl Harbor, attack on 193
Pepper, Thomas 107
periodicals, *see* magazines
Perry, Matthew 27, 43
petrochemical industry 231
Pitau, Father Joseph 56, 64, 123
*Plan for Remodeling the Japanese
 Archipelago, A* 108–9
politics 191–215
 "back money" in 200–1
 campaign financing in 200–1
 corruption in 109, 195, 198, 200,
 201–2
 deficiencies of Western journalism
 on 192
 democracy as practiced in 193,
 194–5, 204–5, 289
 habatsu (factions) in 199–200, 201

politics *continued*
  Japanese intellectuals'
    commentaries on 192–3, 194, 195
  Japanese-style collectivism in 194
  machine 195
  opposition parties in 196–8
  potential for totalitarianism
    in 194, 283–4
  right-wing nationalism and 193–4
  special interests and lobbies
    in 210–11
  surveys of voters' attitudes on 197
  unaffiliated voters and 196
  uninterrupted rule of LDP
    and 193, 195–7
  in U.S. vs. Japan 195, 200, 202,
    204, 206
  vote-buying in 201
  see also bureaucracy; Diet;
    Japanese Government
pollution control 213–14
Pope, Alexander 113
Popiel, Mark 251, 253, 258, 259
Potomac Associates 157
premarital sex 56
press *see* journalism; magazines;
  newspapers
protest demonstrations 145
  student riots and 82, 85, 86, 87,
    129, 283
psychiatry 65–6

Rabinowitz, Richard 215, 226
racism 21, 156, 167, 282
Rashomon 177
reading habits 175–83
  statistics on 183
  see also books; magazines;
    newspapers
Reagan, Ronald 25–6, 52, 204,
    235, 280, 292

real estate speculation 109, 130–1
recreation 135–41
  active sports as 137–9
  eating out as 139–40, 141
  family activities as 141
  festival-going as 135–6
  gambling as 137
  "hanging out" as 139
  hostess bars as 142–5
  income or social status and 135,
    137, 140, 141
  nature-savoring as 136
  spectator sports as 135, 137
refrigerators, U.S.-made, Japan as
  market for 20
Reischauer, Edwin O. 38, 167, 293
restaurants 139–41
  expensive 140, 141
  robot "greeters" in 114, 262
  traditional foods served in 116,
    140
retailing, *see* distribution and
  retailing industries
retirement
  postponing of 133, 223–4
  public assistance programs
    and 245
  saving for 245
retirement communities 120
rice 248, 249–50
  decline in consumption of 116
  farm-subsidy program for 119,
    249, 250
  U.S. production of 248, 249, 250
robots 114, 261–4
  cost of 257, 261
  leasing of 257, 261
  liked by Japanese people 263
  in manufacturing 217, 234–5,
    257–8, 261, 263–4, 272
  in service industries 262–3

unemployment fears and 263, 272
U.S.–Japanese competition
  in 234–5
ronin (wandering warriors) 82
Russo–Japanese War
  (1904–1905) 27, 47

Saar, John 111
samurai tradition, sports drawn
  from 137–8
satellite communications 236
Sato, Eisaku 156, 199
Sato, Komei 247, 248
Sato, Yamahei 247–8
semiconductors 234, 235, 280
sensei (teacher) 74
seppuku (ritual self-
  disembowelment) 66n, 193
Servan-Schreiber, Jean-
  Jacques 216
servants, near-disappearance
  of 115
service industries:
  as labor-intensive 262
  robots in 262–3
sex shops 144
sexual behavior 56, 61–2, 104
  cramped living conditions
    and 120
  of geisha and bar hostesses 93
  unromantic attitudes toward 144
Shimazu, Takako 129
Shimomura, Mitsuko 100–1, 102,
  103, 104
Shinto 41, 64, 136, 192
Shioji, Ichiro 226–7, 263, 272
Shioya, Ken 252–3, 254
shipbuilding industry 208, 231
Shockley, William 238
Shogun 112–13
shogunate 27, 43

Shotoku, prince of Japan 41
Showa 163
Shukan Asahi 100
Sino–Japanese Treaty of
  Friendship (1978) 288
skiing 138–9
sleeping habits, bedding and 115
Sneider, Richard 293
Socialist Party 71–2
Social Security System, U.S. 245
sogo sosha (trading companies) 238
Sohyo 197
Soka Gakkai 196
Sony Corporation 99–100, 128,
  232
Southeast Asians, Japanese disliked
  by 159
Soviet Union:
  collectivism and responsibility
    in 46
  Japanese security and 269, 277,
    285, 287
speed (drug) 146
sports 137–9
  of blue-collar workers 137
  samurai tradition and 137–8
  spectator 135, 137
  upscale 137–9
Starblazers 185–6
status 127–35
  age and 134
  external signs of 134–5
  group affiliation vs. individual
    achievement in 132–3
  inheriting of 129–30, 135
  lack of social elite and 128–9
  meishi (calling cards) in assessing
    of 133–4
  occupational 131–2, 149
  "old" vs. "new" money and 130

status *continued*
  public displays of deference
    and 127
  university admissions and 76–9
  in U.S. 133
steel industry, Japanese 217, 233,
  241
steel industry, U.S. 217, 231
Stokes, Henry Scott 257
stores *see* distribution and retailing
  industries
subcontracting system 257, 258–60
Suharto, President 138
suicide, 66, 82
  ritual 66, 194
supermarkets 252, 254–6
Supreme Court, Japanese 191, 210
Suzuki, Zenko 97, 179, 201–2,
  203, 292
Swift, Jonathan 22
swing music 50
swordplay 138

Takeda, Yutaka 224–5
Takemura, Kenichi 176
Takeuchi, Naokazu 251
Talcottville, Conn., as company
  town 219, 221
Tamayama copperware shop 240,
  258
Tanaka, Kakuei 76, 108–9, 130,
  195
  bribery charges against 181,
  201–2
Tanaka, Yasuo 121–2, 128
tangerine growers 117, 249
tatami (rice-straw mats) 115
taxicabs, automatic doors of 114
teachers
  discipline methods of 74–5
  of English language 89
  humiliated by rioting students 82

party ties of 71–2
public esteem for 74
in socialization process 74–5
see also educational system,
  Japanese; university professors
teen-agers, Japanese
  nonconformist displays by 70–1
  rebellion among 65
  self-gratification sought by 122
  violent and criminal acts of 82,
  146–7
television 121, 137, 183–7
  broadcasting system for 184
  cultural programming on 184,
  186
  educational programming on 184,
  186–7
  entertainment programming
    on 184, 185–6
  news coverage on 186
  quality of, in U.S. vs. Japan 186
  time spent in watching of 115,
  183–4
television commercials 184–5
  escapism in 185
  foreign celebrities in 184, 185
  Western features of models
    in 162–3, 184
television sets 217
  bilingual 114, 188
  proliferation of 114
  U.S. protectionism and 232, 233
Teng Hsiao-ping 198
tennis 139
textile industry 232, 233
Third World, disorderly
  industrialization in 24–5
Thoreau, Henry 152
Tiger, Lionel, 262
Todai (Tokyo University) 77,
  78–9, 80, 202, 207

women admitted to 96
Togo, Heihachiro 47
Tojo, Hideki 158
Tokaido megalopolis 107–9
  boundaries and size of 107
  decentralization plan for 108–9
  population shifts to 108
  as psychic heart of Japan 108
  urban sprawl in 107–8
Tokugawa Era 43
Tokuyama, Jiro 47, 88, 162, 167,
  227, 228, 273, 279–80, 287
Tokyo 167
  air quality in 213–14
  capital-city snobbery in 132
  destruction of, in World War
    II 15
  housing in 111
Tokyo University, *see* Todai
Toyota 259
trade relations 161
  assaults by new Japanese
    industries and 232–3
  charges of free-trade-system
    abuses and 273, 278–9
  Japanese dependence on exports
    and 274–5, 284
  Japanese perceptions of frictions
    in 278–80, 293
  Japanese restrictions in 20, 117,
    249, 250
  mutual dependence of U.S. and
    Japan in 23–4
  suggestions for alleviating tensions
    in 274–6, 291–2, 293
  U.S. protectionism and 217, 231,
    232–3, 273, 284–8, 292
  "voluntary" quotas in 230
transportation system 214
Tsuru, Masato 259–60
Tsuzuki, Kimio 188

Turkey, Japanese loans to 277
Twain, Mark, (Samuel
  Clemens) 156
two-income households 68, 98

Ubukata, Taiji 149, 194, 223
unemployment 256
  robotization and 263–4, 272
unions 222, 227–8, 241, 272
  cooperation between management
    and 224
  U.S. robots opposed by 234–5
United Nations 72, 103
United States
  hostility toward Japan in 156–8
  see also Americanization; business
    and industry, U.S.; educational
    system, U.S.;
    Japanese–American relations;
    Occupation, U.S.
universities 83–8, 108
  academic evaluation of 83, 87
  admission of foreign-educated
    students to 165–6
  Broadcast 186–7
  business recruiting practices
    and 84
  criticisms of 87
  elementary and secondary schools
    maintained by 78
  entrance exams for (examination
    hell) 78–9, 81–2, 83, 84
  in national research effort 88
  permissiveness of 83–4
  personal freedom enjoyed at 83–5
  revolutionary sects at 85, 86
  select list of 77
  social function of 87–8
  state-supported vs. private 77–8
  statistics on application and
    admission to 80–1, 82

universities *continued*
  status determined by admission
    to 76–9
  student riots at 85, 86, 87, 129,
    283
  U.S. vs. Japanese 83, 84
  women educated at 76, 96, 98–9,
    105
university graduates
  establishment values embraced
    by 86–9
  graduate study by 88
  oversupply of 76–7
  recruiting of 77, 84, 88, 98, 105
  starting salaries of 77
university professors
  inadequate salaries of 83, 86
  progressiveness and leftism of 86
Ushiba, Nobuhiko 23, 25, 279
U.S.–Japan Security Treaty 179,
    198, 205

Vander Werf, Pieter 237
Venice Film Festival 177
video systems 189, 232
  Japanese supremacy in 188
  two-way 189
Vietnamese "boat people" 159
Vietnam War 268
Vogel, Ezra 218
Vuitton, Louis 270

Walker, William 160
Wall Street Journal 177
Waseda University 78
Washington Post 179
Watergate 202
welfare system 244–5
  informal 256, 260
Westernization
  of clothing 115

  dual structure of Japanese society
    and 271
  of eating habits 116
  foreign origins disguised in 163
  of homes 115
  Japanese homogeneity and 40,
    42–3
  in mid-nineteenth century 27, 43
  motives for borrowing and 50–1
  subtle transformations in 43–4
  see also Americanization
wholesaleing industry 253–4, 255
Wilson, "Engine Charlie" 230
women, Japanese 91–105
  bolstering of men as role of 93
  changes in physical appearance
    of 117
  changing role of 91–2, 95–105
  clothing of 115
  college- or university-
    educated 76, 96, 98, 105
  continuing education prevalent
    among 88
  as deferential to men in public 59
  discrimination in upbringing
    of 60–1
  educational advances of 97–8
  excluded from husbands' business
    entertaining 140
  household tasks of 98, 115, 116,
    190
  life expectancy of 98
  marriage and childbearing
    expected of 56, 94
  matriarchal nature of family life
    and 58–60, 95
  Occupation reforms and 95, 96
  in political establishment 94,
    96–7
  sexual freedom of 56
  Western views on 58, 59

see also mothers, Japanese
women, working 94–101, 104–5
  desire for material goods and 98
  explanations for increase in
    number of 95, 97–8
  job discrimination against 94, 95,
    97, 100
  marriage and career combined
    by 97, 98–9, 101
  nature of jobs held by 93, 94, 98
  opinion polls on 104
  portraits of 95–7, 98–101
  statistics on 94, 98
  young unmarried 94
Women's Affairs Bureau 97, 103
women's movement 101–5
  disapproval for tactics of 95, 97
  end results of 103–5
  feminist successes in West
    and 51, 102
  government policies and 103
  indirect suasion as tactic of 103–2
  lobby inside government for 103
  men unaware of 103–4
  speed of changes effected by 104
  U.S. movement as model for 95
  U.S. vs. Japanese 104
Women's Wear Daily 128

World War II 30, 51, 66, 159, 193,
  286
  anti-Japanese propaganda in 21
  code-breaking in 168–9
  cruel and brutal behavior in 282,
    283
  destruction wrought by 15–17,
    218
  Japanese surrender in 15, 204
  rapid Westernization and 27, 43
  see also Occupation, U.S.

yakuza (gangsters) 146
Yamamoto, Tadashi 279
Yamashita, Isamu 219, 222, 224
Yayu no Sato, retirement
  community at 120
Yomiuri Shimbun 165, 177–8
Yoshida, Shigeru 202
Yoshitomi, Masaru 190, 243, 245,
  255–6, 260, 261–2, 272, 274
Yoyogi Park, Tokyo, teenagers'
  gatherings in 70–1, 121
Yukawa, Hideki 38

zaibatsu (family-held
  combines) 130
Zen Buddhism 242

David Holden and Richard Johns
The House of Saud £2.95

In 1902, in Riyadh, the desert raider Ibn Saud tossed the head of the town governor from a parapet to his followers below. Thus was the kingdom of Saudi Arabia founded. Two-thirds the size of India, holding a quarter of the world's oil and with six times more overseas assets than the USA.

'Easily the most balanced and intelligent account of the whole Arabian phenomenon' OBSERVER

Brandt Commission
North-South £2.50
a programme for survival

The result of a unique and independent investigation by world statesmen into the urgent problems of inequality faced by a world economic system which favours the prosperous countries of the 'North' at the cost of the poorer 'South'. The report of the Independent Commission on International Issues under the chairmanship of Willy Brandt argues that major initiatives are needed if mankind is going to survive: long-term reforms by the year 2000, priority programmes for the 1980s, and emergency action to avert an imminent crisis. It calls on all countries to make an imaginative response to problems which affect us all.

Michael Kidron and Dan Smith
The War Atlas £5.95
the state of the international military order

The War Atlas illustrates the structures of global competition and collaboration; the nature of contemporary conflict; how war preparations affect lives and livelihoods; who gains, who loses and who opposes – laying bare the economics and politics of armed peace and armed conflict. Using graphics, cartographics and colour, it is a revolutionary extension of the tradition of military atlases in content as well as design, presenting hard information on neglected topics: anti-war movements; terrorism and the internationalization of civil war; China; superpower interdependence; arms-selling and -making agreements.

Fiction

☐ **Options**	Freda Bright	£1.50p
☐ **The Thirty-nine Steps**	John Buchan	£1.50p
☐ **Secret of Blackoaks**	Ashley Carter	£1.50p
☐ **Hercule Poirot's Christmas**	Agatha Christie	£1.50p
☐ **Dupe**	Liza Cody	£1.25p
☐ **Lovers and Gamblers**	Jackie Collins	£2.50p
☐ **Sphinx**	Robin Cook	£1.25p
☐ **Ragtime**	E. L. Doctorow	£1.50p
☐ **My Cousin Rachel**	Daphne du Maurier	£1.95p
☐ **Mr American**	George Macdonald Fraser	£2.25p
☐ **The Moneychangers**	Arthur Hailey	£2.50p
☐ **Secrets**	Unity Hall	£1.75p
☐ **Black Sheep**	Georgette Heyer	£1.75p
☐ **The Eagle Has Landed**	Jack Higgins	£1.95p
☐ **Sins of the Fathers**	Susan Howatch	£3.50p
☐ **The Master Sniper**	Stephen Hunter	£1.50p
☐ **Smiley's People**	John le Carré	£1.95p
☐ **To Kill a Mockingbird**	Harper Lee	£1.95p
☐ **Ghosts**	Ed McBain	£1.75p
☐ **Gone with the Wind**	Margaret Mitchell	£3.50p
☐ **Blood Oath**	David Morrell	£1.75p
☐ **Platinum Logic**	Tony Parsons	£1.75p
☐ **Wilt**	Tom Sharpe	£1.75p
☐ **Rage of Angels**	Sidney Sheldon	£1.95p
☐ **The Unborn**	David Shobin	£1.50p
☐ **A Town Like Alice**	Nevile Shute	£1.75p
☐ **A Falcon Flies**	Wilbur Smith	£2.50p
☐ **The Deep Well at Noon**	Jessica Stirling	£2.50p
☐ **The Ironmaster**	Jean Stubbs	£1.75p
☐ **The Music Makers**	E. V. Thompson	£1.95p

Non-fiction

☐ **Extraterrestrial Civilizations**	Isaac Asimov	£1.50p
☐ **Pregnancy**	Gordon Bourne	£3.50p
☐ **Jogging From Memory**	Rob Buckman	£1.25p
☐ **The 35mm Photographer's Handbook**	Julian Calder and John Garrett	£5.95p
☐ **Travellers' Britain**	} Arthur Eperon	£2.95p
☐ **Travellers' Italy**		£2.50p
☐ **The Complete Calorie Counter**	Eileen Fowler	80p

☐	**The Diary of Anne Frank**	Anne Frank	£1.75p
☐	**And the Walls Came Tumbling Down**	Jack Fishman	£1.95p
☐	**Linda Goodman's Sun Signs**	Linda Goodman	£2.50p
☐	**Dead Funny**	Fritz Spiegl	£1.50p
☐	**How to be a Gifted Parent**	David Lewis	£1.95p
☐	**Victoria RI**	Elizabeth Longford	£4.95p
☐	**Symptoms**	Sigmund Stephen Miller	£2.50p
☐	**Book of Worries**	Robert Morley	£1.50p
☐	**Airport International**	Brian Moynahan	£1.75p
☐	**The Alternative Holiday Catalogue**	edited by Harriet Peacock	£1.95p
☐	**The Pan Book of Card Games**	Hubert Phillips	£1.75p
☐	**Food for All the Family**	Magnus Pyke	£1.50p
☐	**Just Off for the Weekend**	John Slater	£2.50p
☐	**An Unfinished History of the World**	Hugh Thomas	£3.95p
☐	**The Baby and Child Book**	Penny and Andrew Stanway	£4.95p
☐	**The Third Wave**	Alvin Toffler	£2.75p
☐	**Pauper's Paris**	Miles Turner	£2.50p
☐	**The Flier's Handbook**		£5.95p